SNAPPY SHORTS
at
TARRAGON THEATRE

compiled by Andy McKim

Playwrights Canada Press
Toronto • Canada

Snappy Shorts at Tarragon Theatre © Copyright 2004 Tarragon Theatre
The authors assert moral rights.

Playwrights Canada Press
215 Spadina Avenue, Suite 230, Toronto, Ontario CANADA M5T 2C7
416-703-0013
orders@playwrightscanada.com • www.playwrightscanada.com

CAUTION: The plays in this collection are fully protected under the copyright laws of Canada and all other countries of The Copyright Union, and are subject to royalty. Changes to the script are expressly forbidden without the prior written permission of the author. Rights to produce, film, or record, in whole or in part, in any medium or any language, by any group, amateur or professional, are retained by the author. For amateur or professional production rights, please contact Playwrights Canada Press.

No part of this book, covered by the copyright hereon, may be reproduced or used in any form or by any means—graphic, electronic or mechanical—without the prior written permission of the publisher except for excerpts in a review. Any request for photocopying, recording, taping or information storage and retrieval systems of any part of this book shall be directed in writing to: Access Copyright, 1 Yonge St., Suite 1900, Toronto, Ontario CANADA M5E 1E5 416-868-1620.

Playwrights Canada Press acknowledges the support of the taxpayers of Canada and the province of Ontario through The Canada Council for the Arts and the Ontario Arts Council.

Cover photo by Andy McKim.
Production Editor/Cover Design: JLArt

Library and Archives Canada Cataloguing in Publication

Snappy shorts at Tarragon Theatre.

Forty-five 10 min. plays in collaboration with Tarragon Theatre's annual spring fling.
ISBN 0-88754-750-8

1. Canadian drama (English)—21st century.   I. Tarragon Theatre

PS8307.S63 2004   C812'.5408   C2004-903115-5

First edition: May 2004.
Printed and bound by Printco at Toronto, Canada.

dedicated to the memory of Urjo Kareda

Thank You...

Like any book this one owes its life to many people. Angela Rebeiro instantly had the vision to back this idea from the moment I mentioned it to her. Tanya Workman then did all the work to collate the 20 years worth of scripts we had stored away in various places at Tarragon, compiling a cross-referenced list of them all and their writers. Jason Sherman wrote a perfect introduction. Betony Main, using all of her considerable powers, tracked down all these writers and collected their recent drafts. Jodi Armstrong did an amazing job of working all hours to get this book set up and off to the printer.

Catherine May, Rick Sherman, Joanna Miles, Margaret Gobie, Maia Kareda and most recently Kristen Van Alphen were at various times the Producer of the Spring Arts Fair and did more work on it than anyone will ever know.

Marilyn and Robin have stood by me as I buried myself in the Fair every year not noticing that I had a wife and son.

Thanks to everyone who has ever contributed to the running of the Spring Arts Fair and to the production of these engaging plays.

Thanks to the many extraordinary writers at Tarragon who have contributed over the years to the creation of this vast array of wonderful short pieces.

And lastly, I think of Urjo, who was my best friend and workmate. In my first year at Tarragon I created the Spring Arts Fair and I wanted to direct a play in my office as part of the Fair. Urjo didn't like the play I had chosen, but he liked the office idea, so he suggested asking the playwrights in our Unit to write short plays for the office. They took up the challenge, and *Firing Francine*—the first play in this volume—was among them. Those short plays were a huge hit and they soon became the highlight of any Fair experience.

—Andy McKim

Table of Contents

Introduction: *50 Words Per Minute*
    by Jason Sherman   iii

Plays:

Year	Author	Title	Page
1985	Don Hannah	*Firing Francine*	1
1986	Joan MacLeod	*The U.I.C.*	9
1986	Judith Thompson	*A Kissing Way*	13
1987	John Mighton	*Self*	24
1987	Judith Thompson	*Pink*	28
1988	David Sereda	*Salad Days*	30
1988	Mary Ellen Mahoney	*Jane Thompson's Last Dull Day*	38
1989	Susan Coyne	*Typistry*	43
1989	Don Hannah	*The Wall in the Garden*	49
1989	Tom McCamus	*Apoplexy*	54
1989	Bruce McCulloch	*The Two-Headed Roommate*	63
1989	James O'Reilly	*The Bends*	68
1990	Jim Warren and Guillermo Verdecchia	*Philistines and Farmers*	74
1992	Todd Hammond	*Fish*	85
1992	Michael Redhill	*The Hanging Gardens of Willowdale*	92
1993	David Gow	*Listen*	97
1993	Don Hannah	*Aspiring Francine*	103
1993	Michael Redhill	*Information for Visitors to Warsaw*	110
1993	Jason Sherman	*The Merchant of Showboat*	117
1994	Karen Hines	*Telemarketing: The Musical*	125
1994	Jason Sherman	*Equity Rules*	132
1995	Andrew Akman	*The Nose Job*	138
1995	Jason Sherman	*The Poetics*	143
1997	Morwyn Brebner	*Coupe de Ville*	155
1998	Shirley Barrie	*Audience*	160
1998	Michael Healey	*The Button Stories*	164
1998	Kate Lynch	*The Newcomer*	170
1998	Michael MacLean	*The Audition*	176
1999	Kate Lynch	*Ten-Minute Play! (The Musical)*	181
1999	Ivana Shein	*A Doctor, A Secretary and a Bag of Apples*	185
2000	Chris Earle	*Runneymede*	191
2000	Diane Flacks	*Slice of Heaven*	198

cont. on next page

2000	Michael MacLean	*You May Already Be a Winner*	205
2000	Eric Weinthal	*On the Door*	211
2001	Carol Anderson	*Jazz at 3 a.m.*	217
2001	Leah Davidson	*Ladies' Room*	222
2001	Melody Johnson and Bob Martin	*Shoe Store*	225
2001	Eric Weinthal	*Let Me Out of Here*	230
2001	Teresa Pavlinek	*The Weekend*	236
2002	Susan Coyne	*Captive Audience*	241
2002	Sonja Mills	*Mouse*	247
2002	Paula Wing	*Thirty-six C*	252
2003	Richard Greenblatt and Guillermo Verdecchia	*My Cigarette Break with Guillermo*	257
2003	Wendy Lill	*Genie*	262
2003	David Macfarlane	*The Prank*	*268*

Introduction

50 Words Per Minute
by Jason Sherman

There were only two rules, both of them simple. Rule 1: set a play in an office. Rule 2: make it ten minutes long, no more, preferably no less. If Rule 2 was often ignored, and it was, Rule 1 was a little harder to get around, given that the plays were performed in an office. To be precise, in the office of Andy McKim and two other members of the Tarragon Theatre staff who, for a few days every spring, saw their workspace transformed into a performance space where, over the course of an often rain-drenched weekend, up to 60 people at a time would sit and stare at a space to the left of the door, and watch a ten-minute (or so) play.

To be sure, every space in that building—be it an office, a lobby, a rehearsal studio—was considered fair game for the Spring Arts Fair. Plays were staged on rooftops, in courtyards, and twice or thrice in the old box office, which was no bigger than a broom closet, and long-used for just that purpose. It didn't take long before an elevator was installed for someone to come up, and down, with the Tarragon's first elevator play. (And possibly the world's.)

Yet of all the nooks and crannies into which were crammed one-act plays, monologues, readings and performances of plays-in-progress—all of them trying to elbow their way into the consciousness of the mass of humanity wandering up and down stairs, in and out of rooms, clutching their one-sheet schedules, being politely shushed by a cadre of volunteers, trying not to faint from the aroma of smoked hot dogs wafting in from the wagons placed too short a distance from the front door—the nook that perhaps best typifies the experience that was (and, happily, remains) the Tarragon Spring Arts Fair, was the studio office.

Here, brave (or just weary) souls would sit through four miniatures at a time, though, truth be told, once seated, there was little opportunity to leave. The plays played on, every hour on the hour, in a seemingly endless cycle. The door would open, two or three actors would enter, and a scene would unfold inches from where you sat, if you were in the front row, and no more than twenty if you were standing at the back. For the actors, it was an ordeal by fire, performed on fumes of terror and adrenaline. For the audience, it was often a pleasure, and if it wasn't, it helped to invoke the Alberta Weather Principle: "If you don't like it, stick around ten minutes, it'll change."

For the playwrights, it was about taking on a challenge – ten minutes, an office: go. And you'd be amazed, you the playwright, at what you could accomplish within those parameters, even if you did cheat a bit on one of them.

There were two rules for this introduction, too: write about the ten-minute play, and make it 500 words long.

I think I'm over.

Don Hannah   ***Firing Francine***
A Play in Eleven Scenes with an Epilogue Set in Heaven

1985
Andy McKim: Director
June Garba: Francine
Amanda Hancox: Iris

♯ • ♯

An Office: a desk and chair, another chair in front of the desk, a phone on the desk, a door.

SCENE ONE

IRIS sits at her desk, agitated. She opens a large, practical purse, takes a Valium from a pill bottle and swallows it. There is a knock at the door.

IRIS Yes.

FRANCINE *(opening door and poking her head into the room)* You wanted to see me? *(She enters.)*

IRIS Yes. I think it's time for you and me to have a–

FRANCINE *(overlapping)* Little talk?

IRIS No, I was thinking more of a big talk.

FRANCINE That is the way my mother continuously approached things and I shall not have you treat me like a child.

IRIS Francine, I'm not your mother.

FRANCINE Nor should you sound like her.

IRIS Let's try this again, shall we?

    FRANCINE exits.

SCENE TWO

The Same: the purse, the Valium, the knock.

IRIS Yes.

FRANCINE *(poking head in door)* You wanted to see me? *(enters)*

IRIS Yes. Now that you've been on staff for a couple of months, I thought it was time for us to talk about the way things are working out… or not.

FRANCINE I find the job most challenging.

IRIS Yes. Well, I–

FRANCINE I cannot understand when others on staff do not seem to find it so.

IRIS I–

FRANCINE In fact, just the other morning when I was sorting through Accounts Payable into manageable little stacks for everyone, I was thinking that there was no need to have such an horrendous pile-up.

IRIS They do tend to creep up on us.

FRANCINE If we were structured more efficiently, you realise, there would be no need for any of this.

IRIS It doesn't–

FRANCINE Iris, Francine would be only too pleased to reorganise the structure of Accounts Payable into a manner which would render our staff to be more efficient.

IRIS Would you mind coming in again?

> *FRANCINE exits.*

SCENE THREE

> *The Same: the purse, the Valium, the knock.*

IRIS Yes.

FRANCINE *(poking her head in door)* You wanted to see me? *(She enters.)*

IRIS Yes, Francine. I think we should talk frankly about the way you fit into the scheme of things here. We're a pretty small operation and the staff are a pretty decent bunch of people who are a… hell, I hate to use the word "team"… but, anyway, a reasonably functioning team and I'm concerned about the effect you're having on them.

FRANCINE I am being treated like a non-person.

IRIS What?

FRANCINE A non-person.

IRIS *Persona non grata*?

FRANCINE What? No, a non-person. I find that I am being treated like a child with no critical capacities, one who is not consulted on matters of policy, and, thirdly, that I am constantly realising myself in charge of the drudgery. In short, a non-person.

IRIS I…

FRANCINE Who ends up sorting through the immense confusion of Accounts Payable every month?

IRIS *(losing control)* Who makes a beeline for Accounts Paya... *(getting a grip)* This isn't what I had in mind. Would you mind? *(gestures to door)*

FRANCINE exits.

SCENE FOUR

The Same: the purse, the Valium, the knock.

FRANCINE You wanted to see me? *(coming in)*

IRIS Yes, yes, yes. Have a seat, Francine.

FRANCINE I prefer to stand, thank you.

IRIS No, that won't work. *(points to door)* Again.

FRANCINE exits.

SCENE FIVE

The Same: the purse, the Valium, the knock.

IRIS Yes?

FRANCINE *(coming in)* You wanted to see me? *(She sits down.)*

IRIS Yes. Ever since you joined this staff—a time period which seems endless to many but has really been only a couple of months—you have managed to turn a reasonable place to work into a nightmare for all of us...

FRANCINE stands, moves towards the door.

IRIS No. Wait. Stay.

FRANCINE returns, stands by the desk.

IRIS Yes. Ever since you joined this staff you have managed to turn a reasonable place of work into a... into a... into an unreasonable one. You have alienated the rest of my staff.

FRANCINE They treat me like a non–

IRIS No. You alienate them.

FRANCINE And how has this been accomplished?

IRIS Well, take the windows. God knows the windows were filthy, but no one asked you to come in early to clean them. And... no one asked you to bring in your little homemade snacks to pass around and make the rest of us feel lousy because we never bring any. No one wants you to tidy up their desks after they've gone home. And no one has ever asked you to tackle Accounts Payable before it's due and while the rest of us are still up to our armpits with the first half of the month.

FRANCINE I do not care for inefficiency.

IRIS You have an unnatural obsession with inefficiency, as if I were going to present you with an award for fighting it. The staff have taken to hiding out in the corners. When you finally stopped dusting the filing cabinets on your break the other day and sat down for lunch, Louella and Eve took off and I found out later that they've been eating their sandwiches in the Men's Room.... No.... This won't do it. Let's give it another try.

>   *FRANCINE exits.*

SCENE SIX

>   *The Same: the purse, the Valium, the knock.*

IRIS Yes.

FRANCINE *(coming in)* You wanted to see me?

IRIS Yeah, I do.

FRANCINE Yes?

IRIS Oh. Now I don't know where to start.

FRANCINE I have always thought it preferable to start at the beginning. Nine a.m. I am punctual. And I pride myself that I have never been ill.

IRIS God knows you're never away.

FRANCINE I do my job efficiently. I am extremely precise.

IRIS Exactly. Precisely. Minutely. Infinit–

FRANCINE Tesimally?

IRIS To the Nth degree. It drives me nuts!

FRANCINE You shall have to be more specific.

IRIS Please go out.

>   *FRANCINE exits.*

SCENE SEVEN

>   *The Same: the purse, the Valium, the knock.*

IRIS Yes.

FRANCINE *(coming in)* You wanted to see me?

IRIS Yes. You're a lunatic. You're driving me crazy. You're fired.

>   *FRANCINE picks up the phone.*

IRIS You're phoning the Labour Relations Board?

FRANCINE smiles, nods. IRIS sighs, pushes FRANCINE's hand from the phone. FRANCINE hangs up.

IRIS Again?

FRANCINE exits.

SCENE EIGHT

The Same: the purse, the Valium – no. IRIS looks at the Valium, then puts it back in and keeps her hand in the purse. The knock.

IRIS Yes?

FRANCINE You wanted to see me? *(comes in)*

IRIS pulls a gun from her purse, aims, fires, and blows FRANCINE backwards out the door. A pause. The door closes.

SCENE NINE

The Same: the purse, the Valium – a handful this time. A pause, then the knock.

IRIS Oh no.

FRANCINE *(poking her head into the room)* You wanted to see me? *(She comes in.)*

IRIS I did?

FRANCINE Perhaps it was a small matter concerning the reorganisation of Accounts Payable?

IRIS I don't think so, Francine.

FRANCINE You wanted my opinion on Louella's frequent tardiness, perhaps?

IRIS Some other time. No. Come back later.

FRANCINE exits.

SCENE TEN

The Same: the purse, many Valium, the knock.

IRIS What?

FRANCINE *(striding in)* You wanted to see me?

IRIS No. No. Not yet.

FRANCINE exits.

SCENE ELEVEN

The Same: IRIS locks the door behind FRANCINE. She swallows all the pills and lies down on the top of her desk to die. The knock.

FRANCINE *(off)* You wanted to see me? *(She is fumbling with the doorknob.)* Hello? Iris? Yoo hoo? You wanted to see me, Iris? Iris? You wanted to see me? Hello? This is terribly inefficient behaviour, Iris. I'm wasting precious work minutes. Iris! Iris!

IRIS, with a smile and a sigh of relief, dies on her desk. All knocks cease.

EPILOGUE

The Same: Heaven: The sound of a harp. IRIS stirs.

VOICE OF GOD   Iris! Wake up. Wake up beloved Iris Purviance McPhee.

IRIS   *(sitting up, yawning)* Oh, I'm dead.

GOD   There is no death. You are reborn in Me. This is heaven, Iris. Your reward.

IRIS   This?

GOD   We choose familiar surroundings as a part of the orientation process. We find it more efficient. Beyond that door the archangels are preparing to fly you through the pearly gates. And reunite you with your departed ones.

IRIS   Good God.

GOD   Yes?

IRIS   Oh, nothing…. There's no more knocking. It's quiet. It's so nice and quiet.

GOD   Are you ready, Iris?

IRIS   Ready for what?

GOD   For your wish. Everyone gets one big wish as soon as they arrive at my place.

IRIS   Oh, how nice. *(She looks about her. A long terrified look at the door.)* Reunited, you say.

GOD   You will spend endless days with the departed you have known on earth.

IRIS   Oh, dear. Well, can I make a wish about someone still on earth?

GOD   You can have anything you want.

IRIS   Good. Well, do you know Francine from my old office?

GOD   I know everybody.

IRIS   Of course. Well, I wish that Francine may have a long life. A very long life. An abnormally long life. On earth. *(to herself)* I'm sorry, Louella.

GOD   Oh Iris, too bad. You waited too long to make your wish.

A knock at the door.

GOD Just seconds ago, as your dear friend Francine walked from the office steps, she was tragically run over by a moving van.

IRIS Oh, no.

GOD A hit and run.

FRANCINE *(off)* Iris? *(knocks on door)*

GOD Louella is still being pursued by the police.

FRANCINE *(off)* Iris? Gosh, it's terribly bright out here all of a sudden.

IRIS I don't suppose you can put her back.

GOD No. We've exceeded this month's quota for out-of-body experiences already.

IRIS Can I make another wish then?

> *The knocking continues.*

GOD You had better be quicker this time.

IRIS What can I wish for?

> *IRIS looks in panic at the door, where the knocking becomes furious.*

FRANCINE *(off)* Iris! Help! There are big flapping things with wings on all over the place out here! Iris!

IRIS Oh.

GOD We'll have to speed things up, Iris, it's almost time for the pearly gates. I'm giving you to the count of five to make your wish.

IRIS Oh, dear.

FRANCINE *(off)* I thought you wanted to see me!

GOD One...

> *IRIS starts to panic.*

GOD Two...

FRANCINE *(off)* Iris! IRIS!

GOD Three...

IRIS I wish. I wish I wish...

GOD Four...

FRANCINE *(off)* IRIS!!

GOD Iris, I'm at four and a half.

IRIS Oh, I wish I were in hell.

GOD My will be done.

> *A clap of thunder. All knocking stops. Then a very loud knock at the door.*

FRANCINE *(off)* Iris! Open up. It's getting *extremely hot* out here! Iris? Where in hell are you… *(quieter)* Oh, thank you. *(shouting again)* Iris? A funny little red man just gave me the key. I'm coming in.

Key in lock. Door opens.

Joan MacLeod

The U.I.C.

1986
Shelagh Hewitt-Kareda: Director
Lynn Kristmanson: Ms Tricot – thirtyish, U.I.C. clerk
Kris Ryan: Mr. Collie – thirtyish, U.I.C. recipient

⌑•⌑

Opens with Ms TRICOT working quietly at her desk; enter Mr. COLLIE, extremely agitated and hyper.

TRICOT Mr. Collie?

COLLIE Hi Mrs. Tricot.

TRICOT Have a seat please.

COLLIE I want to work. With God as my witness, I am seeking a full-time and permanent position. I'm up with the sun and am always the first person in the entire city to go through the classifieds. If there's a lull in the conversation, I update my resumé. I wear out eleven pairs of shoes a day. I'll re-locate, re-classify, re-establish. I'll change my personality, my sex. *(drops down on his knees in front of TRICOT)* Anything for a job. And in the meantime, I thank God for Unemployment Insurance. I thank God for making you my unemployment officer. *(places head on her lap)* Right now, just at this very moment, I feel very... blessed. Do you feel it too? Ms Treacle? Please, please don't cut me off U.I.C.

TRICOT Are you finished?

COLLIE *(returns to his chair)* Nice dress.

TRICOT I need a list, Mr. Collie.

COLLIE Please. It's been a long time. Call me Bob.

TRICOT I need a list of where you applied for work this week. *(pause)* Bob.

COLLIE Okay.

TRICOT Do you have it?

COLLIE I can tell you.

TRICOT It should be written down.

COLLIE *(writing furiously)* Canada Post, UofT and The United Nations.

TRICOT What position did you apply for at the post office?

COLLIE What?

TRICOT Letter carrier? Sorter?

COLLIE *(pause)* Chief.

TRICOT I beg your pardon?

COLLIE President. It seemed ideal. I'd done some sorting at Christmas, eleven years ago. I have a Masters degree.

TRICOT Do you have a letter of rejection you can show me?

COLLIE Thousands.

TRICOT *(reading aloud from letter COLLIE has handed her)* "Thank you for sending us your poem – 'Love And The Need For Firearms.' Unfortunately, our magazine does not have space for a work that is 83 pages long. In the event…." This isn't from Canada Post.

COLLIE It was on the front page of the *Globe* for God's sake. Donald – Something. He's the new head of the Post Office. It was a political appointment. I didn't have a chance.

TRICOT *(holds up letter)* This is exactly what we talked about last time. U.I.C. isn't meant to subsidise your career as a poet.

COLLIE I know! I even bought a little notebook. Just like you said. Every time I write, I keep track of the hours. See? *(shows book)* "January 30, 10:30-11:15 a.m." I did a little rewriting. Another cowboy poem. Maybe I'm in a rut with them but, you know, sometimes you've just got to write a thing right out of your system. Then, "2:00 a.m. Tuesday." I woke up to take a piss and it hit me like a great fucking earthquake. I mean, I always thought cowboys were just this metaphor for the death of romance but it's way bigger than that. And you've probably been wondering why all the cowboys in my poems are Swiss. Right? Well, frankly Ms Tricot, so was I. The point is…

TRICOT The point is you're supposed to keep track of any time spent writing.

COLLIE I am! Look. "2:00 a.m. to 5:45 or thereabouts." I finished a second draft of "All The Real Cowboys Are Swiss." Then the next night at 8:30 I thought about a new poem. I didn't actually write anything down but got pretty obsessed and thought, right. Better tell Miss U.I.C. Even when you're just thinking about it. She'd want to know.

TRICOT February 13th.

COLLIE Bad day. I know it was a Thursday but it felt like Friday the 13th. Allie and me had this monstrous fight: birth control. I mean she's thirty-three and smokes as though her life's about to end so the pill's out but she got this IUD – behind my back. I don't know. I keep thinking it's like this little copper cockroach that goes roaming around inside her when the lights are out. She says no problem and she definitely says no kids. So what can you do? It gives me the creeps though. *(pause)* What do you use?

TRICOT *(pause)* February 13th you worked six hours for Simpsons.

COLLIE It didn't work out… I don't want you thinking I'm totally irresponsible. We just had this pregnancy scare when I was…

TRICOT You worked six hours for Simpsons and received $18.36?

COLLIE Net.

TRICOT And were actually fired the second hour but refused to leave?

COLLIE Correct.

TRICOT Well?

COLLIE Do you have a good sense of metaphor, Ms Tricot?

TRICOT Mr. Collie! I am very upset about your performance at Simpsons. I felt quite proud that I'd actually found you work as a poet and I understand you were impossible.

COLLIE Writing personalised greetings for Valentine's cards was not a tremendous way of exhibiting my genius. I tried. The night before I couldn't sleep even. I was pretty excited about the whole thing. And I had my own little booth, at mall level, and a hat covered in red cardboard hearts. It looked good on me, Mrs. Trickle, if I do say so myself. I felt good. My pen was loaded. I was going to be a voice for the inarticulate. I mean, that's what poetry is all about. It was like coming home. And functional to boot. I was fucking ecstatic about the whole thing if you want to know the truth.

TRICOT What happened?

COLLIE The customers. Fifteen minutes after opening I was ready to commit suicide. I mean it. You can break down people that need personalised greeting cards into two groups. Either they wanted pieces of air: "I am ME. Thank you for being REAL, etc. etc." or… and this second type is much worse, they wanted nasty stuff. "Write somethun about fat thighs that rhymes." "Do one that's filthy and oral." Can you believe it? I was shocked, Ms Tricot. For your benefit, I hung on as long as possible.

TRICOT January 28th.

COLLIE What a day!

TRICOT You had an interview at Humber College that you didn't show up for.

COLLIE You're asking me about January 28th? You're kidding me. The space shuttle blew up. I thought everyone knew that.

TRICOT I don't understand how a tragedy in Florida would keep you from an interview in Mississauga.

COLLIE I saw it. Me and all the school children in the United States. You think they need counsellors! I mean, the unemployed, we know our television. Watching it is a good way to expose yourself to different careers, broaden your horizons etc. I'd estimate that between noon and midnight on January 28th, I watched the shuttle blow a hundred and twenty times. I'd imagine a lot of the unemployed didn't make their interviews that day. Am I right?

TRICOT You're ridiculous.

COLLIE You're gonna cut me off. Aren't you? Do you have a good sense of metaphor? Do you Mrs. Tricot?

TRICOT You ruined the job I found you. You missed an interview. You have applied for Secretary of State, Vice President of IBM.

COLLIE Regional office. Not the whole corporation.

TRICOT Dean at the University of Toronto. Last week it was something on Parliament Hill that earned a thousand dollars a day. I can't believe you are serious about working and thus…

COLLIE The death of romance. Does it hurt you too?

TRICOT Mr. Collie. I've reached my limit.

COLLIE Do you have a good sense of metaphor?

TRICOT I have no choice…

COLLIE Me either.

TRICOT I'm going to back-date this to January 28th. As of that date you are ineligible for further unemployment benefits.

COLLIE You know what I'm gonna have to do? *(stands, pats pants pocket)* I'm gonna have to kill you Miss Tickle. *(pulls out gun and holds it to her head)* You've broken my heart. *(He mimes pulling the trigger and yells out BANG!)* C'mon Miss Trickle. Can't you even slump over? You're not gonna play fair. I just shot you dead. You're bleeding forms and paper all over the desk. I'm going to back-date your death to Christmas just to make it thoroughly tragic. Fuck it. *(picks up stuff to leave)* I always knew you had a lousy sense of metaphor.

    COLLIE exits; TRICOT resumes filling out forms.

Judith Thompson   *A Kissing Way*

1986
Judith Thompson: Barb
Tim Chapman: Phil

¤ • ¤

Black. PHIL and BARB are seated amidst audience, as if in a cinema. They have just finished seeing an art film, which they did not enjoy. The lights come up. BARB leans over to PHIL.

BARB I guess we missed something. Everybody's so quiet.

PHIL Gee, you know, I don't know if it's just me, being a lowly stockbroker–

BARB No, no, I'm sorry, but when I don't know who's who or where we are or what they're doing, it's them, it's not me.

PHIL I mean WHAT was that bit about the WALL on fire?

BARB Some kind of symbol I guess… everything seemed to be a symbol of something.

PHIL *(standing, getting his coat)* What I want to know is, why can't they just have the something?

BARB Exactly. Is that your scarf on the floor?

PHIL Oh. Sorry, uh. It's… uh… always trying to get away from me.

BARB Scarves and mitts have a way of doing that.

PHIL Indeed. Well. Shall we get out of here before we… suffocate from all the… meaningful air?

BARB Please.

PHIL Whoo. Fresh air!

BARB It's definitely fresh! FREEZING!

PHIL So… can I interest you in a nice warm drink? There're lots of places… around…

BARB OH – uh… thank you. I really have to be getting back, I uh… have a seven-thirty fitness class tomorrow morning… and I want to be… *(pause)*

PHIL FIT for it. I understand completely. You will allow me to drive you home?

PHIL offers her his arm.

BARB I certainly will. Isn't it amazing how empty it is around here. Where is everybody?

PHIL I don't know where everybody is. I often wonder that myself.

BARB Oh it's sooo cold. I wonder how those bag people survive.

PHIL They don't like to be called that.

BARB What?

PHIL Bag people.

BARB Oh yes, just like mentally retarded people have to be called HANDICAPPED, deranged people have to be called SPECIAL. What are we supposed to call them?

PHIL I'm not sure. Homeless, I think.

BARB Oh. I'm sorry.

They arrive at the car.

PHIL Here we are.

BARB Oh yes. Turn the heat on, turn the heat on.

They look around, then get in.

PHIL Radio? Or no?

BARB Whatever you…

PHIL No, then. You'll… ah… have to direct me, having only been to your house to pick you up, I–

BARB Well, just get out to Don Mills, and then I'll tell you… you do know how to get to Don Mills.

PHIL Yes.

BARB Of course.

PHIL Why do you live… so far away?

BARB I like it. It's safe, it's quiet, fairly clean air… it's fabulous.

PHIL I'd hate to live so far out… of the centre…

BARB The centre of what? I mean what's in the centre?

PHIL Not much, really, I guess…

Beat.

BARB So, anyway, what do you… think of the market these days?

PHIL Me? Oh, I think it's going to go higher. Don't you?

BARB Absolutely. The Feds are gonna loosen up the old money supply and we're away!

PHIL So what – what – what do you like this week?

BARB Mines are looking good, VO, the Dump…

PHIL *(laughs)* I've had a terrible month.

BARB Really. How bad is it?

PHIL Unbelievable. I lost my clients a literal fortune.

BARB Options?

PHIL That Ford is tailgating me. Yes, options.

BARB Mmm – It's always a gamble. They'll probably be back.

PHIL I'm going to be in the bottom rung in the brokers' ratings this month. In big print for everyone to see at the bottom: Philip Lambert. Oh well.

BARB Maybe the pit is getting to you.

PHIL Fifty people in a room shouting into phones. You're all doing five grand a day. And today, today, do you know what I did? In the afternoon I did ONE ticket, fifteen shares of Abitibi Price for a Bar Mitzvah. I mean, it's farcical.

BARB Maybe you should take a holiday.

PHIL I can't afford a holiday!

BARB Yeah, it's tough…

PHIL I just seem to have – bad luck – Yeah, I just seem to have bad luck, y'know.

Long pause.

These shoes seem to hold in the cold. My feet are still freezing.

Pause.

BARB It's just around the corner. Take the first left on Freemont, and then right again at the lights.

Sound: Gear change. Acceleration.

PHIL An attractive street.

BARB Yeah, I love this neighbourhood.

PHIL When you get a chance to see it.

BARB Exactly. Sometimes on Sunday for a couple of hours.

PHIL It's an awful profession, don't you think?

BARB And… uh… just right here…. Oh… sorry, you were supposed to turn right back there. Don't worry, I'll just get out…. Philip? I'll just get out here, if that's okay…. Excuse me, Phil? Philip, are you all right? PHIL.

PHIL Just… be quiet for a second…

Sound: Thunder of stock market slides under.

BARB What?

PHIL I said… keep quiet, please…

> *Sound: Squeal of tires, then heavy acceleration. Continuing under:*

BARB Why, is there something up ahead? What is it? Philip, slow down…. Uh, Phil, look, whatever it is… kidding aside, I really do have to be getting home. Philip, where are you taking me? Look, I really have to go home now. It's far too late to go get a Mac. *(beat)* Wait a minute, this isn't…. Rog didn't put you up to this, did he? Oh God, that guy.

PHIL *(looks at her)* I said… shut your mouth.

BARB *(beat)* Philip, let me out of this car.

PHIL "Have to go home early to get up for fitness class."

BARB Uh oh. Oh, no. Oh, no – I'm sorry, I don't mean to hurt your feelings, Phil.

PHIL You? You couldn't hurt my feelings.

BARB I didn't mean that.

PHIL Then say what you mean.

BARB I mean…. If you'd just… slow down… *(beat)* Philip, all I meant was, I wanted to explain it's nothing to do with you, it's just… I have this thing about fitness class, it's very important to my lifestyle.

PHIL You're lying.

BARB I'm not, really, ask my friends, I'm obsessed with it! Phil, look, I'm sorry if I've made you angry…

PHIL *(mock laugh)* You couldn't make me angry.

BARB Then what are you doing? Where are you taking me? *(beat)* Phil, look, I know you've had a bad month, why don't we…. Look, why don't we go back to my place and I'll make us some tea and we'll talk about it.

PHIL We're doing what *I* want to do. *Not* what you want to do, what *I* want to do.

BARB Philip, you do not know me well enough to do this, now turn around the car, and–

PHIL Don't talk to me like that. DON'T EVER TALK TO ME LIKE THAT.

> *Sound: Blare of horn, squeal of tires, moving past.*

BARB Stop it. Just stop it now. Stop this car. Now listen, you're having problems at work, but that's no reason to take it out on me. There are solutions to problems. I have many more clients than I can handle: do me a favour and take on a few. There's a solution. Now stop the car and let me out!

PHIL I don't want your clients.

> *Sound: Blare of horn.*

BARB Well… you're obviously very… upset. Then what do you want? Philip, I'm just trying to think of a way to…

PHIL Get out. Like an animal in a trap. Thinks and thinks and finally has no choice but to bite its leg off…

BARB Philip, don't talk like that. *(She goes to holler.)*

PHIL *(fakes a laugh)* Just joking…. Please! Please listen. Please…. Tell me something. You, someone like you, could never think of me, of… a guy like me… in *that* kind of way…. Could you?

BARB What… kind of way.

PHIL You know what kind of way. A kissing way.

BARB A kissing way? You mean? Oh, oh, oh – of course, of course I could. You're very attractive–

PHIL DON'T. LIE.

BARB No. I'm not, you are – very attractive.

PHIL You're lying, you're lying, you're lying–

BARB Oh Philip, please stop the car. Just stop the car and let me out. Please?

PHIL Stop saying "please," Barbara, it doesn't make sense. See, "Please" means "If you please" and I please to do what I'm doing, or I wouldn't be doing it, get it?

BARB No, I don't get it and I don't…

PHIL Why, do you have to… micturate… or something?

BARB What's… that?

PHIL You don't know? I can't believe it. Aren't you the one that's so clever, winning all the Trivial Pursuit games for your team, roaring with laughter at me when I didn't know where Soweto was? Well I did know, I did know, I just… couldn't say it, that's all, it just slipped my mind, it's in *South Africa*, see? I know, I know–

BARB I was only laughing in fun…

PHIL Micturate means urinate. Pee. *(beat)* Another one for you – expectorate. Come on, come on, guess if you don't know.

BARB I, uh… I don't know.

PHIL Hah, Miss Hot-Shot Broker don't know. Spit. To expectorate is to spit. See? I do know some things.

Pause.

BARB Philip, you may not believe this, but I know what it's like to have a bad month. I've had a few of them myself–

PHIL No you haven't. You're lucky. And luckies don't like unluckies. Unluckies give luckies the creeps.

BARB Philip. Look, I-I think that maybe you're having a kind of minor breakdown due to nervous exhaustion and that you should just…

Sound: Blare of horns.

Look, if you keep running traffic lights we're gonna have a crash.

PHIL Luckies like you feel good in their skin, they know they belong in the world, that they should get up in the morning. Me, I'm… like someone in a… a too… tight suit…. In a too tight, out-of-date–

BARB Oh no! No no no you've got it all wrong, Philip, really, you're… listen, all the girls at work think you're very attractive, really, we all think you must have some gorgeous girlfriend stashed away somewhere–

PHIL You're lying, Barbara, every dip in your voice says lie lie lie–

BARB NO! No, not the highway…. Not the highway. I don't believe this. You're abducting me. I'm being abducted. *(scream)* HELP! *(giggle)* Oh my God.

Sound: Car accelerates. Gear change.

PHIL You don't think I'm handsome, you think I'm soft.

BARB No, not soft. You have those big shoulders. You have… *(beat)* Where are you taking me?

PHIL But you see through my shoulders, don't you? You see right through my shoulder bone into the me, the tiny tiny me who contracts like a snail every time anybody even looks at me coldly.

BARB It's not true…

PHIL You see it, I know you do, that's why you wanted to go home early tonight, because you see what a… suck–

BARB No…

PHIL You… because you're sharp, and the doctor… because he looks in my pupils with the lights and he can see the pressure on my brain, the pressure of being such a… suck, such a…

BARB Philip, you are driving too close to that car.

PHIL I could see it in your face, EVERY time you looked at me, every morning in the elevator, "GOD this guy's a jerk," you were thinking–

BARB I WAS NOT. Philip, I was not. I was thinking, actually, how handsome you were and how awkward I felt around such a handsome guy!

PHIL Bullshit! *You* saw me shaking that day when John Danby brought that big dog into the lobby, you SAW me sweating and–

BARB What, the bouvier? Last week?

PHIL I saw you looking at me.

BARB There's nothing wrong with being scared of dogs. I'm scared of snakes.

PHIL You're female

BARB That makes no difference!

PHIL But it does! You women say it doesn't, you say you want to see us men be soft and cry, but if we do, it's game over, you hate our guts.

BARB PHILIP, there's a car up ahead!

> *Sound: Car slows down. Squeal of tires, gearing down to:*

Where are you taking me? There's nothing down here. Philip, why are you taking me to the country–

PHIL A grown man, PETRIFIED of big dogs, a stupid–

BARB So, it doesn't… who cares, so what's the big deal?

> *Sound: Car pulls over. Engine stops.*

BARB Philip, why are you stopping? Don't stop. Don't stop.

PHIL I'm too… stupid to drive, I–

> *Sound: Car door flung open, scramble of footsteps in snow with BARB screaming as PHIL yells:*

You're not getting away from me now!

> *Sound/Biz: A struggle.*

BARB Oh my God, I pray to you every night. Don't let me down. Please help, please help, please help, please… (screams)*

PHIL You scream again and I'll knock you out. I mean it, Barbara. You're coming back to the car. You're staying with me.

> *Sound: Dragging over snow. Car door slams. Back in the car:*

(struggle) Be still. Be still.

BARB Philip, Philip.

> *Sound: Dashboard struck with fist, with:*

Philip, Philip.

PHIL CHRIST! Just like those sick-faced girls in Grade Six who used to laugh and whisper every time I walked by – especially that one, Marinda, she really thought she was it. You really think you're it, don't you.

BARB *(softer, tearier)* No. No, I don't. I really… really… don't…

PHIL You think you're it because you know my wish.

BARB I don't… know anything about you, Philip.

PHIL Yes you do, you know the worst. You know the most disgusting, sick disgusting thoughts I have, and that's why I have to tell you.

BARB Tell me what.

PHIL What I wish. What I really wish.

BARB I don't know what you wish.

PHIL YES YOU DO! *YOU* KNOW! I CAN SEE BY YOUR LITTLE EYES THAT YOU KNOW. YOU *KNOW* that when I see an attractive woman in the halls that although the outside of me is thinking "Oh yes, I'd like to chat with her," the inside side is seeing her neck, her throat, her neck, snapped, snapped by hands, white bone, falling, falling back, and she's there with her eyes and I give her a kiss, a long French…

BARB NO!

PHIL You can't stand it, the idea of me kissing, because you could never think of me in a kissing way, could you, how could you? Me, the jerk who bled from his fingers in the winter every winter. I had to wear gloves, all day, in school, 'cause I bled from my fingers, from the dryness, the DRYNESS OF WINTER, winter in Winnipeg, everything so goddamn dry you got a shock every time you touched something, really! A shock! And the girls' hair all electric, standing up from their sweaters – set my teeth on edge, that electric hair, with the smiling – I HATE THAT CITY! I hate Winnipeg. 'Cause I'd run outside to get away from the 'lectric and I'd be hit by the cold! Cold so cold it got into your muscles and stayed there and stayed there like insults from guys on the ice, those insults so mean 'cause I kept screwing up, 'cause I couldn't concentrate, 'cause I thought of the ice as a girl, who I skated and skated but she still stayed ice, she still stayed ice you all, you all, you all stay ice…

BARB Some of us… are… nice, Philip…

PHIL You are sharp and frozen, you – you wear sharp high heels, those sharp high heels that crack on the linoleum. Tiny half-moon marks, I saw them once, when I fainted one day. And woke up, and looked and saw tiny half-moon marks. "What the hell are these," I asked the guy and he said… he said, "Oh, those are from the damn high heels the women wear – the damn high heels…"

BARB They're just… shoes… they don't…

PHIL THEY SHOW THE LIE!! THE LIE THE LIE THE LIE, LIKE WATER. Like water…. God. The most prettiest thing I ever saw was in the book place the… library, yes, and sitting with a group of Chinese, doing math, and I saw this girl, this girl from behind, and – and she lifted her arm to reach for a book the – the – the sight of her breast from behind, the most exquisite…. Girls, you girls, like a… pond of water, lapping, lapping, and I'm so glad I'm so tired I'm going to dive in and I run towards it and it laps and it laps and I run and I dive… and it's hard. It's ice, that ice I skated, it's ice. You're a lie, your curves are a lie – your curves…

BARB Philip. Will you… let me show you… that I can be nice?

PHIL What do you… mean? *(beat)* What? What are you doing?

BARB Just touching your hair… you have nice hair. Really nice hair… nice nose… lovely jaw. You know, it's kind of funny, but I'm… sort of… flattered that you chose me... to tell these things to. I didn't think you thought about me one way or the other – and I'm not often chosen for... things...

PHIL That feels nice, the way you touch me.

BARB It feels nice to me, too.

Sound: Rustle with:

PHIL Kiss my neck. Oh yes. Kiss it again. Oh yes...

BARB Philip, this is crazy, but. I'm... getting really... aroused and I... would like – to make love with you. I mean, I would like you to make love to me... please?

PHIL You would?

BARB Oh yes. *(kisses him)*

PHIL *(responds, then:)* Oh God!! OH GOD I CAN'T STAND IT!! I CAN'T STAND IT!!

BARB What's... the matter?

PHIL I know that the only reason you're doing this is because you're scared, you'd *never* have me in any... other–

BARB That's not true, that's not true, Philip, really.... Somehow you taking me tonight has made you very... sexy. I want to make love with you. I don't know why, it's crazy, but I just... I really, really want you. I want to make love with you more than anything.... Okay?

Sound: Rustle, with:

PHIL *(shaking her violently)* Stop lying! STOP LYING!

BARB *(struggling to get away)* YOU YOU LET ME GO!! LET ME GO!!! Oh my God please don't let me down now, please please PLEEEEEEASE...

Sound: A slap.

Oh.

PHIL Why... why do you want to go back so badly... what... makes you think anybody would miss you?

BARB Because they would.

PHIL No they wouldn't. Not really. Oh, I guess there would be a big fuss at first, everybody in the pit talking about it, the women weeping, lots of people at a big funeral, but you know what, Barbara? Most of them, in a small way, somewhere in their being, would be quite pleased. Quite pleased to have something to talk about in the washrooms, at lunch, something new in their lives – quite... pleased. And soon it would all calm down and you'd be nothing more than a thought in your mother's head when she's getting her tea on a Wednesday afternoon. That's all you would be. A name on a old birthday card... a closet of clothes.

BARB So you're... planning... to hurt me...

PHIL I don't know. I can't let you go.

BARB Well then, where are you going?

PHIL We're not going anywhere.

BARB Oh God… what… what pleasure could you possibly get from this? Wouldn't you rather… win my friendship? You still could, you know, I won't tell anybody, I promise…

PHIL When one goes hunting for deer, one doesn't try to win their friendship. I don't want your friendship.

BARB Then what do you want? WHAT DO YOU WANT? What do you want? YOU… YOU have no right, you have no right to take me away to STEAL me, to make me listen to your sick, sick mind. I DON'T WANT TO BE HERE, I HATE YOU. I HATE YOU, I HATE YOU… *(beat)* You're going to kill me, aren't you? We're all alone here in the middle of nowhere and there's nobody around and you're going to kill, you're going to end my life. Oh yes… I want you to put your hands around my throat and snap it. Right now, come on, kill me. I SAID KILL ME!

    Sound: Car door opens.

It takes a second to break a person's neck. Didn't you hear? Just put your hands around my throat / and snap it.

PHIL *(overlapping)* / Oh God. Please go. I'd drive you home, but I think I'm going a long way away…. I'm… so… sorry… God.

BARB No. I don't want to go now, I want… you to kill me. I want you to kill me. Or are you too much of a suck even, *(starts to go)* are you too much of a suck, is that the problem? I think you are. I think you are. I think you are…

PHIL Please… just… go…

BARB I said I want you to kill me. I said I should, I should be killed.

PHIL Why?

BARB I have breasts, I'm a girl, I wear high heels, and I see, I see what a suck you are. I did see you shake at the dog. Because I take up… too much… space. I breathe in… too much… air. I'm too big for a girl. Too smart, way too tall. I should be cut. I'm a… bad… person. I talk about all my friends behind their backs, I… don't visit my parents enough, I don't care about my mother's health, I don't like… ugly people, I want them to leave, I have these dreams where I hurt and I hurt, I don't give to hunger, I've always had everything, I wouldn't hang around with losers in high school, cripples made me sick to look at, I didn't want to be near them, I didn't want to be near you because you're weird. I don't want to be near me, nobody should be near me, I'm bad, I am very very bad and it won't – you're right, you're right, it won't make any difference at all to anybody's life if I'm not there…. None, none, that's right, that's true, so I want… I want… I *do* want to be dead, to be… *not* to be here. I don't like this life. To be nothing, not ME, I don't want to be ME, I am sick – sick of me, I want… to be blackness. Yes. I remember…. Yes, coming out of anaesthetic, yes, and feeling the mask, yes, and wishing I could have just stayed… under. Wishing. Wishing. I want to be under. Oh yes, yes, please. I would love, love that… to be nothing – white sweet – light. *(faints)*

Sound: Rustle with:

PHIL   You've fainted. You fainted. OH GOD, what am I doing here? Philip you were thinking of… I can't believe it. I can't believe it… I was actually thinking of hurting…. It's just, it's just… I couldn't stop thinking about the way you looked when you saw me shaking at that dog. I knew that you knew me and I didn't want… you to tell. Maybe I should try – just… put… my hands… around her… throat…. Ohh!! No!! Of course not, of course not, no, you… couldn't do that, you should have known. You should have known… sucko… from the rabbit, yes. Everybody else knows. Mum, and Dad, and Archie and Linda, Sunday and Dad took us out to catch rabbits and I stand by the rabbit hole, Dad puts in the weasel to chase them out and I'm to catch them one by one and snap their necks. With my hands. And I waited. The weasel went in and the rabbits came out so fast, and I caught one and it… looked at me. With these eyes. And I just let it go. Like an asshole, and then we went home, and I was the joke! "Hey Eleanor, Philip had the rabbit and he just let it go! He had it, right in his hand, and he let it go!" And they laughed all through dinner and I took a bath and my father looked in and he said "Stupid you! You had the rabbit, and you just let it go!!" I had the rabbit, and I just let it go. I had the rabbit… in my hands.

Sound: Stock market ambience, quiet at first but getting louder under:

Oh God – God – now you'll never think of me in "that" way. You'll see me in the pit, and you'll think…. "What a suck." He had me in his hands… and he just… let me… *(in tiny voice)* go!

Sound: Up full.

John Mighton   *Self*

1987
Kevin Teichroeb: Director
Myrna Wallin: Woman
Doug Anderson: Man

⌑•⌑

Lights up. Two chairs, side by side, in an office. A MAN sits in one of the chairs, his left arm on the armrest, his second index finger up, in the "fuck off" gesture. He remains like this. A young WOMAN approaches, carrying Self *magazine. She knocks tentatively.*

WOMAN Is anyone sitting here?

    Pause.

(noticing gesture) I don't have to sit here.

    Pause.

(looking around) This seems to be the only seat in the office.

    She sits. Pause.

I almost missed my appointment. I thought it was at four-fifteen.

    Pause.

Is something bothering you?

    Pause.

I couldn't help noticing… you don't seem to be very happy.

    Pause.

I can understand if you don't want to talk about it. Yesterday I felt pretty much the way you do. I was under a lot of pressure. I had a surprise menstrual shut-down and look makeover all in the same week.

    Pause.

I hope I'm not bothering you. I suppose you're waiting for Dr. Stanley. I don't usually talk this much to people in waiting rooms. I'm very relaxed with you…. Why don't you put your arm down?

    Pause.

You belong to any singles clubs?

Pause.

You look like you work out a lot. I bet I've seen you at Gold's.

Pause.

You probably have trouble making friends. You're a type B personality. It's hard for you to set your love priorities.

Pause.

Self magazine says that if you fake the mood you'd like to feel, you're likely to catch it.

Pause.

Feeling good about yourself isn't hard when you realise that your problems, your little moral dilemmas, aren't the centre of the universe. Ninety percent of the time we agonise over things that the rest of the world isn't even interested in.

Pause.

Why don't you put your arm down?

Pause.

I understand you. You're... I hate to use the word, because it's been so abused... everyone uses it... but you're an artist. You're making some kind of statement aren't you?

Pause.

You're angry, I like you. I like your style. Tepid people are a drag.

Pause.

You remind me of a friend of mine. Recently he threw himself in front of a subway. I didn't keep him from doing it. I couldn't live for him. He was an animalistically sensitive person who no longer wanted to live. He didn't play games with suicide. He died completely untragically.

Pause.

How long have you been seeing Dr. Stanley?

Pause.

He's very good, isn't he?

Pause.

I was a little dubious about coming to see him at first. Maybe it's hard to believe – but I used to have a lot of trouble opening up with people. Dr. Stanley helped me with that. He's probably helped you too.

Pause.

Everyone wants something badly. But no one can see your inside wish. They only see the outward behaviour which gives a clue to the wish.

Pause.

If you could have one wish what would it be?

Long pause.

I wish you'd put your arm down.

Pause.

Negativity is a very expensive habit.

Pause.

I've lost a lot of jobs that way. You have trouble being up front about your needs. I know. I've never been very good at interacting with people. I used to have bulimia. I was down to sixty-three pounds. I almost died twice. If I'd been brought up in a *real home* things might have been different.

Pause.

A person behaves in a certain way. He behaves as if he's stuck with that behaviour. If the therapist treats the behaviour as separate from the person – he's saying I expect you to have no control over this.

Pause.

You're not a therapist, are you?

Pause.

I hope not – because I can tell you something – *it's not working.*

Pause.

I'd like to share something with you: you're making me very uncomfortable.

Pause.

I mean you're not actually hurting anyone. It's not like you're filling up the room with smoke or anything. There aren't any signs that say you can't do that but *I wish you'd put your fucking arm down!*

Pause.

I'm sorry. I didn't mean to yell at you.

Pause.

It's just that. I thought… I thought we understood each other. We've both been through hell.

Pause.

Someone must have broken your heart. I know… I know… You don't have to say.

Pause.

I'll leave you alone. I'll read my magazine. We'll forget each other.

She opens her magazine, the title displayed, tries to read.

What's happened to Dr. Stanley? I'm going to find him.

Pause.

Goodbye.

Pause.

We'll probably never see each other again.

Pause.

Still…… I have the feeling… that if we'd met under different circumstances… we might have been friends.

She knocks tentatively on the doctor's office door, then goes in.

Judith Thompson —   *Pink*

1987
Clare Coulter: Lucy

⌑•⌑

LUCY, a ten-year-old white girl talking to her dead Black nurse, Nellie, shot in a march, in her open coffin.

LUCY   NELLIE I want you to come back, to shampoo my hair and make a pink cake and we can sit in the back and roll mieliepap in our hands see, I told you not to go in those marches, and I told you that what you people don't understand, what you didn't see, is apartheid's for YOU. IT'S FOR YOUR PEOPLE'S FEELINGS, see, like we got separate washrooms cause you like to spit, and if we said, "Wee yucch, don't spit," it would hurt your feelings and we got separate movies, cause you like to talk back to movie stars and say "amen" and "that's the way" and stuff and that drives us crazy so we might tell you you stink and the only thing I don't get is how come you get paid less for the same job my Mummy says it's because you people don't like money anyway, you don't like TVs and stereos and all that stuff cause what you really like to do is sing and dance. And you don't need money to sing and dance I just… I don't understand why you weren't happy with us, Mummy let you eat as much sugar as you wanted, and we never said anything to you, some days, Mummy says it was up to a quarter-pound, but we know Blacks like sugar so we didn't mind, and we even let you take a silver spoon, I heard Mummy say to her friends, "there goes another silver spoon to Soweto" but she never called the police… and you had your own little room back there, and we even let your husband come once in a while, and that's against the law, Mummy and Daddy could have gone to jail for that, so how come you weren't grateful? How come you stopped singing those Zulu songs in the morning, those pretty songs like that one that was about love and kissing, you stopped singing, and you stopped shampooing my hair, you said I could do it myself, and and your eyes, your eyes used to look at me when I was little they would look at me like they were tickling me just tickling me all the time, like I was special, but they went out, they went out like a light does and you stopped making my cakes every Tuesday, every Tuesday I would ask you to make a pink cake and you would always say, "you ask your mummy" and then you'd make it, but you stopped making them, you told me I as too old for pink cakes, that the pink wasn't real, it was just food colour anyway and then, and then you hardly ever came anymore, and when I saw you that day… when I saw you downtown with your husband and four children all… hanging off your arms, I just couldn't stand it! I wanted to yell at your children and tell them you were mine that you were more mine than theirs because you were with me more much more so you were mine and to let go of you to get off you and I hated the way you looked without your uniform, so brown and plain, not neat and nice anymore, you looked so pretty in your uniform, so pretty, but we didn't even mind when you didn't want to wear it.

We didn't mind, but you were still unhappy, and when I saw you in town looking so dusty and you didn't even introduce me to your kids and one of them, one of them did that rude thing that "Amandilia" thing that means Black power I saw you slap his hand but you didn't say anything, so you must have hated me too, I saw that you hated me too and I'd been so nice to you, I told you my nightmares and you changed my bed when I wet it and now you didn't even like me and it wasn't my fault it wasn't my fault it's just when I asked you why that day, you were cleaning the stove and I said Nellie why… don't you like me anymore, and you said, "you're not a child anymore, Lucy, you're a white person now" and it wasn't my fault and I couldn't help it I couldn't help yelling

KAFFIR, KAFFIR, DO WHAT YOU'RE TOLD, KAFFIR OR I SLAP YOUR BLACK FACE, I SLAP YOUR BLACK FACE AND I KICK YOUR BLACK BELLY I KICK YOUR BLACK BELLY AND KICK IT TILL IT CAVES RIGHT IN AND IT CAN'T HOLD MORE BLACK BABIES EVER AGAIN. NO MORE UGLY BLACK BABIES THAT YOU'LL… that you'll like more than me. Even though I'm ten years old I made you die. I made you go into that march and I made you die. I know that forever. I said I was sorry, I'm sorry, I'm sorry, I'm sorry, I'm sorry, but you never looked at me again. You hated me. But I love you, Nellie, more than Mommy or Daddy and I want you to come back, and sing those songs, and roll mieliepap and be washing the floor in your nice uniform so I can come in and ask you to make a pink cake and your eyes will tickle me. And you will say "yes."

"Yes, I'll make a pink cake…"

david sereda

Salad Days
a thirteen-minute opera

1988
Jackie May: Director
David Sereda: Musical Director
Katherine Duncanson: Bess – the wife betrayed
Stewart Code: Robert – the husband caught
Michael McManus: Daniel – the husband's masseur

Note: The score for Salad Days *is also available.*
For more information, please contact Playwrights Canada Press.

♮•♮

"…my salad days, when I was green in judgement, cold in blood."
—Anthony and Cleopatra, William Shakespeare

An office. BESS enters, looks around. She is beside herself. She sings.

BESS No one here… is it so easy
To wipe him from my life?
A leaf or two of poison
Makes a widow of a wife
I looked in his desk this morning
It's something I never do
I only wanted a paper clip
But after a minute or two
I started to snoop for the fun of it
I dropped a file by mistake
And out fell a photo of you with some whore
So this is it, you little snake
Chew on this, my little snake…
To your trendy salad
I add an extra touch
A leaf or two of poison
And you'll feel a deadly rush
You'll feel your death come rush
Fee-ee-ee-eel your death come rush!

ROBERT & DANIEL *(offstage)* Ahhhh……!

BESS Is that him with his whore?

Who could ask for anything more!
May he die in her embrace
Panic on his purple face
May his death be indiscreet
As they screw like dogs in heat!

ROBERT & DANIEL Oh – oh – oh–!

BESS They're coming out, I must go…

ROBERT & DANIEL Ah – oh…!

BESS They're just coming
He never sounded that alive with me

ROBERT & DANIEL Ohh – ohhh…!

BESS No! I'll kill them with my bare hands
Any jury in the world would understand–
They're right at the door–

She hides.

ROBERT Daniel…

BESS Danielle!

ROBERT What hands you've got Daniel!

BESS Danielle!

ROBERT They've really done the trick…

BESS I want a stick

ROBERT A drink, Daniel

DANIEL No thanks, Mr. Case

ROBERT Call me Rob–

DANIEL No – I never drink on the job.

BESS Danielle's a guy?

ROBERT Ha ha ha ha, ha ha ha ha
Ha ha Ha-ha-ha, Ha ha Ha-ha-ha

DANIEL Why do you laugh?

ROBERT I was just thinking.

DANIEL What were you thinking?

ROBERT Of those photographs.

DANIEL What photographs?

ROBERT You know, those photographs.

BESS & DANIEL No – what photographs?

DANIEL I'm in many many many photographs.

ROBERT Where you dressed as a woman–
  Ha! What a laugh!

DANIEL What a laugh?

BESS What a laugh?

BESS & DANIEL Why a laugh?

ROBERT If I wanted a woman
  I'd go home and screw my wife!

BESS Where's my knife?

ROBERT It's been months,

ROBERT & BESS Months and months since we had a sex life.
  Anything resembling sex. Sex… sex… sex…

DANIEL It's been a slice
  But now I must collect and run

ROBERT Oh, come on now
  C'mere a sec
  You know I take my lunch till one…

BESS Poison's too tidy
  I need a gun.
  A large gun.
  A big one.

ROBERT Just hold me for a moment–

DANIEL Just a moment–

ROBERT & BESS Just a moment–

ROBERT Ah, hold me for a moment–

DANIEL Just a moment–

ALL Just a moment – of peace.

  "Secret Lover."

ROBERT I love him, but	**BESS** I still love him…	**DANIEL** Does he love
I'd be a fool	I am a fool	me…
To say "I love you"	To say "I love you"	Oh, say "I love you"
now	now	now
I need to	Part of me wants to	He needs to
be close to him	be close to him	be close to me
But this never could	But this never could	But this never could
work out	work out	work out

ROBERT You don't care, one way or another No passion in your eyes So I leave you as a secret lover You'll never guess my disguise.	BESS You don't care… passion's gone Passion's gone, I realise So I leave you as a secret lover You'll never guess my disguise.	DANIEL I mustn't care one way or another But this time it's hard to lie So I leave you as a secret lover You'll never guess my disguise.

ALL So I leave you as a secret lover
You'll never guess my disguise.

DANIEL kisses ROBERT on the cheek and heads for inner office door.

ROBERT Come back Daniel, please
I'll cancel everything today.

DANIEL Let's send out for Chinese
Or I'll faint dead away.

ROBERT Here's my salad from the deli
We'll picnic in the nude

DANIEL In your office we'll be private
Our agenda: sex and food.

DANIEL & ROBERT Sex and food, sex and food: sex and food.

DANIEL This is really quite a salad
Things I've never ever seen.

ROBERT Boston, Bibb and romaine
Collards and dandelion greens…

DANIEL And this one?

ROBERT Rapini – no, arugula I mean

DANIEL Arugula?

ROBERT & DANIEL Arugula.
Arugula, aru-u-gula.

BESS I hope you're hungry.

ROBERT Are you hungry?

DANIEL I'm so hungry that it hurts.

ROBERT & DANIEL Sex and food, sex and food: sex and food.

BESS Yes, go and eat your just deserts!

ALL Sex and food, sex and food: sex and food.

ROBERT and DANIEL exit to office.

ROBERT & DANIEL *(off)* Ahhh-ahhh-ahhh!

BESS All passion's gone I realise.

ROBERT & DANIEL Ahhh-ahhh-ahh-ahhh!

BESS The one I love I now despise.

ROBERT & DANIEL Ohh-ohh!

BESS Is that their passion, or poison taking effect now?
A common household plant,
No one will suspect how…
How domestic, but deadly, oh yes,
Diefenbachia, no less–
No one will ever guess
They'll never never guess…

ROBERT staggers out.

ROBERT Call emergency – Bess!
What are you doing here?

BESS I just dropped in to see how the rats are racing dear,
But you look preoccupied so I won't intrude–

ROBERT I can explain–

BESS Why are you semi-nude? Semi-conscious?

DANIEL More like semi-dead.

BESS Like a semi drove over your head.

ROBERT & DANIEL Like a semi drove over our head,
Over our head…

BESS They don't know what hit them

ALL It's over our (their) head.

BESS If I wanted a woman, I'd go home and screw my wife!

DANIEL Look at us dying, in our underwear

ALL It's really pathetic

DANIEL Your wife doesn't care
She did this to you and me.

BESS Surprise, surprise!
Like rats you took the bait
Enough to kill a bear

ROBERT But, Bess…

BESS Don't waste your precious air.
Too late for alibis

Seek help from God above
You're finished like our love.

ROBERT Thi-i-i-is is just a little
Mi-s-understanding
Let's discuss this logically like two mature a–

BESS & DANIEL Shut up!!

BESS You disgust me!

ROBERT You disgust me!

BESS You

BESS & ROBERT Disgust me!
A rat right to the end!

BESS You disgust me!

ROBERT You disgust me!

BESS You

BESS & ROBERT Disgust me!
You die without a friend!

BESS Soon you won't make a sound
Your lying tongue will swell and choke you…
How profound!

BESS & DANIEL A liar, strangled by his lying tongue!

ROBERT Ulgh…. Nngh…. Llgh!

ROBERT suffocates ungracefully on desk.

DANIEL I never lied to you, this is my job
I only pleased him for the money–

BESS Sorry, sonny–

DANIEL If you're sorry then let me live.

BESS What's in it for me?

DANIEL Let me live…

BESS What's in it for me?

DANIEL Oh – your life will be lonely
I give a mean massage
I'd clean your rugs and windows
Live above your garage

BESS You mean you'd be my wife?

DANIEL Smooth the wrinkles from your life

BESS & DANIEL Everyone could use a wife to
   Smooth the wrinkles from your life

DANIEL I'd be your houseboy, bedboy
   Employ me in any way, but let me stay alive

BESS I need a

BESS & DANIEL Houseboy, bedboy, employ me (you) in any way

BESS All right you'll stay.
   And you'll begin today.
   What a coup!
   One rat-trap catches two!
   The rat I can't forgive, but
   The mouse is going to live…

DANIEL Help!

   DANIEL gropes for air.

BESS Oh, my God… where's the antidote?
   Here, quickly, down your throat
   You have a lovely throat…

DANIEL Ohhhh

   "Release from Misery."

BESS Oh release from misery
   New life runs ahead
   One man to be buried
   A new lover for my bed

DANIEL I made a last-ditch deal
   to save my mortal skin
   I chose the bigger rat
   Who did the other in

BESS You think this quite extreme
   Beyond what you would do
   Decency's a dream
   Rage can rip it right in two

   And living with a rat
   You learn a dirty trick or two
   You learn to fight to win

ALL You learn to win…

   ROBERT's ghost rises to join the trio.

   Release from misery
   Do what you have to do
   Goodbye to innocence
   These salad days are through

Release from misery
Do what you have to do
Goodbye to innocence
These salad days are through

These salad days are through
These salad days are through
These salad days are through!

Mary Ellen Mahoney   Jane Thompson's Last Dull Day

1988
Performed at the Spring Arts Fair under the title *An Office Romance*
Joanna MacIntyre: Director
Michael McManus: Sam – a payroll clerk with the Ontario Ministry of Community and Social Services. He's an eccentric: a championship-level chess player, married (until recently) to a yoga teacher.
Tanja Jacobs: Jane – a personnel executive with the same ministry, who, after years of being bored out of her mind, has quit her job for a year of travel.

♯ • ♯

SAM and JANE have been stifling a mutual attraction for years.

JANE enters with a package of green garbage bags and heads to the desk, where she proceeds to get rid of the clutter all over it.

JANE *(to audience)* I once bought a package of these things and discovered only *after* the eight weeks' worth of oozing gunk from my fridge was all over the hall carpet that somebody had forgotten to sew up the bottoms. That was a black day.

She briskly continues the purge, opening a drawer, and pulling out a three-inch stack of cards.

Oh my God, these birthday cards, they've been accumulating for decades, I just can't seem to throw them out. *(blithely tosses them into the bag)* In case you were unaware, these are my final hours with the Personnel Branch of the Ministry of Community and Social Services, and I really appreciate you being here because I want to ritualise them somehow, these last moments. We may be in trouble because any ritual in Western culture involves cake, and there *was* one lying around here earlier today– *(She looks around the office.)* well, I don't mean lying around on its side – I mean it was sitting dejectedly on a cardboard thing but, oh hell, Marlene took it home for Pete the pig, I'll bet. That poor guy has finished off more of our office carbohydrates than I care to think about. Well, that's too bad. But you didn't come here for cake anyway; you came to check the pulse of a civil servant and to discover just exactly where those social service tax dollars might be going. Well, forget all that, forget it, forget it, because this is my office, and my ritual, in which you are most graciously participating, and I thank you, but look around, folks, who's the High Priestess here: me. Now, momentarily you will lay eyes, and that's all, upon the four-year object of my unexpressed passion, Sam Nolan from Payroll. He's married to a yoga teacher named Karen who makes him sleep with crystals under his pillow. That explains the dents in his cranium that I've noticed recently – they will likely be undetectable from your perspective, but I wanted you to know they were there.

SAM *(entering, carrying some forms)* You're in here for life if you don't sign these termination papers, Ms Thompson.

JANE Oh, please, no; capital punishment would be so much more humane–

SAM *(pulling out a rope)* Righty-ho! *(He leaps onto her chair and searches for a hook to string it up to.)* Not the latest method, and we may have some trouble with your last meal, but with such short notice– *(pulls a plastic gun out of his other pocket)* actually, would you mind stepping up against the wall? My aim isn't that good–

JANE *(to audience)* These are manly gestures in the impotent atmosphere of the provincial government, wouldn't you agree? *(Sam fiddles with the trigger. She speaks to Sam, reacting with feigned alarm.)* Put that thing away!

SAM *(hopping off the chair)* Certainly. *(indicating forms)* Now if you'll just–

JANE What is the mild-mannered Sam Nolan doing with an instrument of death in his possession?!

SAM Well, you just never know when a field manager is going to step over the line – want his cheque a day early, insist on her overtime without a shred of evidence for it–

JANE *(to audience)* Yes, you wouldn't believe what goes on around here– *(to SAM)* Well, fortunately I'm not going to have to deal with those morons anymore, thank God. *(to audience)* I'm working up to telling him something meaningful and tragic–

SAM Shiite extremists ought to be a pleasant change.

JANE Sam, I'm going to *Europe*. *(to audience)* He's *insanely* jealous.

SAM Well, just remember not to wave your rosary in a Belfast pub–

JANE Uh, just to set the record straight, I'm not in the habit of waving my rosary… it's still in the little case my mother gave me when I was twelve.

SAM Stop! Stop it – you get weird when you talk about your mother – you sag. Stand up! Shoulders back!

JANE *(to audience)* He's right. He knows me too well.

SAM All right, let's balance those chakras.

JANE Oh GOD, Sam, what happened to the good old days when you spurned all Karen's hippie-dippie faux-Hindu bunk?

SAM *(standing behind her, raising her arms over her head)* Up! Palms together – boy, I can tell by looking that your kundalini is just completely out of whack–

JANE My kundalini's just fine, thank you! *(to audience)* I know, I know, but don't tell me you haven't done the ridiculous in the face of hopeless, blind desire…

SAM And reach–

JANE *(to SAM)* Oh *why* do I allow myself to be manipulated like this!

SAM Because you're starved for human contact. And lean to the right–

JANE *(testily)* Whoa, whoa there, buddy; let's just clear this up right now: I am not starved for human contact. *(to audience)* I allow myself ten flagrant lies a year. *(to SAM) Au contraire*, I have *gorged* myself on human contact – it's unavoidable when you're in personnel. I'm going on a fast.

SAM Well, good for your intestinal tract. Now left… and inhale the Prahna!

JANE God help me. Ah, Sam, you are not the rabid cynic I once knew and loved!

SAM Yes, I am. I only do this to torment you. Now back–

JANE *(to SAM)* I mean, I know you and Karen had nothing whatsoever in common, but I must say it was big of you to take up yoga when you could have just given her insult training.

SAM I did give her insult training…

JANE And–

SAM She hurt my feelings…. And down. *(He bends and puts his palms on the floor.)*

JANE *(to audience)* Well, he's sensitive. *(She bends.)* You could've taught her to play chess. Ow! Oh, God, these muscles have been dormant since my last pair of lace-up shoes—black oxfords—Loretto Abbey, circa 1934.

SAM Hmm, so attractive in size ten.

JANE *(standing bolt upright – to audience)* All right, which one of you told him my shoe size?! Come *on*, a little compassion, look at these things! Oh hell, so much for a perfect poignant parting moment.

SAM Get back down here! You've just wreaked havoc on your sacral chakra!

JANE NO! I don't care about my friggin *shockras*; right now all I'm thinking about is the size of my godforsaken monstrous *feet*!

SAM *(his nose is not far from her instep)* Jane, your feet aren't that big. *(He slowly returns to a standing position, gracefully, vertebrae by vertebrae.)*

JANE Oh, yes they are! And they're flat, too, they're flat as a coupla pancakes, only not as lumpy as the ones I make. *(slips one foot out of her shoe)* Well, no they are. They *are* lumpy.

SAM They're slender. They're aristocratic.

JANE Aristocratic?! They're grape tramplers!

SAM *(looking into her eyes)* You have lovely feet, Jane.

JANE *(returning the gaze)* I… I do? I… uh… where are those termination papers? *(to audience, wincing)* That was it, that's as good as it gets, and I blew it, rats, geez.

SAM On your desk.

JANE Right.

SAM I'll be at my grindstone. *(He exits.)*

JANE *(picking up the forms, still stunned by what just almost happened)* It's amazing how one can yearn, hopelessly, for years, for a moment like that only to have some inner demon sabotage it the minute it takes shape in three dimensions. *(pulling herself together)* Well, no point in throwing myself into the arms of unavailable payroll clerks. *(yelling down the hall so SAM can hear her)* What's a person of your intellectual stature doing in payroll with the provincial government anyway, Sam? God, if I can get myself out of this dump, so can you! Maybe if you didn't spend every spare second on a yoga mat or on your burgeoning chess career *(checks her appearance in a compact, reacts with distaste, and hastily applies lipstick to the left half of her upper lip)* maybe you could–

SAM *(entering)* How can you refer to the noblest of games in that disdainful tone, Ms Thompson? How?

JANE *(pause)* Because I see you throwing your life away, Sam. *(She hesitates, then signs the forms and hands them to him.)*

SAM *(icily)* Well, good; signed and sealed. Have a great trip– *(exits)* and feel free to finish your make-up job.

JANE *(wipes the lipstick off; calls through the door)* Sam! Wait – all I meant was that you should get out of this dead zone too, and it just drives me nuts to see a mad genius like you squandering your best years in this bloody salt mine when you could be—I don't know—coming to Europe with me! *(horrified that she's said this out loud)* I mean if you didn't have other responsibilities… which I know you do, good God, what am I saying–

SAM *(enters, pulling a plane ticket out of his inside jacket pocket)* Would you identify this document, please?

JANE It's a… plane ticket–

SAM Very good. Destination?

JANE Uh… Amsterdam…

SAM Quite right. Date of departure?

JANE April 20th—that's this Friday—that's when I'm going– *(to audience)* I'm so glad you're watching this – it proves that it's actually happening– *(to SAM)* Oh God, what about Karen?

SAM She moved in with her Rolfer three days before Christmas.

JANE You're kid– *(He plucks the ticket out of her hand.)*

SAM Thanks to my burgeoning chess career, I've been invited to a tournament on April 20th – something at some Dutch hotel and since, I gather, you're going to be in the vicinity at the time I thought I might arrange something with you over a tulip bulb unless you have any objections– *(exiting)* Have your people confirm with my people in the morning. *Groetjes!*

JANE *(slightly stunned)* Yeah, ccchuchass...! *(to audience)* That's Dutch for gorgeous, or hello, or something.... Uh, well, thank you again for witnessing the proceedings. I must say there were times when I forgot you were even there, which is hard to do in a room this size, but somehow I just got so involved in my – "Have your people confirm with my people in the morning..." the morning? That'll take fifteen hours! What am I supposed to do in the meantime – grow an amaryllis?! *(suddenly gathering up green garbage bags and briefcases and anything else she's left lying around and calling)* The morning? You bonehead, Sam, that's a whole night away! *(exits, bungling with bags; reappears in the doorway, to audience)* Oh, I'd be happy to attend any of your rituals– *(Out of nowhere SAM's mouth is on JANE's, cutting off the emission of all sound, and in a flash he's pulled her through the door and shut it firmly behind them.)*

Susan Coyne *Typistry*

1989
Jackie May: Director
Caroline Gillis: Ashley
Chick Reid: Serena

¤ • ¤

An office. SERENA enters and closes the door, leaning her head against it for a moment. Then she turns briskly and sits down at her desk, rolls a piece of paper into her typewriter, and prepares to type. She lowers her fingers onto the keyboard. The sudden noise makes her jump.

SERENA Damn. Damn, damn, damn.

She goes over to the nearest filing cabinet, searching for something.

W... w... wh... whi... white-out.

She fixes the mistake, blowing on the white-out to hurry up the process. She tries again, but stops after a few words and applies more white-out.

Serena, you idiot. What the hell was I thinking? "Yes, Mr. Finlay, of course, I'll do it myself before I leave, it's not problem at *all*, Mr. Finlay." Oh, God what a mess. I need a Kleenex.

She opens the filing cabinet.

E... F... G, H... K. Kleenex.

Suddenly, the door flies open. A young woman is standing there, a wild look in her eyes. She sees the typewriter and makes straight for it.

ASHLEY Oh thank God. (*She snatches SERENA's paper out and rolls another in.*) Sorry, this is urgent. Roll it up, roll it up. Here it comes, here it comes!...

She types as she speaks.

"Ode to the TTC:
Beautiful tapeworm
In the guts of the city
Swallowing and swallowing
The subway patrons..."

She sits back and shakes the tension out of her fingers.

Whew!...

She notices SERENA.

Oh, hey, backspace, roll it down. Hi. I'm Ashley. I'm the temp.

SERENA You're the *temp*?

ASHLEY Oh, this is very nice. Smith-Corona. Silk ribbon. You know, I can never find the pitch-lever on these things.

SERENA May I see your time-sheets, please?

ASHLEY Sure. Here.

She hands SERENA a sheaf of papers.

SERENA Well. These seem to be in order.... So–

ASHLEY Ashley.

SERENA You're pretty fast on that thing.

ASHLEY Used to be. I'm down to 105.

SERENA *Words per minute???* Oh, my God. Well! I'm Serena. I'm the permanent secretary here.

ASHLEY Hiya.

SERENA I – I – don't know what they told you but I am planning – I am taking a short – vacation, this week and next and so you will be–

ASHLEY Taking your place?

SERENA Occupying this office in my absence. Temporarily.

ASHLEY swivels to take a look around.

ASHLEY Great. Great space…

SERENA Thank you. I like to keep it neat. What – What are you doing.

ASHLEY is taking some things out of her bag: a mug, some tea, a plaque, several small trophies, a plant. She sets these down on a set of files laid out on the desk.

My files!

ASHLEY Oh, jeez, I'm sorry. *(She picks them up.)* No harm! Oh, look! These are beautiful. Alphabetical, double-cut, colour-coded. These go in here?

She opens the filing cabinet.

SERENA Please! I'll do that.

ASHLEY Sure. Hey, you know your kettle's in here?

SERENA Ashley, I would appreciate it if you'd leave the files alone while I'm gone. I've been here for fifteen years and I'm the only one who knows her way around them. Promise me. If – *when* I come back I… I need to know that everything will be in the same place.

ASHLEY No problem. Filing is not my forte.

SERENA It's not?

ASHLEY Naw. Too linear.

SERENA Well, filing is *my* forte.

But ASHLEY is not listening. She is typing another poem.

ASHLEY "White-out! White-out!?
Black keys, like tombstones
in the Liquid Paper meltdown…"

She sits back and puts her head on one side.

What do you think? Too naked?

SERENA Is this how you usually begin a new job?

ASHLEY No. No, it's just lately – I've had this thing with my fingers. Outta control. I go home the end of the day, they won't stop twitching—*typing*—I can't stop. I type on everything I touch – trees, parked cards, doughnut shop counters. Memos, requisitions, and now poems. Covering the city in words – only it's all invisible.

She looks at SERENA.

I'm thinking it's stress-related – you know? The transience of my life, so temporary. Maybe it's time to settle down. Find a place like this. Go permanent. Like you.

SERENA Like me! Well, I have to tell you, you'll never be a permanent secretary without top-notch filing skills.

ASHLEY Yeah, I know… I was gonna give up. But then I found this book!

She fishes it out of her bag.

Fundamental Filing Practices. Listen to this: "The office is the nerve centre of the business office and files are its memory." Isn't that great?

SERENA manages a small smile.

SERENA "Files that are cherished accumulate wisdom."

ASHLEY You've read it!

SERENA Of course.

ASHLEY And do you?

SERENA Do I what?

ASHLEY Cherish your files?

SERENA I don't have feelings about my work. It's too distracting. I have to make a thousand decisions a day. If I'm filing, which folders should I use? Manila, kraft, jute or pressboard? If it's a retrieval, which system is it under? Alphabetical, subject, numerical or geographical, open shelf, soundex or pendaflex. I've got a room in there full of spindle and tilt files, down the hall I've got another with boxes and cards. There are seven floors of lateral files in this building, twelve floors of hanging files and a penthouse full of accordions.

ASHLEY Whoa. This whole building is full of files?

SERENA Of course. This is the Memory Bank. We're a warehouse for the company's inactive files.

ASHLEY I see.

SERENA *The Morgue.* That's what they call it down at Head office. They think that's pretty funny. They all look down on me, see, think anyone could do what I do.

ASHLEY Man, I know what you mean. I go from job to job, no one knows who I am, what I do. Look at these trophies. The Remington Cup, the Legal Documents Festival, the Medical Records Open. No one cares. To them I'm just the temp. It wears you down…. Aw, don't get me wrong. I love the office. Hell, I practically grew up in one. My mama was a steno and I spent mosta my summers hanging out by the secretarial pool. Hey!

She is hit with another wave of inspiration.

ASHLEY "Pencils basking in the fluorescent glare?
An eraser wiggles its fat pink body?
Time gasps like a slaughtered paperweight."

She sighs. Notices a jagged fingernail and retrieves an emery board from her bag.

You don't type much, I take it?

SERENA I type!

ASHLEY Sorry, I just assumed…. With those nails…

SERENA, clearly agitated, picks up the phone and files it under P.

SERENA I type all my own labels and captions and envelopes. And memos, I do memos. Yipes. Memo!

She searches the desk for the memo she was working on earlier.

ASHLEY You know, you seem kinda tense. Maybe this vacation is just what you need.

SERENA What do you know about it? Huh? *Temp?* This place is my *home*. This job is all I *know*. And now they want to take it away from me.

ASHLEY What? Who does?

SERENA Who sent you? Huh? Finlay? *JoAnne?* It's not enough you're going to replace me, you have to torment me first?

ASHLEY I don't know what you're talking about.

SERENA Oh, don't you? Snooping around in here, showing off. You know, typing skills aren't everything.

ASHLEY Okay, okay—

SERENA I've got lots of other qualities. Like loyalty. Neatness. An incredible tolerance for boredom.

> *She has got the memo back in the typewriter. She stares at it a moment, then tries to start typing it up again. Suddenly, she slumps.*

ASHLEY Serena, what is it?

SERENA Nothing. I just have to…

> *She tries again.*

SERENA I can't…. It's no use! I've forgotten it all. Where to put the margins, when to tab, how to double-space. I can't do it anymore. I've lost it!

ASHLEY What are you saying?

SERENA It's gone! Gone from the old Memory Bank. I've looked under typing-dash-skills, under writing-dash-type, under printing-dash-machine. It isn't there!

ASHLEY I don't believe it. You can't just forget how to type.

SERENA It's true. Watch!

> *She tries to type and fails.*

Hopeless!

> *She slumps over the machine.*

ASHLEY It's impossible…

> *SERENA moans.*

Listen to me, Serena…. Remember what the book said? "The office is the nerve centre of the business, office files are its memory."

SERENA So?

ASHLEY So, what does that make the typewriter…?

SERENA Who cares?

ASHLEY You do, Serena, I know you do…. I'll tell you what the typewriter is. The typewriter is the organ that every business needs. Day after day it pumps out memos, letters, transfers, and requisition forms that flow through a corporation and keep it alive. It's the heart, Serena, and yes, the *soul* of the organisation. So you can't forget how to type unless you've forgotten how to *feel* and you haven't forgotten how to feel.

SERENA Yes. I have. I'm numb. Numb.

ASHLEY No. No, you're not. I know you're feeling something right now. Pain. Loss. Betrayal. Go on! Put your fingers on the keyboard. Type it out!

SERENA I can't. I'm afraid.

ASHLEY   I'll help you.

> *She places SERENA's fingers on the keys.*

There. You're on the home row. Feel that?

> *SERENA looks with wonder at the keys.*

SERENA   *The home row.*

ASHLEY   That's right. Now I want you to start, very slowly, with a gentle FJ, just two little fingers… F, then J…. Good Serena! F, now J… F space J space F space J space…

SERENA   *(with great effort)* F space J space F space J space…

ASHLEY   Good! Now try DK

SERENA   D space K space D space K space.

ASHLEY   You're doing great! S space L space

SERENA   S space L space.

ASHLEY   Serena! Look at you! You're typing! Keep going! Now, try the shift key…. Good. *Good.* Keep it light and steady. Caress the keyboard. Wrists down! Shoulders back.

> *SERENA is growing in confidence and speed.*

Now, I'm going to start dictating, Serena. Stay with me, now…. Dear sir comma new line tab… in regards to your letter of August the seventh new paragraph tab space space… I will be in Denver May twelve and thirteen semi-colon new paragraph and would be glad to meet with you at a mutually convenient hour to continue our discussions with regard to our new product line full stop respectfully yours comma J period A period Finlay

> *ASHLEY begins picking up her things and packing them in her bag.*

Now you try one.

> *SERENA tackles the memo from before.*

SERENA   Dear sir comma please be advised that as of June first my secretary…. Hmmmm hmmmm hmmmm. Yours truly comma yours *very* truly comma yours sincerely comma kindest regards comma *warmest* wishes!

> *She pulls the paper out of the typewriter in triumph. ASHLEY slips quietly out the door. SERENA puts another piece of paper in the typewriter.*

"Life is a blank sheet?
Of 84 bright?
We type
Without carbons ?
Changing ribbons as we go."

> *She sits back, looks around and sighs.*

Don Hannah
The Wall in the Garden

1989
Andy McKim: Director
Carole Galloway: Lisa I
Janese Kane: Lisa II

The Wall in the Garden is for Janese Kane and June Garba,
with many thanks for their stories.

¤•¤

Although both actors are playing the same woman, it is not essential that they look alike or be dressed alike. The fact that this is a piece about one white South African woman should be made clear in the direction. Both actors speak the words that are <u>underlined</u>.

LISA 1 I spent the entire summer of 1956 in a tree,

LISA 2 A jacaranda tree. There was a crook in the trunk where I could sit,

LISA 1 and a limb stretched out just above it

LISA 2 like a little shelf. We could balance <u>the tea set</u> on it. My best friend

LISA 1 Helen and I felt

LISA 2 <u>very private</u> up there,

LISA 1 <u>very safe</u>. Of course, our mothers were probably always watching from the back of the house, but

LISA 2 we didn't think about that. We pretended that we were very alone. Helen had very blonde hair

LISA 1 and I adored her. She decided who would pour the tea and who we would have over. She was eight that Christmas,

LISA 2 a year older than me, and she got crushes on people before I even heard of them. Her mother took her to the Bioscope

LISA 1 where she saw Cary Grant, so we always had to have him over. When we got hungry,

LISA 2 I would climb down and pick fruit from one of my mother's trees. We'd throw the pips towards the

LISA 1 big wall by the maids' quarters. Everything was always in bloom and there were

LISA 2 thunderstorms over the mountains. On the days when Helen didn't come over, I climbed up in my tree

LISA 1 and just sat looking around me. From up there, my whole world was spread out

LISA 2 like a big green map. The house, with myna birds on the red tile of the roof,

LISA 1 the fruit trees, the aloes. I could see over the walls that

LISA 2 went all around the yard. The street beyond the concrete fence in front,

LISA 1 where Daddy opened the gate every morning

LISA 2 and drove to his big office downtown in Johannesburg.

LISA 1 There was the park beyond the street,

LISA 2 and the brick wall in the back,

LISA 1 and just past it,

LISA 2 the dark, flat roof where Miriam lived

LISA 1 and the others…

LISA 2 Daniel walking about slowly, watering the yard in the shade…

LISA 1 If I was up there long enough, everyone would forget about me.

LISA 2 Sometimes I could hear them talking about me.

LISA 1 Sometimes Miriam said nice things about me to Daniel because she

LISA 2 knew I was listening. She teased me to make me

LISA 1 laugh out loud. Once a mossie flew into the tree and sat on a branch right by my hand.

LISA 2 I sat very still.

LISA 1 Mommy's friends were always dropping by and I could hear them laughing *(LISA 2 laughs.)* from the other side of the garden.

LISA 2 People were always dropping by. They would sit in the little white chairs under the fruit trees and

LISA 1 drink all those pretty things,

LISA 2 mysterious things.

LISA 1 Gin fizzes.

LISA 2 There was always lemonade for me and Miriam squeezed orange juice, but what Helen and I loved most was Coca-Cola.

LISA 1 Miriam too.

LISA 2 Canada is not my home.

LISA 1 I miss the sun on my skin. The dry air, the clean air,

LISA 2   the sun on my skin. The rain was so soft and warm that of course
LISA 1   you walked in it. And there was so much time,
LISA 2   all the time in the world
LISA 1   to drop in on people and <u>relax</u> and drink things.
LISA 2   Of course, you never went out by yourself. And everyone had a gun.
LISA 1   But there was so much time
LISA 2   to drop in on people and relax and go camping in the mountains,
LISA 1   go to the beaches. Helen's mother and my mother on their towels calling to us,
LISA 2   laughing,
LISA 1   So much time.
LISA 2   but then, servants give you time.
LISA 1   We were very good to them. Miriam loved me.
LISA 2   She made my lunch every day. Sometimes we ate <u>mieliepap</u>–
LISA 1   you didn't eat it with a spoon, you used your hands. It was wonderful.
LISA 2   She had her own little girl, but I never saw her.
LISA 1   Sometimes Miriam went home to visit her.
LISA 2   She took the <u>bus</u>.
LISA 1   One day Miriam took me for a long walk and we went sliding down the gold sand at the mine dumps.
LISA 2   The yellow light was coming through the window of my room that evening.
LISA 1   Yellow sand, soft and warm. All warm on my legs.
LISA 2   The sun was just setting behind the wall in our garden.
LISA 1   Miriam laughed when she shook the sand out of her clothes.
LISA 2   I could see it glinting on the pieces of glass that were stuck there, all jagged and sharp.
LISA 1   "Shake it, shake it," she laughed and we wiggled our hips like dancers.
LISA 2   I saw his shadow first, stretching long over the top of the wall
LISA 1   Miriam hugged me and told me I would like her little girl.
LISA 2   his shadow across the dark green of the grass.
LISA 1   She called me "Darling. Lisa, my Darling."
LISA 2   He jumped into the flowers
LISA 1   Her little girl lived far away,

LISA 2   I could tell from the way he moved that he had torn his skin on the glass.
LISA 1   Far away, she said, with her grandmother.
LISA 2   Suddenly there was shouting from the front of the house.
LISA 1   I thought how wonderful it would be to live with my grammy.
LISA 2   He started to run towards the window, then he saw me
LISA 1   Presents all the time, never having to finish my food…
LISA 2   He was shining, blue black and shining.
LISA 1   Miriam smelled different, all warm and strong.
LISA 2   His torn pants were covered with blood, his shirt was soaking.
LISA 1   I asked her if she would let me play with her little girl.
LISA 2   Mommy and Daddy were in my brother's room.
LISA 1   "No," she said. She said, "No."
LISA 2   My brother had the measles, he'd been crying all day.
LISA 1   "Miriam, why not?"
LISA 2   The man saw me.
LISA 1   "Because she is far, far away."
LISA 2   I did not know him.
LISA 1   "Can I go see her?"
LISA 2   He was running towards the window and he saw me.
LISA 1   "She can play with me and Helen."
LISA 2   He turned and ran towards the garden.
LISA 1   "No." Miriam said, "No."
LISA 2   He jumped up and caught a branch of the jacaranda and swung himself up into my tree.
LISA 1   She said "no" and we went back home.
LISA 2   I ran through the house to the back door and out into the garden.
LISA 1   We didn't talk all the way home.
LISA 2   There were policemen with knopkieries and sjamboks.
LISA 1   Miriam sang a little song. Very, very quiet.
LISA 2   Daddy came running out the door behind me.
LISA 1   We didn't talk all the way home.
LISA 2   I thought Daddy would be in trouble. I thought we would all be in trouble. The policemen were running about the garden. "Where is he?" they shouted,

"Have you seen him?" I thought we would all be in big trouble. "He's in the tree!" I said. "He's climbed up into my tree!" Two policemen climbed the tree and the threw him down and dragged him into the front yard. He didn't move. They dragged him like he was a big sack. I thought, "Why isn't he screaming? If I was him, I'd be screaming for help." They made a circle around him and hit him with sjamboks and knopkieries. Nobody ever told me who that man was and why they were chasing him. I didn't want to ask.

LISA 1 I was afraid.

LISA 2 One time my mother was talking to Miriam, Mommy was talking to her about

LISA 1 her family.

LISA 2 About

LISA 1 the government. We all hated the government.

LISA 2 Mommy said,

LISA 1 "Miriam, if there was a revolution, would you kill us all?"

LISA 2 Miriam said,

LISA 1 "Madam, if I didn't, they would kill me."

Tom McCamus — *Apoplexy*

1989
Lloy Coutts: Director
Don Adams: Matthew
Stephen Ouimette: Warren

¤ • ¤

> *MATTHEW—late forties—chases WARREN—early thirties—into a washroom. MATTHEW, livid, begins to pace outside the door.*

MATTHEW This is it… this… this… this is it. They can't do this. They think they can… but no… they always think… or they don't think… this is it. This is the point. Well… there's got to be a time. They never think anyone's going to… you see… they never think. Again. Well… it's come to this… this time.

> *WARREN sticks his head out.*

GET BACK IN THERE!

> *WARREN quickly ducks back into the washroom.*

And you DON'T come out…. EVER!

WARREN I can't. There's no fucking way out of here.

MATTHEW I'm not listening to you. I'm not listening to a word you're saying. Because most of it is filth. And most of it… you don't know what you're saying!

WARREN I don't know what you're talking about, man.

MATTHEW Shut up!

WARREN Why are you doing this?

MATTHEW SHUT UUUUUUUP!

> *There is a silence, with the exception of MATTHEW's panting as he stares at the closed door. He waits.*

WARREN Look man, if I did anything…

MATTHEW NA NA NA NA NA NA NA NA NA NA…

> *Pause.*

WARREN I think that…

MATTHEW NA NA NA NA…

> *Pause.*

WARREN Will you just…

MATTHEW NA NA NA NA…

> *Silence.*

WARREN I'm sorry.

> *Pause.*
>
> I'm going to come out now.

MATTHEW Try it and you're dead.

> *Pause.*
>
> I'm waiting…. Not so tough, eh? When it comes to meeting somebody face-to-face.
>
> *Pause.*

WARREN Listen man… I'm at a loss here. I've obviously done something to offend you, and I don't know what the fuck it is.

MATTHEW Filth. You are filth. You are all filth.

WARREN There's only one of us in here, mister. Perhaps…

MATTHEW I know how many are in there. I chased you in there, didn't I?

WARREN Yes, you did. You did that. And now that we're on the subject, I'd be interested to know why.

MATTHEW You really don't know? You don't know what it is that you did?

WARREN No, I don't.

MATTHEW No, I guess you wouldn't. Why should you? You don't think. Your type never thinks. But that's no excuse, buddy. That's what makes you dangerous. I've been waiting for years to get one of you in the open. So I can tell you exactly what I think. That's right: think. Because, unlike you, I exercise my brain. But all it takes is one stupid punk with mush for brains and I'm wiped off the face of the earth. And that's why you're in there and I'm out here.

WARREN Okay. It's a bit clearer. But I'm still foggy on the particulars.

MATTHEW Don't get smart with me.

WARREN Sorry.

MATTHEW You see, I've been waiting for years…

WARREN Yeah, I know, you've been waiting for years to get me in the open. Well let me tell you something, there are no washroom doors in the open, okay? So why don't you let me come out and then the two of us can talk calmly, man-to-man.

MATTHEW You're not a man. You are SCUM!

WARREN Okay, we're not ready for calm yet. You mind if I ask you a question?

MATTHEW What?

WARREN Are you married?

MATTHEW What's that got to do with anything?

WARREN I thought maybe I'd fucked your wife or something. Inadvertently, of course.

MATTHEW You probably would have. If I had a wife you would have done that too.

WARREN So, it's not jealousy. You just don't like the way I look? Right? Is that it?

MATTHEW No. I can't believe this. I can't believe you don't know what you did.

WARREN All I know is… I turn on this street with you right on my tail, leaning on the horn, yelling "fuck you" out the window. Then you try to run me over and chase me into this bathroom. Will you just tell me what I did?

MATTHEW I didn't say "fuck you." I don't swear.

WARREN Oh, for Christ's sake!

MATTHEW You thought I did, because those are the only words your tiny little brain can understand.

WARREN It sounded like "fuck you."

MATTHEW It wasn't. I don't say those words.

WARREN Okay, you don't. I don't care.

MATTHEW That's right, you don't. That's your problem.

WARREN It's one of many. But my big problem, right now, is my inability to understand why I'm in this washroom.

MATTHEW You really don't know?

WARREN Okay, I admit it. You weaseled it out of me, I don't know.

MATTHEW I'm going to have to tell you, aren't I?

WARREN It would help.

MATTHEW Not only do you threaten my life; I've got to tell you that you did it.

WARREN I threatened your life?

MATTHEW You threatened to take away my life, and not only that, you threatened countless other lives along with it.

WARREN Oh that!

MATTHEW And don't think I'm letting you off the hook because you happen to think this is a minor infraction. Because it's more than that. It's the reason our city is falling down around our ears. It's an erosion of the basic principles – the foundation. Are you aware of what that is? Have you any idea of how important a solid foundation is in maintaining the quality of life we enjoy here? I don't think so. I don't think you give a tinker's damn about that. To people like you, Toronto the Good means Toronto the Dull. Well let me tell you something… move to New York if that's what you want! You want excitement? All those little rules get in the way of your personal freedom, eh? You're a big-city boy, you want the freedom to do what you want when you want. Well that happens when you want to get down Bloor Street as fast as possible but some free-thinker's parked his car in a no parking zone at rush hour? Try keeping your cool then, mister. Right?… You see in my own way I'm trying to do some good here. I'm trying to rebuild the foundation. But it won't work unless people like you listen to people like me. So are you listening? Am I getting through?

There is a pause, then WARREN cautiously sticks his head out.

Well, it's about time. Get out here.

WARREN hesitantly moves out of the washroom.

Okay, let's have it.

WARREN And what's that?

MATTHEW The apology.

WARREN Uh…. Before we go any further, I think there's something you should know about me. I'm kind of stupid, slow on the uptake? So most of the stuff you've been talking about hasn't really clicked in. And before you punch me out, or whatever it is you plan on doing, I think you should spell out exactly what it is I did.

MATTHEW I just told you.

WARREN You did? It must have gone over my head. Could you put it to me in layman's terms?

MATTHEW Scissors and knives.

WARREN What?

MATTHEW Scissors and knives. What do they do?

WARREN They kill people.

MATTHEW That too.

WARREN Uh huh.

WARREN starts to inch away.

MATTHEW What are you doing?

WARREN I'm moving away from you. You're dangerous. I don't like danger.

MATTHEW Stay where you are.

WARREN No, I'm going to my office, where I work, this was my lunch hour… but hey, that's not important. What is important is that if you so much as look at me the wrong way, I'll have the cops down here so fast you won't know what hit you.

MATTHEW I already called them.

WARREN What?

MATTHEW I called the police. They should be here very soon. They are the law, and if you choose to break that law you must pay the consequences.

WARREN You didn't call them. I would have heard you.

MATTHEW I called them from my car.

WARREN You have a car phone? You're more dangerous than I thought.

WARREN starts to move away.

MATTHEW Just stay where you are.

WARREN Why?

MATTHEW Uh…

WARREN Tough question, huh?

WARREN starts to move.

MATTHEW Don't move!

WARREN Fuck you!

He tries it again.

MATTHEW I said don't move!

WARREN Try and stop me.

WARREN starts to move, MATTHEW makes a jerky movement towards him. WARREN, startled, makes the same kind of jerky move back.

This is ridiculous! I'm not afraid of you.

MATTHEW I'm not afraid of you, punk!

WARREN Oh yeah? Then what's that wet spot on the floor?

WARREN screams and moves away. MATTHEW jumps in front of him and screams. WARREN jumps back, screaming and flailing his arms about his head. MATTHEW is doing the same thing.

MATTHEW HOLD IT!

They both stop.

Let's just calm down.

They calm down.

There's a simple solution to this.

WARREN Yeah? What is it?

MATTHEW You apologise to me.

WARREN I don't think I can do that.

MATTHEW And why is that?

WARREN YOU HAVEN'T FUCKING TOLD ME WHAT I DID TO YOU!

MATTHEW Don't you dare talk to me like that. You know what you did.

WARREN I don't! There're lots of things I don't know. Like, I don't even know your name.

MATTHEW It's Matthew. Wait a minute! Why do you want to know my name?

WARREN I don't really. You can take it back.

MATTHEW Don't think you can scare me. I know what your plan is. First you find my name, then my address, and then you terrorise my house because I humiliated you.

WARREN No I…

MATTHEW Well think on this, punk. I've got the finest collection of guns this side of the Don Valley.

WARREN Hey, wait a minute…

MATTHEW And I'm an excellent shot.

WARREN There's no need for threats.

MATTHEW Shut up, pig!

WARREN I'm not a pig, I'm a person! And I'm a pissed-off person. I've been pretty calm up until now, but I'm ready to fuckin lose it unless you… you fucking asshole… you let me have my say!

MATTHEW Watch your language, buddy.

WARREN screams.

WARREN You don't have ears, right? Is that it? If somebody says something, it just sort of bounces off your head. Except for the bad words, they kind of stick, like all over your face and up your nose and… stuff. Fuck!

Pause.

MATTHEW Hey, buddy. You okay?

WARREN No, I'm not.

MATTHEW I believe you, okay? You don't know what you did. So I'll tell you…

WARREN No, no! Don't tell me! I wanna guess.

MATTHEW Don't get smart with me. I'm telling you. It…

WARREN NA NA NA NA NA NA…

MATTHEW ALL RIGHT! GUESS! But when you get it… I want an apology. And I want a good one. And I don't want any more games.

>   *WARREN, slightly manic by now, starts to mime driving a car.*

WARREN Okay, I'm driving down Dupont. I'm coming from downtown, where I've just picked up a nice lasagna for my lunch, which is now lying upside down on the floor of my car, getting cold. Anyway, I'm driving defensive, I'm in no hurry. I'm letting the assholes use me for slalom practice. I don't yell, as a matter of fact I'm whistling. I'm whistling a very nice tune that I made up all by myself in my head. I get to bathurst, I stop, even though the light is green. I look both ways and then I turn right. No sooner am I around the corner than Matthew is on my tail. I don't know his name is Matthew yet, I find that out later. I continue up Bathurst Street for about a block…

MATTHEW You've gone too far.

WARREN No, it's only a block.

MATTHEW You've already done it.

WARREN You mean the thing?

MATTHEW That's right.

WARREN Okay, okay, we're getting warmer. Back up, back up… Bathurst… Dupont… downtown… lasagna. Lasagna! I bought the lasagna from you. Now I remember. I forgot to pay you! Holy shit, why didn't you say so!

MATTHEW That's not it.

WARREN Oh. Okay, it's after that?

MATTHEW Right.

WARREN While I'm driving along Dupont.

MATTHEW No.

WARREN And Bathurst is too far?

MATTHEW Yup.

WARREN So it's got to be… when… I… turned the corner.

MATTHEW Yes.

WARREN Okay, wait a sec, I'll get it.

MATTHEW God, you're thick.

WARREN I turned the corner. What's wrong with that? Did I hit somebody?

MATTHEW No.

WARREN I know. I clipped the corner too close and started off a nuclear reaction.

MATTHEW You're pathetic.

WARREN A little smaller than that, huh? Okay… I'll get it…

MATTHEW You cut me off.

> *Pause.*

WARREN What?

MATTHEW You cut me off. When you turned the corner you cut right in front of me.

> *Pause.*

WARREN That's all?

MATTHEW That's all! Haven't you been listening to a word I said. The foundations of our society, that's what we are talking about here, I thought I made that clear.

WARREN But the light was green.

MATTHEW So.

WARREN You were coming up Bathurst?

MATTHEW Where did you think?

WARREN You went through a red light.

MATTHEW I knew it! I knew you'd try to get out of this. Well it's not going to work. You can't even remember what you did, how are you going to remember what colour the light was.

WARREN You remember?

MATTHEW I remember seeing you at the corner and I remember thinking, I'll bet this guy's going to cut me off. And I remember I sped up so that you wouldn't have the chance. And by the time I got to the intersection… the light was red.

WARREN YES! YES!

MATTHEW Son of a gun, I went through a red light. Get a load of that eh? I don't think I've ever done that before.

WARREN So that's what this was all about.

MATTHEW I feel like kind of a fool. Wait till the guys at the office hear about this. Oh God, I'll never hear the end of it.

> *MATTHEW stands lost in thought.*

WARREN You must have been going pretty fast, cause I didn't see you.

MATTHEW Hey, don't you go making any accusations. I make one little mistake – that doesn't mean my life is riddled with them.

WARREN Sorry.

MATTHEW That's all right… Jesus, a red light… oh well. You live and learn. And speaking of living, I've got to make one. I better run.

MATTHEW starts to go.

WARREN Don't you have anything you'd like to say to me.

MATTHEW Oh yeah. Forget about the apology, it's not necessary. Take care, buddy.... Oh and buddy.... Keep your eyes open from now on, eh.

MATTHEW leaves. WARREN watches him go.

WARREN My name is Warren.

WARREN starts to whistle a little tune he's made up in his head.

Bruce McCulloch

The Two-Headed Roommate

1989
Catherine May: Director
Tom McCamus: Guy

Later produced as a full-length play at the Tarragon with:
Andy McKim: Director
Albert Schultz: Guy

♫ • ♫

GUY We are not alone… although is anyone really alone anymore? People in groups, large similarly dressed groups, getting away from it all, together. Like being a black sheep, in a HERD of black sheep. Still, we are not alone. On the other side of that curtain is something so horrible, so disgusting, breathing smoke, menacing… between that curtain and us lurks "my roommate…"

He butters some toast.

Maybe you've heard of them? Maybe you remember them from fairy tales you were read as a child? You may have lost sleep over them, thoughts of how they make life miserable for little children, or perfectly normal, or trying to be normal, grown-ups or trying to be grown-ups… *(beat)*

Turning away from the audience.

He sits on the other side of that curtain, brandishing boredom. Having no idea how the world feels about him. Well, me… a small part of the world. But I'm a large part of MY world, not that I think I'm the centre of… *(trails off)* I can feel him there… just knowing he's using the floor, walking on the floor, taking steps adding nothing…. Just looking at his gross bulbous futon turns my stomach… thoughts of him sleeping, gape-mouthed snoring, naked, that meatless white-ass…. No wonder I can't sleep…

Surveying the place.

It's not much is it?… Sometimes the less it is, the more men fight over it…. But I don't fight, I'm fought with. It's like I'm an innocent bystander… with my fists wailing… *(beat)*

When I wake up and look in the fridge, I'm not just looking in the fridge – I'm surveying the DAMAGE… it's more than him taking my food, it's like he's taking my MOOD. Most days I open the fridge and it's "my mood is missing!" …well bits of it, tiny knife marks on my cheese.

He opens the fridge, revealing its pathetic contents. He seems repulsed to even go near where the roommate has been. He opens the bread bag.

(*counting*) Seventeen pieces of bread... there were 19 this morning... sounds like a sandwich to me...

He opens the bargain peanut butter and shows the audience.

The knife marks in the peanut butter seem to indicate movement. Maybe someone was moving it around, rotating it... or... taking some?... (*beat*) I've started buying foods I don't even like – breads so hard they're going to make you rethink your whole life. Doorstop hard. I'm on the verge of buying tofu. Tofu and nothing else. Meals of just tofu, so you have to get the taste from somewhere else, another place, another meal you had, a sandwich from a couple years back maybe.

The smile fades from his face.

Although that would probably just backfire. He'd be sitting there, wolfing down raw tofu, entranced by some garage sale book that he'd meant to get around to reading, that he actually got around to reading. I hate everything he has ever read... or is likely to read! His books smell! Just the titles, pompous and old, turn my stomach, make a bright yellow bile come halfway up my throat and just hover here below my jaw.... He has spoiled all literature for me.... He sits around all day in these brown sweat pants, "brown sweat pants," I've never heard of such a thing.... If it would serve him he would take the light bulb, the mustard, the cold from the crisper and the marrow from my bones. I would be sitting there soft-boned, slumped, and he would say "So how's it going man? Want tea?" Want tea? He obviously confused me with someone who actually DRINKS tea.... So I sit, perched over a chipped mug of instant coffee. Hating him with every instant of every sip. I hate him as much as I hate that coffee without milk, Christ there hasn't been milk in here for 4 months...

He slams the fridge door. Turning back like he'd seen the face of hell.

The dishes, the dishes... the dishes have been in the sink for... (*lunging*) The sink? Let's just say that I wouldn't let a child play near there. The blood of those who fought for our land remain on those dishes. On those MISMATCHED dishes, the unwanted children of past relationships, cast-offs from parents and... cups from Fran's. A motley set even if clean... even if taken and hosed down, filed, rubbed, scored, rinsed, waxed... (*lunging*) and that saucepan! I hate it like the bastard that stands over it, slurping, stirring, scratching his ass. The pan like the man, thin and misshapen. Made of the very cheapest materials that would take.

The pan bent like it had been the weapon of a thug who waited with it, in some alley... a pan not to be trusted... even at room temperature the handle seems to burn your hand... caked with tomato soup, reheated like his boring stories of how the income tax people "rooked him." Income tax people don't have the time to bother to rook hovel-dwellers like you! They have bigger fish to fry!... Circling his phone calls on the phone bills, is not the way I want to spend MY

Sunday… the numbers he has called long distance, disgust me. (613) 693-3821 would disgust anyone!

He pauses to consider where he is.

(starting softly) What he does to the air is a crime…. His lungs warm it up, take what they need and cough it back up. The air that was once mine and MINE alone… his lungs warm up MY air, so when I get it, it's mildewy and soggy. Not virgin-crisp the way I like my air. The way I LOVE my air. The way I enjoyed air as a child…

The broad weight of the thought hits him, he sits.

I am sharing air with someone…. That's it. That's what it's come to… OF COURSE that's what you're doing when you get a roommate… *(beat)* When you consider getting one, all you think about is how he'll pay half of the rent for a third of the space… but really, you're putting an ad in the paper for someone to breathe the same air as you… *(beat)* I don't think this is what my mom had planned for her baby boy when she held me, firstborn, 6 pounds, 11 ounces, in the hospital room… that hospital that is listed on my birth certificate but the name now escapes me…. Nope, this isn't what my mom had planned for her little baby holding me in her arms, dizzy from screaming.

She didn't think "I hope one day this child will share space with a loser, haggle, fight over clean-up schedules, and end up drinking from a measuring cup as the dishes in the sink are the site of the stand-off." *(beat)* I want him dead. Not just dead, but I want him to die and have an out-of-body experience and watch me rent his space… *(beat)* But it's a jungle out there, I'm as about as far from a "feminist non-smoker" as it gets. I don't want to be part of a caring, sharing household… I just want a place to crash and collect my phone calls. The more I know him, the more I just want to keep him from knowing me. I'd feel safer if he'd never seen my face. If I could just dart in with a newspaper or some burlap over my face "mornin" through a sack. I shouldn't have used my real name.

Looking at the newspaper or NOW *magazine on the table.*

But how do you pick a roommate? You don't want someone that's like you and you don't want someone that's UNLIKE you…. The whole idea of me picking makes me nervous anyway, I just hear this voice, whining, obvious, authoritative… and I realise it's mine!… *(transition)* "So… are you reliable?" "Yes, I am reliable, very reliable." "Ah, I see… good, good… but are you clean?" "Yes I'm clean… *(quickly)* but not TOO clean…." "Clean but not TOO clean… I see." *(transition)* They sit and tell you about how they take up hardly any space and that they work all the time. They should just sit there and and let you watch them breathe… *(beat)* They work all the time yet somehow they quit, or are laid-off a week after they move in. When I go to the curtain to listen…

He goes to the curtain to listen.

Instead of hearing a good sturdy silence, I hear the steady brain-dead din of game shows. People jumping up and down and winning jukeboxes they have no room for. Why aren't they working? Why isn't he working? Since he moved in I'm now cheering for "THE SHOW" not the contestants…. He watches TV on his side, he turns the TV sideways and lays there… like a fucking "*Pud* cartoon…." *(beat)* If I knew what he did for a living, what he is BETWEEN doing, I could suggest some jobs to him. It's pretty hard to just open the want-ads and say "my my my… dive in. Take a walk on the working side…." *(beat, softly)* If I could help him, I've got more going for me than he must realise. I know people… they don't always know me, but… I could make the calls on his behalf, talk him up… *(transition)* Did you know that there are over 100,000 parasites in each of your eyes? I retained that from school, nothing else, just that. I think back on what I learned in high school, and I have a vague memory of colouring some map with pencil crayons and that there are 100,000 parasites in each of your eyes. I used to think about it every time I looked in the mirror. I had almost forgotten, but when I saw "him" I remembered… "of course, 100,000 parasites are crawling around, right now in my eyes…." And every time I look at him, I think about it again, he's that type of guy… I just know that he's doing something to my lightbulbs! It sounds crazy perhaps, but I know it's true. My lightbulbs are burning out at an unprecedented rate. Either he's not very good with lightbulbs or, it's the way he's pussing up the air. I wouldn't put it past him to buy used lightbulbs. I wouldn't, he's just the type. Or to buy some, and just before they burn out, come into my space, quietly, get up on the chair while I sleep and switch them. Then a couple of days later, my life has to be shattered in darkness… *(now convinced)* Of course… it's SO obvious now… *(transition)*

It makes me want to live with "Her" and carry "Her" over the threshold of some new house in some new place. A place where the lawns have yet to be unrolled off the back of trucks, by guys who live somewhere else…. Just me and "Her" looking up at our own cupboards, no judgement, no regret. To be with "Her" away from "Him…." *(beat)* Men have those fantasies too, but we're real quiet about it. 'Cause if it ever got out…

Shakes his head contemplatively.

…there would be mayhem.

Again he thinks about the prospect. Obviously he is having trouble getting rid of the thought.

…mayhem…. He makes me want to live with "Her" and have sets of towels, not just one stolen from a hotel that fully expected it. The only trouble is I don't know who "She" is… there is no "She" in my life…. God it sounds so heavy and corny to say it. "There is no 'She' in my life…." *(beat)* But it's more than that, there is more light in my phrase than my uttering it might seem to allow…. But not enough to light a new room, a new house, on a new street that had just been named. More like a naked bulb hanging near your head, but for some odd reason, out of reach. Swinging, slashing for that twine… *(beat)* I look at him look at me, and I know what I am to him. What I have BECOME to him, what I have been forced to become because of him… *(vulnerable)* but I tell you it's him. To him the world must be a complaining grumpy place, but hate is in reaction to HIM… well to ME the world seems like a complaining grumpy place, but it's somehow different. What I'm trying to say is that if this were a movie I'd think the smell from the sink was funny. Broad comedy, but funny.

But when the light goes on and the bugs run back to wherever it is that bugs run back to when you click on the light and your yawn becomes a scream, it's hard to share that laugh. I hate him for making me hate him, maybe if I were nineteen, I would just let it roll off my back, when you're young and can work and puke and forgive in the same shirt… *(beat)* If I were 19 I wouldn't care if a good friend of his from out-of-town wants to crash on the couch… *(beat)* When I look at him, or even his hangers that dangle, a clump of three in the closet, I am reminded that I… do not have a maverick outlook on life. I look at him and I know that I… am not a fun guy. I can HAVE fun but I am not a "fun guy.…" I never start the fun, I can merely keep it going, but I can't churn it out. But now, in a way I can never be FUN again, because I know how he can make the world smell… and I hardly know him.

James O'Reilly — The Bends

1989
Julian Richings: Director
Gregory Nixon: Producer of Flexible Packaging Plant – co-producer
James O'Reilly: David the waiter; Narrator
Edward Glenn: Johnny McLeod, 8 years old
Michael Lamport: Sieu the salad man; Sammy McLeod, 12 years old
Roger McKeen: Francis Triggerman
Alison Sealy-Smith: Judy

¤ • ¤

The set is an open courtyard which is broken into a number of playing areas in and around a small restaurant: the alleyway behind the kitchen, the dining room, the parking lot and street corner, an adjacent empty schoolyard playground.

SIEU makes a vat of salad in the kitchen of a busy downtown restaurant. He stands under a fan to catch the cool outdoor breeze. Just outside, in the alleyway, a little boy, JOHNNY McLeod stacks a few milk crates and climbs atop, undoes his fly, then urinates into the fan separating the kitchen from the alleyway. SIEU feels a mist coming in through the fan and tries to cover his mixing bowl.

DAVID We join an arcing stream of urine at the peak of its amplitude and jump across in one direction to the freckled face of seven-year-old Johnny McLeod. The child is hypnotised by the amber core of the urine jet as he bends his mind towards other things like skipping ropes, and streams. He farts, then shudders, sending a ripple through the wave. His hair flaps around as if he were in a speeding convertible on the highway, it smacks him about the forehead, then snaps straight out into the suction draft of a large fan at the other end of his arcing sine wave. A meat delivery truck pulls down the alleyway. The driver blows his air horn. The blast shatters the meditative whirr and flutter of the urine-fan ensemble, along with the child's concentration, sending him backwards, off the upturned milk cartons, to the pavement. A second later he is up and running, hastily tucking in his spout as he goes.

> *An impatient FRANK Triggerman and his secretary JUDY wait at the door of the restaurant for a table.*

FRANK Two for lunch, by the window.

DAVID Certainly sir. And how are you today?

FRANK Well, I guess I could be dead, so, I'm okay under the circumstances. How's that for an answer?

DAVID Just fine… I guess. And you ma'am?

JUDY *(shy)* It's good to be alive. Sure.

> *DAVID presents them with menus and a wine list, then exits as they seat themselves. After a minute, DAVID returns to take their order.*

DAVID Can I bring you something to d…

FRANK The lady will have a spritzer and I'll have a P–

DAVID Perrier with lime and a couple drops of bitters.

FRANK *(to JUDY)* Say, *he's* sharp isn't he? *(to DAVID)* You know, you should be running this place.

DAVID *(extravagantly)* One day, all of this will be mine.

> *DAVID exits for the kitchen.*

FRANK You look good today, Judy.

JUDY Thank you, Frank.

FRANK Judy, I think Rod's turning commie on us. Did you catch that bullshit about the plant at the meeting today?

JUDY Of course, I was right th…

FRANK Do you know how much it would cost to put air conditioning in a plant that size? I've told him before. Get rid of the problem. If they won't work in the heat, fire 'em and find someone who will. The streets are crawling with refugees and vagrants who'd be only too happy to work for the money I'm paying out. Half!

JUDY Frank, he wasn't that bad.

FRANK Like hell he wasn't.

> *DAVID returns with the drinks, then exits.*

JUDY Don't forget, he has to listen to their complaints all day long, and most of them don't even speak English.

FRANK Judy, what's the man being paid for? To listen to complaints, whatever language they're in, and run the plant as efficiently as possible, *that* is his job. Don't get me wrong. I like Rod. I think I understand him. He started out just like me: right at the bottom. But that's where the similarity ends. To be honest with you, I don't think he's got the jam to make it. And I'll tell you another thing, this is as far as he's going to get if he pulls that shit on me again. Imagine, calling *me* out in front of the board. My board. My goddamn company. I built that place from dust.

> FRANK *accidentally knocks his Perrier off the table.*

FRANK Shit!

JUDY Relax, Frank.

FRANK I'm sorry Judy. Waiter! *(finger snap)* Waiter!

> *JUDY's heart sinks as she watches the earth absorb the Perrier bubbles. She slips into a reverie as a hedge against total self-loathing.*
>
> Action in the restaurant freezes while the next scene plays out.

•

> Under the following text JOHNNY meanders about the outdoor playing space in a rough mime version of DAVID's narrative, while his older brother SAMMY enters with his skateboard, then hangs out on a fire escape. SAMMY is stoned and playing with glue-sniffing paraphernalia. He is unseen by his younger brother, JOHNNY, until the last possible moment.

DAVID Johnny McLeod walks down an alleyway behind the IGA, throwing stones against the wall and buzzing his lips to mimic the sound of urine passing through a fan. He spots some garbage against the brick wall below a loading dock and zeros in on a green cigarette package – his mother's brand. The smell of menthol smoke in his memory makes him stop for a moment and walk over to the rustling garbage. He picks up the faded green box and thinks about last New Year's when his mother made him go to the store and buy two packs so she could sit up all night with his grandmother. The night her boyfriend didn't show up. His mother and grandmother just sat up all night drinking, crying, talking, and smoking cigarettes. Most of the time though they just sat, saying nothing, with the lights off, curling the ashes from their cigarettes against the lip of a huge, green, porcelain ashtray shaped like a bird. Johnny used to call it "the duck ashtray." He remembers playing "duckpond" on the living room table, the one his mother used to rest her feet on when she watched TV. The wood-grain looked like cat's eyes and the sea to him. The current runs swiftly through his mind now as he clutches the empty green cigarette package. From beyond the periphery of his attention, his left hand opens to release three warm stones to the ground. As they hit, the child envisions green ripples, concentric circles, forming on the surface of a wood-grained sea mapped out over the seamless expanse of a menthol cigarette package.

JOHNNY So many things are green. Jello. Martian blood. Lizards. Dishwashing liquid. *(mimicking the old Palmolive commercial)* "Dishwashing liquid? You're soaking in it."

DAVID …jewels, jelly bears…

JOHNNY And Jaques Cousteau under water, breathing into a machine that makes bubbles.

JOHNNY daydreams. He picks something from his nose, rolls it between the fingers of one hand, then drops it to the earth as he did with the stones.

DAVID More ripples, and one last reminiscence about New Year's, the next morning, coming down the stairs, and the whole place smelled like cigarettes. His mother and grandmother were asleep on the fold-out couch together, and three of these empty packages were on the kitchen table.

JOHNNY finds a bug on the back of his hand and drops the cigarette pack. He pokes at the insect.

JOHNNY Oh. A ball-up bug. *(poke)* Go on. Ball up.

He lets the bug roll off his hand and drop-kicks it away from him, then takes off running as if in a war movie.

The Germans are after me. The Germans! I gotta escape.

JOHNNY runs a circuit of the playing space while performing a number of movie-stunt maneuvers until he finds himself defusing a bomb, which happens to also be his brother SAMMY's skateboard. SAMMY hardly notices his little brother because he is absorbed in his glue-sniffing ritual (squeezing glue into a baggie, smoothing the plastic over his cupped fist, bringing it to his mouth, then inhaling deeply for four cycles). JOHNNY stops daydreaming after defusing the skateboard, after receiving the imaginary thunderous applause of a packed football stadium, and stands watching his brother get high. JOHNNY scratches at an eczema rash on the inside of his elbow. SAMMY pulls his fist clutching the sticky baggie from his glazed mouth then exhales a thin jet of air.

SAMMY *(after a beat)* Here ya go runt. Go ahead. Give it a shot. *(offering the glue bag).*

JOHNNY No way. Smell uh that stuff gives me a *headache*.

JOHNNY scratches at his arm vigorously, to the point of hurting himself as his brother reclines on the fire escape with the spent baggie still clutched in his fist. After a beat, the brothers freeze as action resumes in the restaurant.

•

At the restaurant, DAVID presents FRANK with the bill, then clears the table.

FRANK Unlike the rest of these clowns, I got half a day's work waiting for me back at the office.

DAVID takes the plates away, says "Thank you", and "Goodbye", to an imaginary couple of exiting customers, as FRANK reacts to the bill with anger, snapping his fingers and yelling.

Waiter! Waiter!

DAVID I can hear you. You're not my only table. And it's no good waving your arms around like that because I don't understand sign language.

FRANK You should be able to. It's *primitive* enough. Look, how come you charged me for two Perriers? I only drank one.

DAVID I brought two to your table. Do you expect me to pay for the one you knocked over?

FRANK *(demonstrating)* Look at this table. It's wobbly.

DAVID The table does not wobble. I checked it before my shift. I could build a playing-card castle on…

FRANK Are you calling me a liar asshole? Get the manager over here.

> *DAVID tenses, seethes with anger, then turns to the audience with both hands behind his back and speaks like a circus ringmaster.*

DAVID Ladies and gentlemen. I give you the one, the only, Mr. Francis Triggerman, world-renowned cheapskate and asshole, who prides himself—and rightly so—on his ability to thoroughly decimate the small, the insignificant, the working class, with a shrill command and a deadly hand-held Platinum card. Take it away Frank.

> *DAVID bows deeply, then leaves the dining room while loosening his tie. He sings the Gershwin standard "I Got Plenty o' Nuttin" as he exits to the side of the playing space and changes into his street clothes.*

FRANK *(furious)* I wanna see the manager! Get the manager over here!

> *JUDY shrinks in horror as FRANK continues his tirade. After a beat, she rises to her feet and bolts for the door. FRANK gets flustered, fumbles for a few loose bills and change in his pants pocket, counts out the sum on his cheque to the last penny then heads out after his secretary. In his haste to clear the door, he snags his jacket pocket and rips it open.*

Shit!

> *FRANK heads to the parking lot after JUDY. She waits stone-faced at the passenger door. FRANK tosses his newly-torn jacket in the back seat, jumps into the driver's seat, then lets JUDY in. FRANK jerkily starts the engine and slams the vehicle into gear. They freeze as the next scene, between the two brothers in the adjacent schoolyard plays out.*

•

SAMMY Come on ya little peckerhead, just one more time, that's all.

JOHNNY No way. I told ya. They know *me* too at the store. And don't call me a peckerhead.

SAMMY Why not? That's what you are.

JOHNNY Don't!

SAMMY Peckerhead.

JOHNNY I mean it!

SAMMY Mean what peckerhead? What're ya gonna do pecker-boy. Come on. What's a few more tubes of glue?

JOHNNY Forget it because ya keep callin' me that.

SAMMY *(play-smacking his brother)* Fuck you peckerhead.

JOHNNY STOP!

SAMMY Peckerhead. Peckerhead. Peckerhead.

> *JOHNNY, in tears, lashes out at his older brother who continues to rant sleepy-eyed. In a rage, JOHNNY grabs the skateboard and tries to whack SAMMY with it. SAMMY knocks the skateboard out of JOHNNY's hand sending it out onto the street. SAMMY gets up to go after it. Freeze. Action resumes between FRANK and JUDY in the jeep as they pull out of the parking lot.*

•

FRANK What do you mean you were embarrassed? By that *puke*?

JUDY Just watch the road Frank.

FRANK Why do you think he's working as a goddamned waiter? Because he's a no-brained *puke* that's why. A lazy puke with no *ambition*.

> *SAMMY stumbles out onto the street after his skateboard, directly in front of FRANK's vehicle. DAVID, in his street clothes, is off to one side of the playing area with a ticket in his hand, waiting for a streetcar. SAMMY looks up in time to catch the following:*

JUDY *(yelling)* Shut up Frank! Frank! Watch the road!

> *SAMMY bounces off the car and hits the earth in a heap. FRANK jumps out of the vehicle.*

FRANK My God. Honest, I didn't see him coming. That's impossible. I couldn't've... couldn't've been going any faster than fif... ten miles an hour. I just pulled away from... you saw the whole thing didn't you Judy?

> *JUDY is out of the vehicle and at the dead boy's side.*

JUDY Frank you bastard. You killed him. When does it end with you?

> *JOHNNY, devoid of emotion, rehearses his next action—a phone call to his mother—aloud.*

JOHNNY Mom, I was on my way to swimming but, don't cry but, Sammy is dead. He got hit by a jeep on the street. I'm all right. I was on the sidewalk. I was on the sidewalk honest.

> *DAVID walks towards the young boy for an explanation.*

Jim Warren and   *Philistines and Farmers*
Guillermo Verdecchia

1990
J: Jim Warren
G: Guillermo Verdecchia

⌑•⌑

J Geoffrey, where are you?

G I'm here, Jeffrey.

J Do they actually expect us to perform out here?

G It's a suitable metaphor for the state of theatre in this country. Appalling.

J After a lifetime in the theatre they expect us to perform in a parking lot.

G Absurd. Shakespeare did say all the world's a stage, but this is ridiculous.

J Appalling. I won't stand for this anymore. I quit.

G So do I. *(looks at audience)* What are all these people doing here?

J Go away, the show hasn't started yet *(looks at public, no reaction)* Philistines.

G Farmers. Probably some of those people come for that pay-what-you-can thing.

J What the devil is that supped to mean anyway, pay-what-you-can?

G Then they say minimum $5.00. Well that's a–

J & G Contradiction in terms.

G It's either pay-what-you-can or it's $5.00.

J I hate that.

G Weird custom.

J Who comes to those performances anyway?

G Take a look. *(They stare at the public.)*

J Philistines.

G Farmers.

J The dregs of society.

G People should dress up to come to the theatre.

J That's what theatre's all about, after all.

G Dressing up.

J Going out to dinner.

G Having a few drinks.

J Paying lots of money.

G Being seen.

J And going home.

G Pay-what-you-can? Well you know what I say to that? If it's pay-what-you-can then it's act-what-you-can. *(Much laughter from both, and then they go off into separate comas.)*

J Did you say something?

G Hmm?

J What do you think of this nose? *(referring to large putty nose covering his face)*

G Magnificent, reminds me of Oliver's Richard.

J Ah Larry. He's dead now.

G Yes. *(pause)* Well I didn't really like him.

J As a person, no.

G Did he leave you anything in his will?

J Autographed first folio edition of all the collected works.

G Ah Shakespeare, the greatest writer that ever lived.

J Ever. And you?

G Pair of socks.

J Yes, well he's dead now. Do you remember his Romeo?

G No.

J Nor do I. Here's to Larry. *(They drink, "Cheers.")*

G Here's to the Bard. *(They drink "To the Bard.")*

J Here's to the bar. *(They laugh and drink.)* That reminds me of the first time I worked with the then young and upcoming Larry Oliver. It was the Old Vic in '34 or was it in the young Vic in '43? Anyway he was playing some young porter in one of the Henrys and I could tell even then that this boy had some talent buried deep inside.

G Deep deep inside.

J Anyway *(begins to laugh)* he came onstage carrying *(laughing so hard he can hardly get the words out)* this tray at this crucial moment *(He laughs so hard he's unable to continue. GEOFF joins in, they laugh uncontrolled and then lapse into coma.)*

G Jeffrey?

J Hmm? Make-up is a lost art. What do you think I should use to play this part? *(shows him various teeth prosthetics, then speaks to audience)* What are you laughing at? I'll have you know that I wore these at the Whitehall in '32 in the most sensitive and compelling performance of Quasimodo ever to grace the British stage.

G It was magnificent, Jeffrey.

J Thank you, Geoffrey.

G But you know, Jeffrey, this is Canada in these postage-stamp-size theatres.

J Yes of course, subtly. *(puts smaller teeth on)*

G Yes, much subtler.

J Or my favourite. *(puts in gums)* I wore these to play the fool to Sir Ralph's Lear in '44 at R.S.C. *(quotes)*

G Ah, Shakespeare, the greatest playwright that ever wrote.

J Ever.

G I like those. I mean what's this unnecessary Canadian consternation about characterisation.

J Choose a prosthetic and it's all decided for you.

G Absolutely.

J *(to audience)* What are you staring at, haven't you ever seen an actor prepare?

G This is Canada, Jeffrey.

J Philistines.

G Farmers.

J Ridiculous.

G No one understands make-up anymore.

J To mould your face.

G It's art and the face is your palette.

J No one understands.

G Especially the actors in this country.

J They don't use make-up because they just play themselves all the time.

G That's not acting.

J Some people believe it is. They call it behaving. I've actually heard directors say "don't act."

G Well, what's the point of being on stage if you're not going to act.

J They don't know any better.

G They don't.

J They have no tradition.

G No training.

J No diction.

G No diction to speak of.

J Actors mumbling, walking around in jean jackets.

G Speaking gibberish.

J Essentially it's gibberish.

G There's no poetry, no rhythm, no lyrical intonation.

J No eloquence, no sense of style.

G No sense of heightened, heightened, heightened…

J Anything.

J & G GET OFF THE STAGE!

G Canadian Theatre, contradiction of terms.

J And the names of these theatres. Tarragon? What's that, some sort of vinegar?

G Factory? Who wants to go see theatre in a factory?

J Now the Globe was a theatre.

G That was a theatre.

J & G Yes.

J Not like these theatres where the audience has to follow you around.

G What?

J Yes, some Necessary Leaves company has the audience follow the actors around this big house.

G That's absurd. Who wants the audience moving around?

J It's bad enough that they're there in the first place. Keep them in their seats where they belong but for God's sake don't let them move and don't let them talk, just have them sit quietly and applaud at the appropriate time. *(to audience)* Are you getting any of this? Perhaps you should be taking notes? *(pause)* Philistines.

G Farmers.

J And the names of the plays, there was that weird thing called *A Movie the Play*. Now isn't that confusing? Are you going to a movie or are you going to a play? *A Movie the Play*, what does that mean?

G I have no idea.

J   Well, I didn't either, so I didn't go.

G   Of course not. I never go to the theatre. I hate the theatre. Or that thing called *Unrecognizable Human Remnants*.

J   Uhh, sounds like a news report. What, did they have human remnants on the stage?

G   That no one could recognise, I suppose.

J   Frightening, different parts of people lying around on the stage.

G   *(high voice)* Yes, yes, yes.

J   Mutilated things?

G   Yes, yes, I suppose, I suppose, who knows? Apparently lots of nudity.

J   Oh splendid. If you don't know how to act, take off your clothes. Show your private parts and they'll line up around the block.

G   I saw something recently called *Blue Amigo's Mandolin*. Well first of all there was no one called Amigo in the play, there was no mandolin, and the only thing that was blue was the poster.

J   What was it about?

G   Some foreign lad refugee or something from one of those countries. Could barely speak English, dreadful accent.

J   Oh who wants to see that? We don't want to actually see other cultures onstage.

G   No, that's what make-up is for.

J   There is the art of illusion, after all.

G & J   GET OFF THE STAGE!

G   Theatre is about Kings and Queens. Shakespeare knew that.

J   Greatest writer that ever lived.

G   Ever.

J   No one knows how to do Shakespeare properly anymore.

G   Did you read where some foreigners were doing LEAR played by a woman?

J   Women in the theatre, absurd. Ah, for the days when men played women. Queen Lear? Ridiculous.

G   Absurd. I mean, I've known a few queens who have played Lear but none of them were women. *(Both laugh and lapse into coma.)*

J   Did you say something?

G   Hmm? There's a company that has even done a clown version of *Twelfth Night*.

J   Good God, clowns. I hate clowns.

G European clown technique.

J Those bloody Europeans.

G Adult clown, they call it.

J As if adults are interested in that sort of nonsense.

G Of course not, children don't even like clowns.

J Red-nosed lunatics with orange hair running about in tiny cars squeaking at you.

G Children scream at clowns.

J Children hate clowns. Gives them nightmares, they run screaming into the street.

G Clown theatre, contradiction in terms.

G & J GET OFF THE STAGE!

G That reminds me of a story John told me.

J Gielgud?

G Is there another? The entire cast was sitting around during rehearsal on one of those concept productions of the Bard and the director was doing one of those psycho internal ooga booga exercises.

J I hate that.

G And he asked everyone to tell him the most frightening story they could imagine, and of course they all went on about some macabre childhood trauma or some such drivel and when it was John's turn, he said, and I quote, "We open next week." *(Much laughter from both and lapse into coma.)*

J Did you say something?

G Hmm? Well I suppose we should run our opening scene. *(J starts writing on props.)* What are you doing, Jeffrey?

J Writing my lines on props that are strategically placed all over the set.

G Good idea.

J Well, surely no one expects us to remember all this drivel. *(They get into position to rehearse.)* What's my first line?

G Wind.

J Oh yea. *(to audience)* Pay no attention to this part. This is called a rehearsal. This is where we practice what we are going to do before we do it. *(waits for response from public… none comes)* Philistines.

G Farmers. Well let's get on with it.

J Wind.

G Wolves.

J Water.

G Wild.

J Whippoorwill.

G The days are bad, the nights are worse
   They struggle on, under their breaths, they curse
   This cold and bitter land
   If they'd gone to Peru, they'd be tanned

   They look at each other. JEFFREY has been placing his line-covered props around the area.

J A land untouched, glorious, and free
   A home to caribou, rock, and tree
   They plough the earth, cut down the trees
   To build a home for the great Gretsky

   They stare hopelessly at each other.

J Appalling.

G Hopeless.

J Who wrote this drively drivel? *(gets script, reads title)* History of the Hamlet of the Tiny Tents: A Poetic Exploration of the History of Canada by James G. Verdeccia.

G Wasn't he that weaselly-looking, emaciated, pock-marked ferret sitting at the back of the theatre during the first read-through, clearing his throat every 15 minutes?

J Proudly announcing that his play has been workshopped 18 times.

G Workshop? What the devil IS a workshop?

J Some small room in your basement where you build shelves with carpentry tools.

G How can you work on something that isn't finished?

J Exactly. But, they say, that's why we need a workshop to see what direction the play is going in. What they mean is they can't write the bloody thing so let's get some actors together and improvise.

G Improvising. The death of the theatre. You get up there and say whatever drivel comes out of your mouth and the playwright copies it down and you end up with a big pile of drively words that needs to be workshopped again.

J Explore the characters' life outside the play. The character has no life outside the play. What was your character doing right before the scene?

G Well I don't know about anyone else, but my character was having a cigarette and waiting for his entrance. Explore the character through movement.

J That's the influence of that dreadful French physical performance style by that Lepage Derosier.

G The French always jumping about, picking up things that aren't really there.

J And this director.

G Going on about his vision. His concept of the play. Vision, concept. Should be shot.

J The play has its own vision, just do the bloody thing.

G Explore this.

J Explore that.

G Stop exploring. *(imitates director)* Let's explore your character as an animal. You be a bear.

J The character's name is Clifford, but then they say that Clifford's really a bear.

G Yes, what the devil is that supposed to mean?

J *(overlapping)* What's that mean. I'm supposed to growl when I say the lines? They say no, of course not. I'm supposed to get up and be a bear, then sit down but retain that bearness when I say the lines.

G Ridiculous, everyone knows that bears can't speak.

J Retain the image of the bear. You must find the bear within.

G Release your inner bear. Observe the bear so you can find accurate bear movements.

J Why don't they just give you a costume?

G There're no costumes anymore. Have you seen the costumes in Canadian plays? Modern dress, real life. They wear what they wear on the street.

J Street clothes. Who wants to see that?

G & J GET OFF THE STAGE!

J They don't even have proper dressers, you have to change yourself. You're supposed to know where you come on.

G Know where your costume is, know what you wear at what given moment in time and where you enter from.

J A good dresser puts your costume on, relaxes you, hands you your brandy, points you in the right direction, and tells you your first line so you know what scene you're going into.

G Here you go off stage.

G & J IN THE DARK.

G Probably bump into something.

J Possibly hurt yourself.

G Get changed into your next dreadful costume by yourself.

J By then you've missed your entrance, you have no idea what you're supposed to be doing, so you come on and look foolish.

G It's no wonder there are plays where people don't wear any clothes.

J It's probably because they couldn't get changed fast enough.

G Probably.

J So they came on semi-naked and there they were.

G And the bloody director said, "Keep it, it's brilliant."

J Wonderful.

G As a matter of fact, we'll have everybody take their clothes off.

•

G & J   THE CONCEPT

G The text is so moronic that we'll have the actors take their clothes off to distract…

J Distract the audience from the fact they they're speaking drivel. Saying those drively words that no one understands. That's it, Geoffrey, I can't go on.

G Nor I.

J No Geoffrey, I mean it. I'm through, I'm retiring.

G Now?

J Yes. I can't bear it any longer. I'm going to change careers.

G Jeffrey, don't be ridiculous, what could you possibly do?

J I've been thinking of buying a farm.

G A FARM!

J Yes, a farm.

G You mean a farm farm?

J Yes, Geoffrey, a farm farm.

G *(laughs)* Very amusing, Jeffrey, but really it's almost time to go on, don't you think you should finish writing your text on that ashtray.

J No, Geoffrey, I'm through with the wooden O. I am weary of this artifice.

G What artifice?

J The theatre, I want to do something real.

G Jeffrey, whatever for?

J To see what it's like. I want a little farm, raise corn, milk cows, walk pigs. I want to rise with the sun, till the land, get my hands dirty.

G Really, Jeffrey, one might think you've gone a bit soft.

J *(increasing madness)* I am soft, Geoffrey and so are you – soft, soft, soft what light through yonder window breaks?

G Jeffrey, Jeffrey, you can't be serious.

J *(coming back to himself)* Hmm, no of course not. A farm? What a terrifying thought. No. *(pause)* What I'd really like to do is write.

G Write? What?

J A play.

G You know I've written a play.

J You have? What about?

G My life, the roles I've played, my struggles as an artist, my search for truth and beauty.

J Oh dear.

G It's called, *AY, THERE'S THE RUB*.

J Smashing title.

G Yes, I thought so. It's just in the idea stage at the moment. I'm having it workshopped actually.

J WORKSHOPPED!

G There's this marvelous scene in it where I take a friend to the theatre. I've told him that they play is quite dreadful, but there's one moment in it that is worth the price of admission alone.

J I remember, that was me. There we were. We had sat through the first act, which was fairly dreadful but not completely awful and during the second act I turned to you and asked "When is this wonderful moment?" and you, you sly boots, said nothing and then suddenly you turned to me and said, in hushed but dramatic tones, "This is it" and you pointed to the stage "in exactly 10 seconds…

J & G I'm supposed to make an entrance through those doors." *(They laugh and go into comas.)*

OFFSTAGE VOICE Places please, gentlemen.

G Did you say something, Jeffrey?

J Hmm? Must almost be time to go.

G I suppose we must.

OFFSTAGE VOICE Places please, gentlemen!

J Yes, yes. I'm not ready and I shan't be rushed.

G I don't know why we bother, Jeffrey.

J Nor do I, Geoffrey. A Life in the Theatre.

J & G Contradiction in terms.

G Philistines.

J Farmers.

    They exit.

Todd Hammond *Fish*

1992
Andy McKim: Director
Todd Hammond: Performer

♯ • ♯

A single light up on stage. A man enters wearing a turtleneck. He addresses the audience.

I was born, which in itself is not unusual. The circumstances surrounding it, however, are; so much so in fact, that a certain person has recommended I talk with you about it. As you can see, I've taken up this person's advice—for posterity, I suppose— in the event that in my old age I will require some refreshing, or perhaps to immortalise myself by planting my stake inexorably in the annals of human history.

Pause.

According to my mother, I was conceived on a late August night on a deluxe coiled-spring mattress in room 13 of the Silver Saddle Motel, outside the town of Conwright, Alberta. The prairies: a two-tone land of gold and blue, sprawling effortlessly for miles, victim of the sun's range, parched beyond recognition, breathing shallow. The moon that evening was full which, according to my mother, is the worst of all omens. My father skillfully executed the "out of gas" trick a mere five metres from room 13. He coaxed, she coyly refused, he persisted, and in the heat of the evening, and governed by forces too mysterious to understand, she appeased him. The deluxe coiled-spring mattress creaked, a moan and a shiver, and, well, the rest is history.

Soon after the swelling in my mother's belly, my parents were married. The few photos I have of the event seem to suggest firstly, that my parents had very few friends, and secondly, that it was a hastily arranged ceremony; cheese and crackers served as the celebratory feast. Also, both sets of in-laws seemed quite displeased with the event, as they all had twisted, miserable expressions of one afflicted with severe constipation or some other equally burdensome malignity.

As my mother was a very forthright person, she never hesitated telling me I was hated from the very moment a certain Dr. Kelpak, I believe, gave her the grim news that no, she was not getting fat, and no, her vomiting problems were not due to a lack of bran in her diet.

Her first act of kindness towards me was by sliding into a very warm tub of water with a very large jug of brandy at her side. The abortion proved unsuccessful, as is evident, and it merely exacerbated her vomiting problems.

In desperation, I suppose, she took up the fine art of walking on her hands. She gained some notoriety with this activity and several of the neighbours would gather in the backyard and clap as she practiced. She grew so adept at this activity that she even mastered hopping around on her hands, much like an inverted rabbit. Again, the neighbours would gather and cheer, throwing small amounts of coinage in appreciation. One woman baked her a cake. Many suggested she should audition for the circus the next time it came through town. A gift, they said. Natural talent.... My father saw this, but he, he knew better. He knew that the pleasure she derived from the applause and the spare coinage, which, by the way, was welcomed, was actually secondary to her true motivation.

Trying hard to make the best of a sorry situation, my father tried to support my mother during her nine-month incarceration. He took the requisite prenatal courses with her, and painted the room pink and blue to herald my imminent arrival. He even recorded my first moments of life with a small tape recorder and a camera. The photos have since been destroyed, apparently by way of a fire, more likely by garburator, but by good fortune I happened upon the tape recording which is to this day in my possession. The event goes as follows: *(He pulls out a notepad.)* My mother is breathing hard *(He breathes hard.)* and yelps with pain. *(He yelps.)* My father says "You're doing fine, honey. That's right. You're doing great." My mother says, "Shut up, you idiot." My father offers no reply. The doctor says, "You're doing great. Yes. Yes, that's right, Mrs. Parkinson. That's right, just push a little harder." My mother moans. *(He moans.)* My father says, "Breathe, honey. You remember. In two-three, out two-" "Shut up, you idiot." Again, my father offers no reply. The doctor then says, "Yes, that's right. Great! That's right. Good. Good. Just push a bit more. *(He grunts.)* Good. Good. Yes, that's it. One last time. *(He grunts.)* Great. Great. Now I can see...." At this point the volume gets surprisingly low. "Holy mother of God. What the..." "What!" says my mother. "Push, 2, 3, honey." "Uuggh," screams my mother. "Nurse?" asks the doctor. "Jesus Christ. What the hell... is that a..." "Oh my!" says the nurse. "Great. Just great," says the doctor. "What?" says my mother. "It's out now. Relax. Nurse, I want you to.... Where the hell.... Get over here. Wrap this up." "Oh no, if you please, I'd rather...." "Just wrap it up and keep your mouth...." "What?" says my mother. At this point you can hear my father start to chuckle, and then break out into a hysteric macabre laugh. *(He imitates his father's laugh.)* He then collapses on the ground, mute. "This is my moment, Harry. My moment." "Don't just stand there. Wrap it up." "What's wrong?" "Please, no, I can't." "My baby. You have to slap my baby. It has to breathe." "Ah, yes, right, slap it. I forgot. Hmm. Yes...." You then hear what sounds suspiciously like the sound of two hands coming together in a clap, and the doctor going "WAAA!" "What? What the hell are you doing? Give me my baby. I want to see my baby!" "Ah, I think, Mrs. Parkinson, that under the circumstances...." "I want to see my baby. Give me my baby! My baby! My baby!" "Yes, yes of course, but...." The nurse weeping in the background. "Give me my baby!!" "Yes. Of course, but, ah, Mrs. Parkinson, I'm afraid you've, well, you've just given birth to a... a...." "A what? Is it a boy or a girl? A boy or a girl? A boy or a girl?" "Ah, geez, I, ah... Nurse?" "I just wanted to help people. That's all. I just wanted to help." "Let me see it!" "Yes, of course you do, but under the circumstances...." "Let me see it!" "Well, if you insist...." There is a brief pause and then my mother screams. It's really quite horrible when you hear it on the tape. "Okay, who's the joker, huh?" She wails, and over her lamentation the doctor can be heard to say, "It would appear, Mrs. Parkinson, that you've just given birth to a, a…. It would appear, Mrs. Parkinson, that you've just given birth to a fish." A Fish.

And so, I was born. Actually, my feet were partially formed and a tuft of hair sprouted from my pate. But it was undeniable. I was, for the most part anyways, a fish.

Needless to say, my mother didn't want a shower. What would she do with the obligatory gifts of sweaters and booties? Diapers? How does a fish soil itself? Can they be breast-fed? Can they be…. My mother would never dare.

In front of the hospital, the doctors and nurses cheerfully waved as my mother slipped into a waiting taxi with her now-born… whatever. My father was unable to drive her, you see, as he was admitted into the regional psychiatric facility. He remains there to this day, mute. When we arrived home, my mother placed me on the counter, drew a shallow bath, and then threw me in. I suppose I flopped around a bit, hitting my head on the cold enamel.

No doubt my mother had a terrible time eradicating the rumours, which were in fact true, about her wretched little spawning. The rumours were made to fester, however, by my mother's refusal to let anyone see me. Not even my grandparents saw me until much later. Taunts of "fish lady" and "salmon head" followed her wherever she went, but she would protest, upon entering the pet store, that the fish food she was purchasing was indeed for a pair of Brazilian goldfish she had won at a pie-eating contest. The hearsay persisted, however, and my mother was forced to relocate to the town of Lethbridge, to the south.

I lay in an enamel tub for the first four years of my life. My mother would only appear during feeding times, as prescribed by her fish-care book. I was weaned on a steady diet of worms and tinned fish food, which she would sprinkle on the surface. As I was something of a hybrid, I could breathe both by way of gills, and out of my mouth. In an attempt to make my life a bit more tolerable, I suppose, she placed in my tub two miniature ceramic figurines: a submerged castle, and a pirate skull. I would pathetically flop about, ravenous for food. Without so much as a word, she would sprinkle my meal and exit. Sometimes I could see her crying.

Strangely enough, during my early years I slowly developed the anatomy of a human. By one year of age, my feet blossomed like those of a real baby. Twinkly toes and all. No legs, though. Just feet. Next, hard bumps appeared just below my lateral fins, and my head changed from an angular, to an oval shape. My eyes came together and my large, gaping mouth grew smaller. Scales still covered the entirety of my body.

By my second and third years, those two little bumps had developed into small hands and arms. My head, for the most part anyways, looked like that of a child, except with a severe skin disease, eczema or psoriasis perhaps. I had no nose, just two holes. My feet were now well-formed and the beginnings of legs could be seen. Also, and this is very important, I now had two sprout-like ears. My mother, who was now resigned to her fate, spoke to me. Her tones were never pleasant, but at least she was speaking, and I could hear! In the privacy of my tub, I would desperately try to form words with my mouth—to imitate her—but to no avail. I could only manage a hapless "glug, glug."

By my fourth and fifth year, I was getting too big for the bathtub and was placed downstairs in the basement in what I fondly call the "holding tank" – a converted trough. My legs were now formed up to the knees. I had the full arms of a child my age and my fins had fully receded. My tail was now a large bump where my rear should have been. I had a head now and my eyes were only slightly askew. I even had a nose, though small. My lips were light and full, and my thick tongue had thinned, allowing me to train it into a dexterous tool for speech. I could now lift myself up the ledge of the tub and call, "Mommy." She would never come, of course. Only at the time prescribed by her fish-care book.

Some time toward the latter part of this period, I can remember feeling terribly hungry. As was often the case, my mother would either leave for extended periods of time without providing adequate food, or just plain forget to feed me. In desperation, I ventured for the first time out of the tub, lifting myself up and over the ledge, flopping onto the floor. My feet and legs were useless and weak, so walking was out of the question. I heard something upstairs. What was that? Something. A noise. People? I'm not sure. But… using my spindly arms I dragged myself along the floor, exploring as I went: the coolness of concrete, the roar and warmth of the furnace, the *(knock, knock)* crispness of the wood stairs. All was new and mysterious. Tactile sensations.

Scaling the stairs, of course, was a formidable task, and I had to use every ounce of my strength to lift and pull myself up, up into the light of day. Heaving and pulling, I got to the second-last stair, and…. What was that? Yes. Yes. People. Living human beings, more distinctly now. With a tremendous effort, heaving and pulling and grasping and stretching, I reached up, up to the last stair, but, my weak arms gave and I tumbled, tumbled, tumbled, tumbled, tumbled, tumbled, tumbled, tumbled, *(He stomps.)* hitting my head on the concrete. The door at the top of the stairs opened with a bright shaft of light, and there stood my mother. She gave me a look, a look which I can't even try to describe, and then she whimsically turned to her audience and quipped, "Oh nothing, just the belching of the furnace. Another drink?" The door closed, and the light receded.

As I'm sure you can imagine, my early years were devoid of the pleasures commonly associated with youth. I attended Fleetwood Bawden Elementary School, and was blessed with the tutelage of a certain Mrs. Provan, who never hesitated reminding me (in front of others, by the way), that my patchy skin could be improved with a good washing and some calamine lotion, and that my fish-like stench was inhibiting the academic performance of those that sat around me – within a "barns width," as she was fond of saying. One morning, after a particularly bad day, I called the school saying that I was ill and couldn't make it in, as I had risen too quickly from the tub that morning and was suffering from the "bends." It didn't work, and Mrs. Provan often publicly cited my attempt as an excellent example of poor reasoning. Most children learn the sweat of self-consciousness in the latter stage of puberty. Most.

Winter proved a relief as I could hide my deformity behind a heavy coat and a full-faced balaclava. Wearing the balaclava indoors, however, which I was apt to do, proved difficult, and it only worsened the jeers from my classmates. I can remember one time in grade three math class, when the teacher left the room to attend to some business at the front office, leaving us to work on some math problems. Bradley Shidell, a horrible example of the species with a pitbull disposition, started with a few cracks about my smell. I tried to ignore him, but his taunts grew louder and louder. In indignation I defended myself, saying "I didn't know what he was talking about." You see, I was immune to the problem by now, the smell, so technically speaking, I wasn't lying. I knew with this defiance, Young Bradley would either cease, or that it would catapult him to another level of belligerence. A tactical error on my part. He rose with a huff and approached my desk. I tired to ignore this escalation in the conflict by burying myself in the assignment. Two times two equals four. Four times four equals – "Hey guys, check this out." Please. Please. Just go away. And the next thing I knew, several had gathered around my desk, jeering and taunting and poking and prodding…. Then one grabbed the balaclava on my head. I tried to hold it tight. Please, just leave me alone. Just – But then another grabbed, and then all, all these hands. These hands grabbing and clawing and wrenching and… prying it off. *(pause)* I cried. *(pause)* But that was then.

I'm sorry. This is difficult. You understand? It's funny really. I mean, why am I here? Right now. In front of you? I'm standing here and you're sitting there, and… quite dutifully I might add. It's good of you. *(pause)* You see, we're searching, aren't we? I mean you and I, all of us, for something. We're all searching for something that can't be grasped, or placed in a box, or held in our arms. For a place where no one knows us, free of names or titles or histories.

I remember once, I had to do some shopping, for something. I don't know exactly what, and there was an old woman on the corner selling poppies, you know, the poppies that you buy to support the veterans, and I went up to her, offered her ten dollars and asked for one. She smiled and said my contribution was more than enough. And behind her, in this parking lot, I could see these two boys peeing on the front wheel of this parked car. Right there, peeing for the hell of it. And, well, I thought it was pretty funny. The old woman pinned the poppy on me, and there walked by these two young people, a greasy boy with the remnants of acne and a smiling girlfriend with too much make-up on, clinging to his arm. And he was so, so proud, and she was so beautiful, awkwardly trying to place her head on his shoulders as they walked. And the old woman going on about the generosity of my contribution and how most would have offered much less, and those two having a hell of a good time at the car, and I suppose I thought in that moment, that in some way or another, it was all going to be all right. We were going to be all right.

    Pause.

I actually made it through school, and my skin, the skin of a fish, cleared to what it is now. I left home after graduating, getting a job at the city hall as a clerk. A tedious job, I know, but it was welcomed, as few of the people there had ever heard of me. I loved the anonymity, I suppose.

I didn't have much luck with women, as I'm sure you might imagine. It's hard for me, you see. Often I would meet a woman, and summoning all my courage I would ask her out. Often she would say no, but sometimes they would say yes. I was very awkward, and, well, often they would leave immediately after the movie. I spent many hours alone, and still don't talk very much.

I once met a woman named… well that really doesn't matter. She worked in the cafeteria downstairs. She was very friendly, and to me, very beautiful. I would go out of my way to visit the cafeteria, often just sitting, silent, staring, as she flipped her grilled-cheese sandwiches. I couldn't bear to talk to her, only sit and be enamoured by her culinary expertise and gentle disposition. One day, and I couldn't believe it, she came up to me, at the table where I was sitting, and asked why it was that I always wore turtlenecks. You see, I have to, as they cover up the remains of what I am: one gill on either side of my neck. I said that my father wore them and that I always sought to emulate him. A stupid reason, I know, but it was the only thing I could think of at the time. She said that she had always found men handsome in them. I didn't know what to say. I mean, could this perhaps be construed as meaning she found me handsome? That was a pretty ridiculous thought. Then, to further this momentous exchange, she said that she preferred white, but that dark blue was still nice. And when she said this, she smiled, how can I say, with this innocence. I came back for the next while with the same sort of regularity, and again, we would talk. Sometimes about everything, the world, and sometimes about nothing at all. And then on a Friday afternoon, when I came in for a coffee, she paused and quietly asked if I would like to go out with her that weekend. We did. She said that she had always liked Walt Disney films, and I think that under any other circumstances I would have found those seven dwarfs unbearable, but I loved it. We went for a walk. For miles. We talked and talked, and then sometimes, as we strolled through the crisp spring air, we said nothing. Nothing at all. The third time we went out, she even took my hand. And nothing was even said.

I was worried, though. I had to tell her about myself. Who I was, what I was. I was sitting across from her in a dimly lit restaurant. I had to tell her. I wanted her to know about me, and everything I was, or loved, or feared, or hated. And that perhaps, perhaps if she could accept…. I told her I had something to tell her. She smiled and said that she couldn't imagine anything about me that she didn't know. But you don't know, you have to know this…. And I pulled down the neck of my turtleneck. Please. Please, just… I don't want to be let… I just want… she just looked at it a moment, saying nothing. It's me. Remember. Me. Please. Oh God please. I didn't say anything to her. I didn't know what to say. What more could I say? Then, no no please, she stood up, quickly, saying she had to go. To a meeting or something. I'm not sure and… she was gone.

And at that moment, at that pinpoint moment in time and space, where everything just stands still, so still, like an echo frozen in air, at that moment I was all alone in my life. Terribly alone.

Pause.

Well, what could I expect? Right? I mean, really. What could I expect? *(pause)* I didn't visit the cafeteria much after that.

All I ever wanted in my life is…. Have you ever wanted to fly? Just to fly away, governed by the wind's currents and the will of your arms. Driven, driven on by a contempt, a rotting, gnawing contempt for yourself, and everything you are or ever will be? Just to fly away, or, yes, yes, to swim, swim the seven oceans and the countless boundless seas without ever needing a breath, to swim away beyond this, the dominion of the senses. To a world, far away, once known but forgotten, like a hazy dream, a world where the sea, the sea refuses no river. Not a drop. And I am that driver. We. We are that river. What have we done? What have we lost? What have we…. I'm sorry. I'm not making very much sense.

Pause.

Three weeks later, I was looking out the window of my office, in a reverie no doubt, musing on what I was, or what I wasn't. I saw a yellow Volkswagen drive into the parking lot. It was her car. She must have been late for work. I turned away. I didn't want to see her. I… I sat back at my desk and tried to concentrate on my work at hand. And then, a few minutes later, there she was, standing beside the partition that separates my space from another clerk's. I was… I'm not sure. It was like– "I want to take you somewhere." For lunch, I supposed. I cleaned up my desk and left with her. Without saying a word, we got in the car, and she started to drive. We passed where one would normally stop for lunch, and then on to the outskirts of town. "Ah, where are we going?" She just turned to me, gently putting her finger on my lips and said "Sshh." We spoke no more after that. We headed into the mountains. I had never been to the mountains before. They were beautiful. Through the windy passes, on and on for miles. The only time we stopped was for gas. And further into this land I never knew, until night fell, and still on, on, without ever saying so much as a word. And then as the sun began to rise, I could smell something. I didn't know what, but it was something I knew, or felt I knew, or once did. A familiar, sweet smell. And as the morning sun crested over the land, we arched over a hill, and there before me was the sea, the endless expanse of water, in constant motion, and infinite depth. We drove down to the beach and parked. She got out, came around the car, opened my door, and said, "Come." She led me down to the water. And then just a few feet from the shore, she turned me to face her, and then, she undressed me. I didn't know what to say. You see, I've never been without my clothes, I mean, in front of anyone. And then she took off her clothes and she was… beautiful. So beautiful. And we stood there facing each other. Then with a slight, gentle smile, her smile, she took her index finger and gently stoked my gills. Like this. And then she held my shoulders, turned me towards the sea, and said "Go home." Home. I was afraid, you see, as I don't know how to swim. I know that sounds ridiculous, but it's true. I don't know how to swim. It's deep, very deep, and… I've always been afraid of water. Very, very afraid, and… and I went in. To the water. And at that moment, I suppose I discovered, for the first time in my life, what redemption was. Redemption. And what it was to belong. To belong to something, something greater, far, far greater than ourselves. Than you or me or any of us. Something wondrous and large and fearful and wondrous. The water is cold, but good. We swam. I was home.

Michael Redhill   *The Hanging Gardens of Willowdale*

1992
Richard Greenblatt: Director
Andrew Akman
Diane Flacks

¤•¤

A play for two actors. One actor will play the role of MORDECHAI. The other actor will play all the other roles.

Lights up.

YIDDISH GOTHIC   A man of perhaps 25 stands in a yarmulke and shorts holding a rake.

MORDECHAI   Yea, verily I toiled in the gardens of the Lord. I toiled in his vineyards, I toiled in his orchards, I toiled like never has a twelve-year-old with buck teeth so bad he bites his chest every time he sneezes toiled.

The second man enters.

RABBI   Verily shalt though prune this bush, and thou shalt rake out this pond and so wilt thou also make like a monkey up this tree and there shall you pick apples and pears receiving unto yourself tremendous cuts and bruises so you may never forget that the Jews suffered in the land of Pharaoh and did not eat unto themselves any manner of fruit salad. And for this we shall pay you a sum of no less than two dollars an hour. So now, Mordechai, what do you say?

MORDECHAI   The closest experience I'd ever had to gardening was eating salad. I was in a delicate moral position. Should I allow myself to be trusted with the types of tools that cause the cessation of fun by the poking out of eyes? Or should I continue in the Hebrew lessons I was to be excused from if I took the job?

MR. GREENBERG   Repeat after me: *sh'chall v'chach chlach chhachh chh chhh chhachhl.*

MORDECHAI   I prayed many nights to God, hoping he would tell me what to do.

GOD   Well, Mordechai, let me put it thusly unto you: I did not bring you out of the land of Egypt so you could live like some lazy yutz out here in the promised land. Okay, Willowdale, so it's not the promised land, so sue me. Still, I caused you to be born to loving parents, this is true – all right, so your mother doesn't know from haircuts. *Still*: a nice package, don't you think? What am I saying? Yes – Mordechai: as your God, as the one and only God, to whom you ask this question vis-a-vis your job, I say: don't be a putz. Two dollars an hour is not for sneezing at. I have spoken.

MORDECHAI Thank you, oh God.

GOD And Mordechai: remember I am watching everything you do and can hear everything you think and know what is going to happen to you for the rest of your life, including the awful things your children are going to do to you. Have fun!

MORDECHAI In this way it came to pass that I was a gardener. And the head gardener was Joe, brother of Al, brother of Harry who drank so much it looked like his eyes stayed in his head by sheer suction. Joe was a good man, patient, gentle.

JOE How'd you like me to kick your butt for you?

MORDECHAI When Joe was around I daintily plucked weeds or looked tenderly at saplings, but when alone, I took my revenge on Joe the head gardener and hacked at the evergreens with a rake until the gardens looked like a topiary from the third circle of Hell. I hacked at the vines running up the gazebo, I hacked at the chokecherry tree, I hacked at the tulips. I was a young Turk with that rake. I had something to say with that rake. What I was saying was this: if you are in the right place at the right time, you can get out of Hebrew lessons.

RHONDA How come you're not in class? Mr. Greenberg says you're not coming back.

MORDECHAI OH! I… I… I'm… look at her. Isn't she something? Look at that face. Rhonda Eisenstatt. I hated Hebrew lessons, but I could think of no crueler fate than having to drag the pond for green scum while inside she sang traditional Hebrew songs in a sweet lilting voice which sometimes gave me a terrific boner. Rhonda. Rhonda. Rhonda.

RHONDA Why didn't you come back to Hebrew classes, Mordechai? Because of you, I sat beside Shane Resnick the whole year and eventually I married him and had three *meeskite* children.

MORDECHAI RHONDA! Can you still respect me that I returned to the land while you fell for that fat pig Resnick? I had to take that job to send my father to medical school, else I would have been in there with you singing "*Cheery Cheery Bim*" in four keys all at once. How I wanted to present you with a gift of pears from the temple orchards! How I longed to grow a tall red rose to show you my undying affection! How I wished you would grow breasts already so we could see how this could all turn out!

RHONDA (*fading away*) Mordechai! I loved you—only you—and you abandoned meeeeeeeeee.

MORDECHAI I hacked and hacked! I hacked at everything – clear it away! I hacked a path clear into the future where Rhonda Eisenstatt would have breasts and we would be married with beautiful children. But who was I fooling? I knew nothing about girls. Nothing about gardening. Nothing about life even.

RABBI Mordechai! Come here, Mordechai. Come into this little house of mine and let me impart unto you the wisdom of the ages. Come!

MORDECHAI I walked into the Rabbi's house.

RABBI No, here – come through the door.

MORDECHAI I walked through the Rabbi's door. He took me and sat me down in the special room with all the fish tanks. As usual, he offered me things without yeast in them.

RABBI Have a macaroon? A Swedish toast? A little wood? No? Fine. Listen, Mordechai–

MORDECHAI –He said to me–

RABBI Mordechai ben Shmuel ben Yosef ben Zeitel ben Ben, these are carp. And these over here, these are carp as well. Do you know what this tells us as Jews?

MORDECHAI It tells us… that our suffering is like these carp, which swim unaware that they are surrounded by enemies and that the only way they will survive is if they band together and only marry other carp.

RABBI No my boy, my *shaneh punim*, it doesn't tell us anything. Now if the gardens look *os gemachte* next week, you're fired.

MORDECHAI Fired! I was in a quandary! If I got fired my father would never let me forget it.

FATHER I won't let you forget this.

MORDECHAI But if I kept working at the temple not only would I have to continue doing something I had no skill at, but I would also have to keep eating the Rabbi's Swedish toasts. I decided to confront my elders with this difficult problem. Buby, I said, what should a man do if he is involved in something that makes him feel like he is not living up to his potential?

BUBY Potential shmotential! Feh!

MORDECHAI Buby, I want to know what is the moral thing to do if you're doing something you don't enjoy. Should you quit?

BUBY Quit shmit! You had supper?

MORDECHAI Buby! I have a moral problem. (I'm thirteen and I have a moral problem!) Listen to me – what is the right thing to do?

BUBY Your mama didn't make you no supper. So, okay, I'm making you supper. Then we'll have maybe an enema and you'll see things are going to come out okay.

MORDECHAI Things weren't going so well with my grandmother. So I went to my grandfather and I said, Zaida, should I keep my job?

ZAIDA coughs, a prolonged rheumy cough.

Said my grandfather.

ZAIDA Listen, when I was a boy, my family didn't have what to eat, so I was lucky I should make five shekels what is now maybe half a dollar, and if I wanted to see a show, I couldn't eat supper, and if I wanted to eat supper, I couldn't see a show. Sure – once I saw half a show and I had half a supper, but that was no good because all the night I'm hungry and I don't know what is the ending of the show. I didn't have even a crust of bread, and if you went into the orchards to pick yourself an apple maybe, the *rushess* would come with a gun and shoot you.

MORDECHAI But Zaida! What about my question?

ZAIDA Ah, my *shaneleh*, listen to me. My faddah was a Cohen and my faddah's faddah was a Cohen, and me, I'm a Cohen too. So be a good boy and get me a Coke.

MORDECHAI I was running out of elders. I went to my bar mitzvah teacher.

JACOB *(chanting)* A-men!

MORDECHAI Jacob: will quitting my job interfere with my becoming a man?

JACOB Chanting! Chanting!

MORDECHAI *(chanting)* Can I quit my job at the temple?

JACOB *(chanting)* Why should you quit your job at the temple?

MORDECHAI *(chanting)* Because I *want* to quit my job at the temple.

JACOB What? And bring shame to your parents?

MORDECHAI I'm already bringing them shame.

JACOB But that's because you hardly cross a room without your breaking something. But a job they're proud of!

MORDECHAI I'm never going to be a man at this rate.

JACOB Don't break out in a sweat. I'm here to teach you. Let's hear you recite.

MORDECHAI *(chanting) Chachll b'chach v'chach–*

JACOB No! Like this: *(chanting)* A-Men! Please God I shouldn't get an erection in front of the congregationnn…

MORDECHAI I was no good, but they bar mitzvahed me anyway.

RABBI And let us say, as a congregation, *oy vey*.

MORDECHAI I was scared out of my wits, but everyone was so proud–

ZAIDA *Oy* my *pitzeleh*! You chanted like a man! Everyone was crying like a river! Everyone loves you! Now we're going to give you lots of money! *Vavoy!* *(sings) Mazel tov* and *tzimmin tov* and *tzimmin tov* and *mazel tov* and *mazel tov* and *tzimmin tov* and *tzimmin tov* and *mazel tov*!

MORDECHAI So now I was a man. Yet I did not feel like a man. The only relative I had my age was my simple cousin Moishe, who spent his days trying to suck his face into jam jars. Moishe couldn't tell me about manhood–

MOISHE *(voice reverberating inside a jam jar)* Hey! Look at this!

MORDECHAI –then it hit me: so, okay, Moishe's an idiot, but at least he has a skill! I went back to the Rabbi's house with new resolve. They'd tried to make me a man by giving me a job. That didn't work. Neither did making me yodel in Hebrew. I had to become my own man.

RABBI Hello, Mordechai – how is it with you! Have some of this sponge cake what is made from potatoes and water.

MORDECHAI Rev: this is not my calling. I was made for something bigger. I want to become a carpenter! I want to build things with my hands that people will be proud to put inside their home.

RABBI This is good news! This is wonderful news! I am happy for you, Mordechai ben Shmuel ben all those other people! Now maybe you will find yourself and the temple grounds will stop looking like some giant cow grazed here! I give you my blessing!

MORDECHAI And with that he lay his hand on my head, but he was just getting some leverage so he could turn around and shut the door.

The second actor vanishes.

And so I left from that place, and I did not look back unto that place, and the Rabbi's words to me at my bar mitzvah reverberated in my head:

RABBI *(voice)* If a man steal an ox, or a sheep, and kill it, or sell it, he shall pay five oxen for an ox, and four sheep for a sheep.

MORDECHAI –which to this day, I still don't know what it means. That summer I did my job at the temple and I went finally to Israel – The Promised Land! The Land of Milk and Honey! The Home of The Chosen People! – and there I met some lovely Mormons. Then I came back and went into grade seven where God caused me to suffer greatly, or at least I thought it was God, but it turned out to be my haircut, which was my mother's fault.

David Gow   ***Listen***

1993
Performed at the Spring Arts Fair under the title *Do You Have a Moment?*
Hamish McEwan: Director
Andrew Miller: Brian – in his early twenties.
He is good-natured, somewhat shy, which he tries to compensate for with a bravado that is not convincing.
Ron Lea: Alex – in his late thirties.
He has a large personality and presence, he seems to be full of confidence and certainty, at times this is contradicted by his impatience and temper.

¤ • ¤

The two men are in an office which is very simple. They each have an office phone and papers, perhaps electric pencil sharpeners,

BRIAN   I'm not selling anything. I'm not selling a goddamned thing. Jack said to talk to you, and watch.

ALEX   Why? Why aren't you selling anything? That's what you've got to examine.

BRIAN   No one's interested. They're practically hostile. They got screwed on a scheme. Can you believe this Publisher's Bookrack thing? Ten magazines a month for four years. Twenty dollars a month, they get from these people. That's five hundred bucks over four years and then we call.

ALEX   Yes…

BRIAN   Well, there's no way we're gonna sell to these people.

ALEX   I'm using the same deck as you. So many bought from the magazine, so many this, so many that.

BRIAN   I don't think so, these people are hostile.

ALEX   What area code are you in?

BRIAN   Why?

ALEX   What area code are you in?

BRIAN   Five One Nine.

ALEX   Get out of it.

BRIAN   Why?

ALEX Am I talking for my own benefit here, or are you listening to me? Because if I'm talking for my own benefit, I'd prefer to complain, like you are. *(beat)* Very few people want to hear someone else complain, if you're asking. People hate whiners. People like winners.

BRIAN Yes, I know, people have become tired of detail.

ALEX What?

BRIAN You heard me, that's what I think.

ALEX What are you, a demographer? Did you just recently get laid-off from a pollster's job?

BRIAN Ya. Ya I did. I just left a job, at sixty thou a year and took my Beamer back to the dealership. I'm a repentant baby boomer fallen from the dizzying heights of the latest boom, practicing a peculiar blend of Zen Buddhism and Amway sales. Taking from life…

> *ALEX stares darkly at BRIAN for a moment. He stands up, walks over to him and swats him with something.*

ALEX *(starting to laugh)* You little pipsqueak. You've got quite a mouth on you, don't you? You should be selling like crazy; that was quite a pile of sarcasm came spewing out there. If I were a little more macho, I'd give you a shot in the mouth for that.

BRIAN Ya, but you're not, you're a very sensitive individual.

ALEX Shatup. Sell some product, ya wuss.

BRIAN I will. I will. *(beat)* Why should I switch area codes?

ALEX Watch. (*He picks up the phone and dials. He waits a few moments.)* Four O Three, Alberta…. Hellooo, Mr. MacGuigan. How are ya today, sir? (*He hits the mute button.)* They love talking out there, too cold to do anything else. (*He hits the button again.)* Good, good. Listen, listen. *(pause)* It's Alex Majors callin' for *Cottage and Country Magazine*, and we've had a little problem with 'r mail-outs, on the renewal forms. This isn't just a problem in Red Deer, but in Lethbridge, Fort McLeod, Edmonton, all over Alberta, can you believe it? *(pause)* Yes they are. Well that's Canada Post for ya', ah ha ha ha. Would you believe this? All through November and December they were taking our mail for Alberta and shipping it out to Chatham, Ontario, of all places, and just leaving it there, ya, in those big canvas mailbags, in a giant deserted warehouse. Ah ha ha ha. Three, four thousand pieces of mail a month. Ah ha ha ha…. Well that's what I said; give me fifty thousand a year plus benefits, I'll throw away the mail. Thaaat's right. Ha ha, so anyway we're calling to apologise for that little mix-up, oh jeez, I forgot to mention the free book, we've got this book deal all about cottages, it's coming to ya' free, don't even worry about it…. Ya! ya, that's included. Uh huh. Are you still on Kincardine Road? Okay, that's it, Mr. MacGuigan, it's on the way out to ya sir. *(long pause, then very genuinely)* Well thank you very much, and you have a good evening too. Bye now. (*He hangs up.)* Thank you, Mr. MacGuigan, under two minutes, loves the magazine, can't imagine what he'd do without it. Pleased as pie.

BRIAN Hmmn. You don't feel bad telling them all that mail story?

ALEX What's to feel bad about, it's true, I read it in the *Star*. Happens all the time.

BRIAN Ya, but you make it sound like it just happened, just now, to us.

ALEX That man just had the best laugh he's had since God knows when. He was dying over the mail stuff. It's a universal Canadian experience.

BRIAN Ya, but it's not true.

ALEX I am trying to show you something here. You think Toshiba actually boils their computers in saltwater to test them? No, it's an isolated instance, it's something that happened once, but they put it in the ads in such a way, you'd think it was their testing procedure.

BRIAN *(pause)* Ya, I guess, but people know that's an advertisement.

ALEX Mnn hmnn. What were the first words out of my mouth after "how are ya'?" I said, it's Alex Majors calling for *Cottage and Country Magazine*, they know I'm calling to sell something, they buy it. That's a relationship on top of which, when one has personality, we build rapport. People don't want a stunned, twenty-year-old, just got kicked out a' Forest Hill, guilt-ridden bum clod on the phone, they want entertainment. And you're an actor. Ha.

BRIAN So you're entertaining them, is that it?

ALEX Yes, I goddamn am. Make a call, I want to see what you're doing.

BRIAN Now?

ALEX Yes now, right now, let's go.

BRIAN All right, all right, I'm calling. *(He picks up the receiver.)* Four O Three, these people lo-ove to talk. *(dials, to himself)* Mr. O'Malley. *(into phone)* Hello Mr. O'Malley, it's Brian Stevenson here. I'm calling for *Cottage and Country Magazine*. Yes…. Oh you do, that's nice yes, yes, oh all right, all right then. Bye now. *(hangs up)*

ALEX What was that?

BRIAN His brother gets it, they read it together so…

ALEX So: *(laying on a bit of the brogue)* is that subscription up to date now, Mr. O'Malley? I know it may sound ridiculous but these are skills. Skills which could stand you in very good stead in the real world.

BRIAN You seem to have the impression I come from a pampered background, where do you get that idea?

ALEX The way you hold yourself, the way you seem to find this just a tiny little bit of a pain. If you came from a less privileged background, you'd either get angry and walk out, or you'd get on with it.

BRIAN I think you're making generalisations, I also think you're taking about yourself.

ALEX Oooo. *Touché. (beat)* Good, very good. To succeed at anything, the first thing is to get the fists up. Now, stop apologising on the phone and try another one. If you don't sell a couple tonight, you'll be encouraged nicely to leave.

BRIAN I need this job, I have to make a little money…

ALEX In the programme here, we generate funds for Jack, we do that by selling.

BRIAN Would you please cut the sarcasm, it's not helpful in any way, so cut it, Alex.

ALEX Very good, fists up. Now tell me off some more, sting me…

BRIAN Shut up.

ALEX Thank you.

BRIAN Welcome.

ALEX Go at it tiger, sell some product.

BRIAN I will.

ALEX Good. Do it.

BRIAN Fine.

ALEX I'm watching

BRIAN Great. Great, to have you watching.

ALEX What area code?

BRIAN I'm going to try local.

ALEX Local is good.

BRIAN Here I go.

ALEX GET ON WITH IT FOR CHRISSAKES, this is the longest build-up in the history of telephone sales.

BRIAN Hello, Mr. Ferrar. Yes, it's Brian calling for *Cottage and Country Magazine*. We're just calling because your subscription has just recently run out and we'd like to see if we can take care of it for you. We have a free book and ah…. You would, that's great. All right, are you still on Dufferin, no. Brunswick, well let me take that address down. You're kidding, for your brother too? Both of you at the same address, oh I see. Well this is great for me. Two years, forty-nine, ninety-five? Perfect we'll send them both out. *(pause)* All right, thank you, Mr. Ferrar. (*He hangs up.*)

ALEX Could you hear his breathing? What did you sell, two two-years? (*BRIAN nods.*) That's rare. Very rare.

BRIAN How do mean? What do you mean about the breathing?

ALEX You couldn't hear it?

BRIAN NO.

ALEX You weren't listening. Once you have the party breathing correctly, the sale is done.

BRIAN What are you talking about?

ALEX takes a sharp inhale as though about to say something.

ALEX That. Seventy percent of the time that's *large inhale*. I'm not interested, but at least thirty percent of the time, it's YES, YES, YES. No breathing is usually very good news. Like a slide, a steady downhill slide is what no breathing means. The resolve sliding away. Steady relaxed inaudible breathing, that's best, breathing that you hear on "oh ya," "sure," "yup" this is: finish me off breathing. This is: I'm yours breathing.

BRIAN I don't see how this relates to my sales average. I don't notice much of anything about other people's breathing, I'm not really that interested. Most of the very few sales I've made are, I think, because the person at the other end happened to want the product, and we called.

ALEX Well you should be dialing like all hell then, because that is not an efficient way of selling. It's not about what the other party wants. It's about what you want. It's about two points of view and how you can make "them" see "yours." That's what it's about.

BRIAN I don't agree with that.

ALEX People fear the intimacy of sharing a viewpoint with someone else. You can almost see them at the other end of the line, looking down at the floor, twirling with the telephone line in their fingers. "Ya, ya, okay, you're right take me with you."

BRIAN Please Alex, I appreciate that you're trying to help me to sell, however I don't subscribe to your…. Your particular view of human interaction as a series of manipulations with winners and losers is…

ALEX What?

BRIAN I don't like it.

An awkward pause.

ALEX I've told you what I think works. We've been talking for too long, and I've been wasting my time.

BRIAN I agree. You have. And so have I. Tell Jack when he comes back, I left, I'll give him a call.

ALEX All right. Bye. *(BRIAN goes to shake his hand, ALEX turns to his work.)* See ya. *(dialing, then looking back)* Hey, you made that sale on Brunswick, two two-years.

BRIAN It was my answering machine.

Pause.

ALEX You're a good kid; but this isn't for you.

BRIAN Bye.

ALEX Hello, Mr. Peters, how are ya. I'm calling from Toronto, what's the temperature out there. Oooooh, that's cold. Listen, listen.

Don Hannah   *Aspiring Francine*

1993
Richard Greenblatt: Director
Nancy Palk: Iris
Chick Reid: Francine

⌑ • ⌑

FRANCINE backs out of the inner office with a paper in her hand; on her head she wears an absurdly large radio headphone set of the sort that joggers use. She never faces the audience and does not notice them. She speaks loudly because the headset is on.

FRANCINE   YES, YES, YES, MS MCPHEE. YES, I'LL POST IT RIGHT AWAY. YES, YES, I'LL LET YOU KNOW THE MINUTE THE STOCK REPORT IS ON THE RADIO.

She shuts the door.

Idiot.

She realises that she has spoken out loud. She glances back to the door, waits a moment, then shrugs. Her back is constantly to the audience as she pins the paper to the wall. The large type at the top of the page reads "HOW TO NAVIGATE YOUR FUTURE" and, below that, "LET MOTIVATIONAL SPEAKER TONY ROBBINS TEACH YOU TO WALK ON FIRE." She turns the radio up louder and she half sings, flatly, along with "Memories" as she reads the paper. Her pantyhose is riding up her bum and she starts pulling at it through her dress. She bends her left leg and pulls at that side of her seat. Then her right. She wiggles her bum. All the while she moans and sings.

"MEMRIES do do do do MEMRIES do do do do do Memries da da da dada daaah" – God, I hate this song.

She isn't getting anywhere with the problem with her panties. She glances towards the inner door, then reaches up inside her dress.

Damn cheap supermarket pantyhose! Aaah.

She gives the panties a sharp tug, wriggles her bum, and breathes a sigh of relief. She turns to go to her desk when she sees the audience.

(screams) AHHHH!

For a split second she stares at them, stunned and embarrassed, then she runs to the inner office. She fumbles with the doorknob and falls inside.

IRIS *(off)* Francine what's—

FRANCINE *(off)* Who are *they*?

IRIS *(off)* Who are who?

FRANCINE *(off)* What are *those people* doing out there?

IRIS *(off)* What people?

FRANCINE *(off)* SSHHH.

IRIS *(off)* Don't Sshhh me! There's people out there?

FRANCINE *(off)* Yes.

IRIS *(off)* Where?

FRANCINE *(off)* In my office.

IRIS *(off)* How many?

FRANCINE *(off)* Twenty, thirty!

IRIS *(off)* In your office? Where are they – pinned to the walls?

FRANCINE *(off)* Rows of them, row after row, they saw me…

IRIS *(off)* In that crummy little office? Oh please. Get back to work. *(beat)* Now!

> *FRANCINE's head appears a couple of feet from the floor, looking out the door. She sees the audience and jerks back inside.*

FRANCINE *(off)* They're still there.

IRIS *(off)* Let me see.

> *IRIS stands in the door and looks about the room.*

FRANCINE *(off)* See?

IRIS Where? I don't see anybody.

FRANCINE *(off)* What?

> *IRIS moves into the centre of the office.*

IRIS Where?

> *FRANCINE's head appears low at the door frame again.*

FRANCINE *(beat)* They're still there.

IRIS Are they hiding?

> *FRANCINE shakes her head and withdraws.*

IRIS Come here.

FRANCINE *(off)* I don't want to.

IRIS Come here!

FRANCINE timidly comes out.

IRIS Where are all these people?

FRANCINE stares around, rather stunned that IRIS doesn't see them. She slowly moves over to IRIS and whispers in her ear.

FRANCINE In the chairs.

IRIS In the chairs.

FRANCINE Yes.

IRIS You mean this chair?

She points to FRANCINE's chair, which is empty.

FRANCINE No, not that chair.

IRIS Oh. Well, which chair then? That one?

She points to a chair in the front row. FRANCINE nods.

There's someone sitting in that chair.

FRANCINE *(hesitantly)* Yes.

IRIS That one.

FRANCINE nods.

That chair that I am pointing at – you see someone in it.

FRANCINE Yes.

IRIS looks at FRANCINE, then at the chair, then back to FRANCINE.

IRIS There is a person sitting in that very chair.

FRANCINE nods.

And ah, what is that person doing?

FRANCINE *(beat)* Watching us.

IRIS The person sitting in that *empty* chair is watching us.

FRANCINE nods.

FRANCINE *(beat)* I don't think that chair is empty.

IRIS Francine doesn't think the chair is empty.

FRANCINE shakes her head.

These people, are they, by any chance, little? Are they little people?

FRANCINE *(whispers)* Normal size.

IRIS What?

FRANCINE *(timidly)* Normal size, I said they're normal size.

> *IRIS sighs, goes over to the chair and, taking no notice of the person sitting on it, she sits down.*

IRIS See?

> *IRIS bounces up and down a few times.*

Lumpy but *empty*. Francine, come here.

> *FRANCINE shakes her head.*

Come here!

> *FRANCINE timidly goes to IRIS. IRIS pats the thigh of the person sitting next to her.*

Sit. Sit down.

> *FRANCINE looks in horror at the person sitting in the chair. She shakes her head.*

Why? Ooh, is there someone in that chair too?

> *FRANCINE nods.*

That *empty* chair?

FRANCINE *(timidly)* It's not... empty.

IRIS Well, then...

> *IRIS pats the thigh of the person sitting on the other side.*

Here. Sit here. *(beat)* Francine, we both know you're on probation in this office. Sit down!

> *FRANCINE moves timidly towards the chair.*

Now!

> *FRANCINE turns and lowers herself gently onto the audience member's lap. She hovers over it. She turns away from IRIS and whispers.*

FRANCINE Sorry.

IRIS What?

FRANCINE Nothing.

> *FRANCINE turns her head and timidly surveys the people behind her.*

IRIS Tell me. Are you on medication?

FRANCINE Not that I'm aware of.

IRIS Francine, you have snapped.

FRANCINE *(beat)* You really can't see anyone?

IRIS Just you. You can still see them?

FRANCINE And hear them.

IRIS Oh, they're talking?

FRANCINE No, laughing a bit. Rustling about.

IRIS "Rustling." "Rustling" what? Paper? *Cattle?*

FRANCINE Just themselves.

IRIS This crowd of immense proportions that only you can see, they are rustling *themselves?*

> *FRANCINE says nothing. IRIS stands up and when FRANCINE starts to follow her:*

Stay!

> *FRANCINE remains sitting, making furtive glances beside and behind her.*

Francine, you're only at this job to support your hobby, aren't you?

FRANCINE Um...

IRIS Yes or no!

FRANCINE Yes. But it's not a hobby.

IRIS Francine, is your name William Shakespeare? Is it Andrew Lloyd Webber?

FRANCINE No.

IRIS An obsession that isn't a *living* is a *hobby*. Ships in bottles, decorative plates from the Franklin Mint, writing for the theatre – these are hobbies. Am I right?

FRANCINE If you say so, Ms McPhee.

IRIS And all that big talk when you're down on the street smoking. About the crisis in theatre, about finding your audience – all that moaning about busloads of "fools" on their way to a *perfectly respectable evening* at *Phantom* – I think it's all caught up with you.

FRANCINE You do?

IRIS Yes. You used to fantasise about phone calls from producers. Yes?

FRANCINE *(meekly)* Not quite.

IRIS When little Darth Valinsky phoned up from the mail room, you got all excited because you thought it was someone else, didn't you?

FRANCINE Please...

IRIS And someone you'd previously said unkind things about. But yet when you thought he was phoning you to talk about your little script on the evils of corporate Bay Street – what was it called?

FRANCINE Please...

IRIS What was it called?

FRANCINE *Facilitator 2.*

IRIS *Facilitator 2.* Based, I might add, on a weekend that you were sent to at no expense to yourself and no small cost to this firm. A motivational seminar with a very great human being and, had you paid attention to Tony Robbins, you might start getting somewhere in this life. Well, when you heard Darth was on the phone that day you were pretty excited, as I recall. I recall the phrase "That She-Bitch can kiss my butt goodbye." Am I right?

FRANCINE Um, maybe…

IRIS I don't think it's a maybe, Francine. I know it's a yes because I wrote it down. But it was just little Darth from downstairs calling to tell you that a stack of very important letters had come back due to insufficient postage.

FRANCINE *(meekly)* They keep changing the rates.

IRIS Who is talking here? I believe She-Bitch has the floor. *(beat)* And now you're so desperate for attention that you're actually imagining that there is an audience in your office.

FRANCINE But…

IRIS But what?

FRANCINE But there is.

> *IRIS scans the office.*

IRIS If I didn't dislike you so much, this would be sad.

> *She moves towards her office.*

Very sad. Get back to your desk and stop wasting my time.

> *IRIS leaves. FRANCINE stands and turns to the person she has been sitting on.*

FRANCINE I'm very sorry. If you exist. I mean, I'm not sorry that you *exist* I'm sorry that, well, if you are there and I sat on you, that, well, it isn't very polite to sit on someone. Even if they are invisible. To the corporate sector, at least. Are you here? God, I hope not. I hate audience participation. I'm always afraid that I'll get dragged up in front of people and humiliated. Like my Aunt Marsha at Raveen that time. He had her crawling around onstage on all fours, barking like a dog. Then she took out her teeth.

> *Shakes her head and, going to her desk, tries to work. But she keeps making furtive glances at the audience. She stops trying to work.*

Five nights a week my boyfriend Danny and I get drunk and complain about the fact that no one gives a damn about theatre. That there's no money. That there's no audience anymore. And now, maybe I have an audience, but I'm not sure you exist. And even if you are there, you didn't see my work. You saw me struggle with a second-rate pair of pantyhose, and be humiliated by a woman who thinks Tony Robbins will convince me that Andrew Lloyd Webber is right. Tony Robbins. That sleazeball couldn't convince me to go to the toilet after a Prune Bake!

She is standing now, she tears the paper off the wall and crumples it up.

If you are here, if you are truly here, please vindicate me! Show Ms Iris McPhee that you exist.

She goes towards the door.

You will know what to do. You are an audience.

She enters the inner office.

IRIS *(off)* What now?

FRANCINE returns dragging IRIS. She stops inside the room, lets go of IRIS' hand, faces the audience, and bows.

Michael Redhill — *Information for Visitors to Warsaw*

1993
Rick Sherman: Director
Ruth Marshall: Bella
Michael Redhill: Irving

⌐•⌐

IRVING, a male airline steward of 65 and BELLA, a stewardess a little younger than IRVING, address the passengers of Flight 5730, bound for Warsaw. From behind the door to Tim's office, we hear IRVING singing a show tune, then we hear BELLA's voice.

BELLA OY!!! Irving!!!

IRVING What? What?

BELLA Look at the time! And you sitting there playing cards like a bus driver! You couldn't look at the clock!

IRVING Stop with the shouting!

BELLA Get up!

IRVING Such a mouth on you!

She busts out of the office, still fixing her cap.

BELLA Ladies and gentlemen… excuse me – hello – HELLO – ladies and gentlemen, we are making our final approach into Warsaw and on behalf of Captain Greenstein—whose mother is very proud of him—I want to thank you for flying Yiddish Air. We're sorry for the turbulence–

IRVING *(off)* So sue us!

BELLA –But we trust that you've been comfortable. Now before we land, we'd like to offer you some advice and information to make your stay in Warsaw as enjoyable as possible.

IRVING comes out. He's done up his shirt wrong.

IRVING See what you do to me?

BELLA Are you finished already with the interruptions?

IRVING Sorry, sorry. Okay, ladies and gentlemen, we're nearing the end of our flight, and before we land we'd like to offer you–

BELLA I said that.

IRVING —Some advice and information to make your stay in Warsaw as enjoyable as possible.

He looks at her. Pause.

BELLA Once you come out from the airplane, you go and get your things–

IRVING *Your* things, remember! I knew once a man took the wrong bags and he had the whole time in France nothing to wear but little poodle sweaters!

BELLA Shame!

IRVING Hand-to-heart, the truth!

BELLA Okay, so let's hope it's your things and not some little dog's… what kind of dog is going to France?

IRVING What? Poodle's a French dog. What's with you?

BELLA Fine, whatever. Take your things and go through customs where God knows they'll treat you like a criminal–

IRVING Go get a cab, lie back and enjoy the drive into the city.

BELLA Or at least don't not enjoy it, God knows some of these taxi drivers wake up in the mornings just so's they can make you soil your pants you're so scared from the driving!

IRVING Okay! So you get into the hotel – it's not such a bad idea you should have a light meal and then take a nap. Why wear yourself out on the first day?

BELLA Don't be a mad person! You've been in the air for ten hours, so okay, you played bridge the whole time, but believe me, you're gonna be tired. So go easy why don't you, eat something sensible.

IRVING Some herring in sour cream or a few cabbage rolls.

BELLA Or maybe a dozen pierogies with cheese and bacon.

IRVING Tomorrow, you'll wake up refreshed and ready to go, trust me!

BELLA So here you are in Warsaw, it's a dream come true, what's to do!

IRVING First, when you're walking around Warsaw there will be plenty to do and see. But be warned: there are people who will try to sell you a hat. If this happens, ask yourself what hat is this hat this man is trying to sell to me? Is it a nice hat? Do I look good in a hat? For what do I need another hat? And what of the material?

BELLA Remember this is a hat what you have to wear on the top of your head!

IRVING You think people are not going to see? God forbid you should have a hat so ugly you have to buy another hat just to wear on top!

BELLA And then, should this hat also be ugly–

IRVING You could have fifteen hats on your head before sundown. Just think of the shame! Plus, it'll give you a hunchback.

BELLA Don't get me started.

IRVING So, when you have considered all these things, you will be able to make a informed decision on if you should buy yourself this hat. Also, try to catch a opera.

BELLA Who doesn't love a opera?

IRVING Believe me, the opera is a night out like you never seen. Everyone is wearing at least four hats, the women push up their chests to their noses and everyone is having such a good time.

BELLA It's like a bar mitzvah but everybody kills themselves at the end.

IRVING It's beautiful. You'll cry.

BELLA Because it's so expensive.

IRVING Sure, but also it's beautiful.

BELLA Plus, in the intermission you can go out in the lobby and drink a coffee or have a turnip.

IRVING But do yourself a favour and at least spit on it and wash off some of the dirt. Okay, so other things to know in Warsaw:

BELLA If you have some dirt in your nose, so leave it there already and don't make everyone sick.

IRVING For those of you who will be travelling into the Carpathian Mountains, can I just ask what kind of *meshuggena* you are? What person needs to walk up a mountain? Do you see me walking up a mountain like a goat?

BELLA Ask me, you want to climb a mountain and get eaten by wolves *if you're lucky*, why waste your time, I might as well give you a gun so you can shoot yourself right now.

IRVING Try writing once in a blue moon a letter home, you're on vacation granted, but at least think of your poor parents sitting at home watching the microwave because they don't got no television.

BELLA You couldn't lend your mother a television, you're going away on a trip? Shame.

IRVING Don't let a cossack buy you a glass of wine. This is a very very bad thing, but if this is something you have to do, at least try a red.

BELLA I ask you, what's wrong with having a glass of red wine in the middle of the afternoon, nothing, that's what! But you have to sit with a cossack in plain view? What's wrong with you?

IRVING Don't wear your underwear too tight or you'll cut off the blood to your feet, then what will you do?

BELLA Don't come crying to me if your feet turn black and fall off.

IRVING Have some sense in your head! Buy some underwear that fits.

BELLA On these things you shouldn't scrimp.

IRVING If you're in the market, remember nothing's written in stone–

BELLA Unless you're buying the Ten Commandments!

IRVING Don't be afraid to haggle. Watch, we'll show you.

BELLA Hello.

IRVING What's so good about it?

BELLA Fine, thank you.

IRVING So, enough about me. How can I help you?

BELLA I would like to buy that piece of sausage.

IRVING It's not for sale.

BELLA I will pay you in zlotys.

IRVING Zlotys! Well, why didn't you say. How many zlotys will you give me for this little piece of sausage you don't know how old it is?

BELLA I will give you 500 zloty!

IRVING 500 zloty! Why don't you just shoot me in the head! 500 zloty!

BELLA Then I will give you 600 zloty.

IRVING I would rather be torn apart by mink!

BELLA I will give you 650 zloty and not a zloty more.

IRVING For 650 zloty you can smell this sausage.

BELLA You are a cruel and unpleasant-looking man!

IRVING This sausage is like a brother to me. 150,000 zloty.

BELLA 150,000 zloty! I should be trampled by bears before I pay 150,000 zloty for that sausage!

IRVING Why are we arguing like this?

BELLA Because we love to say the word "zloty."

IRVING That's true. Zloty zloty zloty.

BELLA So. Really, how much for that sausage?

IRVING 200,000 zloty.

BELLA Done.

IRVING See?

BELLA It's as easy as it looks.

IRVING BUT! If you're gonna eat sausage, do us all a favour and turn your face, we shouldn't have to smell the air what comes out of you after.

BELLA Please be a gentleman and eat it alone in your hotel room with the lights off!

IRVING I know a man ate a Chicago 58 in 1972 and twelve years later you still couldn't share an elevator with him. Nice man, though.

BELLA Sure! A salami doesn't have to make you a bad person.

IRVING Unless it's a fried salami.

BELLA Don't get me started. Fried salami, you should push me first out of a bus!

IRVING People who eat fried salami should have to live in Egypt under the ground!

BELLA What kind of a person is this person who puts a piece of salami into a pan and fries it until all the people around him are crying out for air to breathe the whole place is filled with salami smoke? I ask you, would Hitler fry salami even? Have some dignity. Slice it—it's already cooked for crying out loud—put it between two pieces of bread with mustard already, have maybe a pickle and that's it.

IRVING Very reasonable.

BELLA Okay, let's move on. There's nowhere to dance in Warsaw, so I suggest if you have to dance, and let's face it, some people do, if you have to dance, what you can do is fill the sink with hot water and let from the tap come a little drip–

IRVING Don't knock it, it's a beat.

BELLA Put on a nice pair of shoes–

IRVING And you should wear some pants too–

BELLA And have a lovely time.

IRVING Okay. Some problems you might encounter while travelling in Warsaw. First, should you get stepped on by a horse, the best thing is to lie very still.

BELLA Very very still.

IRVING Then say to the horse: "*Chlachl v'mishtenach genem telachem*" which means "I am fond of millet" and he will understand and remove from upon you his foot.

BELLA Be also careful not to laugh out loud in the streets. This is a bad thing to do because people will ask you what's so funny and even if you should have something to tell them, they will disagree with you and they will strike you on the head with rocks.

IRVING Try for once also to breathe through your nose. You think it's a nice thing to have to look at, a person who breathes through their mouth? I don't want to look down your throat!

BELLA God made you a mouth so'd you can eat–

IRVING But not fried salami–

BELLA Not to hold your mouth in the air like a fish. Be a person! Do you see me putting food in my nose?

IRVING Not on purpose! A person doesn't do such thing. So why breathe through your mouth?

BELLA Have some priorities.

IRVING Okay. I see the Captain has put on the No Kvetching sign.

BELLA Those sitting in the Arguing Sections of the plane, please stop it already with the was it a Tuesday or a Wednesday, what does it matter?

IRVING When the airplane lands, will everyone please stay in their seats until the pilot has a chance to look for some parking. In two minutes, Bella and I will be coming around with some duty-free items.

BELLA Who ordered the pastrami toasted? I also have two hot turkey and one doesn't have a name. Is that your writing sir?

IRVING And I've got two sides of coleslaw, but only one pickle – did someone ask for no pickle?

BELLA There was no egg salad so I got the tuna and they were out of Fresca. *And* Coke, but we got Pepsi.

IRVING Who had the ham and cheese with milk?

BELLA reacts.

Please! I'm just joking!

BELLA Thank God! Also: we did separate bills, so you don't have to ask.

IRVING As you know, the emergency exits are here and here–

BELLA And here and here and here and here. You can't be too careful.

IRVING For our descent, Bella and I will be bringing around Tums and little glasses of tomato juice so you should have something to spill on your shirt if we have a rough landing.

BELLA For those of you who will be returning with Yiddish Air, please try to be on time for the plane or at least call ahead if you're going to be late, so's we're not waiting up the whole night for you.

IRVING The film on the way back is incidentally the classic Yiddish film noir "The Man With the Golden Gun Only It Wasn't Gold Because He Didn't Buy From a Reputable Jeweller and it Turned His Whole Hand Green." You shouldn't miss it.

BELLA Also, those passengers who finished their carrots can get their dessert on the way out.

IRVING So, thanks for flying Yiddish Air and we hope you'll fly with us again or at least drop by if you're in the area, it was a pleasure to have you, blah blah blah, okay, come on, we're missing "Lucy."

> *He goes, she mouths "have a good time" blows a kiss, and exits into Tim's office. As she's closing the door:*

BELLA You want a coffee?

IRVING Does the Pope shit in the woods?

BELLA Do you have to answer a question always with a question?

IRVING Do you?

> *She shuts the door.*

Jason Sherman   *The Merchant of Showboat*

1993
Colin Taylor: Director
Marium Carvell: Politician
Ron White: Businessman

¤•¤

The POLITICIAN is Black. The BUSINESSMAN is white. The setting is an office.

POLITICIAN You have–

BUSINESSMAN Yes.

POLITICIAN You have–

BUSINESSMAN Yes.

POLITICIAN You have to see–

BUSINESSMAN I do.

POLITICIAN You have to see it–

BUSINESSMAN I *do*.

POLITICIAN You have to see it from *my* perspect… from *my*, from my…

BUSINESSMAN Angle.

POLITICIAN My, no, not my… my point of *view*.

BUSINESSMAN Your point of, your point of… okay, and I do, I *do*–

POLITICIAN No.

BUSINESSMAN I *do* see it from your angle, and that is why I invited you into my office, I *do* see your take on this, and that is why I *defended* you at the council meeting, defended your your integrity, said you *said* some things you didn't *mean*, didn't under*stand*, because of the anger, the emotion of the situation, which I under*stand*, and I defended you, yes, against the *accusations* of the Jewish Congress, to keep you from being…. I protected you from being censured, protected you from charges of racism, of–

POLITICIAN Protected–?

BUSINESSMAN You don't know how close you came, and I was the one, okay, and, understand, no one else could have had the desired effect: I afforded you some measure of, listen, because I understand where you're, I understand your angle. Your angle is this. Your angle is... okay? ...your angle is "you have no *right*" to do–

POLITICIAN Now just–

BUSINESSMAN –to do this.

POLITICIAN Just a, *no*, just a min–

BUSINESSMAN Am I–

POLITICIAN This *isn't*... no–

BUSINESSMAN Then–

POLITICIAN That isn't what I'm saying.

BUSINESSMAN That isn't what–

POLITICIAN What I'm saying–

BUSINESSMAN What you're saying.

POLITICIAN I'm saying...

BUSINESSMAN What is your angle.

POLITICIAN My point is... my point of view is... my point of view is that what this represents, what this "play" represents–

BUSINESSMAN This "musical."

POLITICIAN This is...

BUSINESSMAN This "entertainment."

POLITICIAN ...this is reprehensible... this is – what you are undertaking–

BUSINESSMAN Okay.

POLITICIAN What you are attempting to, I see those billboards and, okay, and I see the, I hear the *songs*, the, and the *images*, of, of a past that, I hear and see the images of enslavement, of, of oppressions–

BUSINESSMAN Now–

POLITICIAN No–

BUSINESSMAN Now just–

POLITICIAN Listen, of...

BUSINESSMAN I don't think–

POLITICIAN Of *enslavement*–

BUSINESSMAN It isn't–

POLITICIAN Let me finish.

BUSINESSMAN What is your *angle*?

POLITICIAN And it is *hurtful*, all right, don't you, can't you *see* that, how it could be *taken*, a *musical treatment of our enslavement*, of… how can I make you *understand*?

BUSINESSMAN I understand what you're saying, and I'm–

POLITICIAN You *don't*.

BUSINESSMAN I understand *exactly*, "you don't have the right," and what–

POLITICIAN *No*.

BUSINESSMAN I have, okay, I'm a businessman, an entrepreneur, this is–

POLITICIAN No.

BUSINESSMAN This is my angle, I listened, okay, to yours, please, then, okay, listen to, okay? Because here is what I see… what I see is this: an entertainment, a, a romp through… look… I understand your "feelings must be hurt," I understand that and, yes, I understand that there are instances of, there are, in the book, in the lyrics, in, yes, the musical, examples of what might be construed, *in our time*, as racist beliefs, but, and here is the point I am trying to make, we have the benefit of being *in this time*, of, what *hindsight*, we can look back and say to ourselves, "this is not right, to treat people in such a manner, to *demean* people in an artistic representation, is not right–"

POLITICIAN That's–

BUSINESSMAN Okay?

POLITICIAN That's what–

BUSINESSMAN And my answer, my response, my position is this: let us not judge the mistakes of the past with the knowledge of the present. Let us – that's right – let us, instead, as an *example* of behaviour which we find offensive, let us hold this musical up, let us put it upon our stage and say: "*this is how it was, let it never again be this way*." That is my position.

POLITICIAN How can I make you understand?

BUSINESSMAN I–

POLITICIAN How can I get it to you that–

BUSINESSMAN I have heard you.

POLITICIAN "Look at her shuffle."

BUSINESSMAN Yes.

POLITICIAN That is a line from the play.

BUSINESSMAN That's right, and those words, that word–

POLITICIAN "Niggers working on the river."

BUSINESSMAN Okay, that's, all right, are you saying… what… are you saying the word, the word you used, was never uttered, are you saying, let us not put upon our stages representations of that which is *real*?

POLITICIAN You don't understand, you don't *hear* me.

BUSINESSMAN I–

POLITICIAN You're Jewish.

BUSINESSMAN That's right.

POLITICIAN You're a Jewish man.

BUSINESSMAN I'm a Jewish person, what's–

POLITICIAN Then–

BUSINESSMAN What's that–

POLITICIAN You take that play, *The Merchant of Venice*, and you, okay, what about, what if, let's say, would *you* produce *that* play?

BUSINESSMAN Would I?

POLITICIAN A play that shows Jews to be usurers, a play that–

BUSINESSMAN I would, well, I'd have to, I do of course entertainments, I do, not the classics of course.

POLITICIAN Let's say then, what I want to know is, let's say a *German* producer, okay, were to–

BUSINESSMAN That's–

POLITICIAN –were to–

BUSINESSMAN That's a ridiculous–

POLITICIAN Listen–

BUSINESSMAN I don't see the point to–

POLITICIAN If a German producer were to, were to produce that play, all right, what would you–

BUSINESSMAN I find it–

POLITICIAN Yes.

BUSINESSMAN I find this line of reasoning, this comparison, this–

POLITICIAN Your reaction is right.

BUSINESSMAN I–

POLITICIAN Your reaction is my reaction, is our reaction, that's what I'm *getting* at, that's my, that's my *angle*, my *angle* on this enterprise, is this: it is *offensive* because of a certain history, because of what has occurred, because of the way we have been regarded, and continue to be regarded, because we have been without power, and powerless to stop you, because we have had no lobby, no voice in the abuse we suffered, and continue to–

BUSINESSMAN You're calling me a Nazi? Is that what you're doing? You're saying I'm a Nazi like that German producer of *The Merchant of Venice*?

POLITICIAN No, I'm–

BUSINESSMAN You *said*–

POLITICIAN Listen, because I grew up, I grew up without power, without privilege–

BUSINESSMAN And you assume, what, I *did*, because, *why*, I'm Jewish?

POLITICIAN –The privilege you, *yes*, enjoy, that you have enjoyed, that you, in this office, you exert influence, over the people, the thousands of people who see your entertainments, who, and the dangerous thing, the dangerous part is that they regard it, as you do, as entertainment, nothing more, and they wonder, as you seem to, where is the offense in this, they wonder, where is the crime being committed when all we are presenting, as you will say, as you have said, is an entertainment, not to be taken seriously, a representation of that which has occurred in time and place, but I am here to tell you, take *me* seriously, take *us* seriously, because I grew up *without* power and I wanted change, I wanted to make change, and I am here to make change, to tell you, this entertainment, this musical, this offence, must not be committed, that a stand must be taken, by you, to say: it is not acceptable, these views, this treatment of a people, it is not acceptable, because if it was *wrong* then, it is *wrong* now, and if it is not acceptable to you, when you see a depiction, of your people, that is, to you, inflammatory, then it is equally so to *us*.

BUSINESSMAN You're comparing, what, *my* history with yours? *My* history you're comparing *my* history with your history? What is the basis for that? What are the grounds for that?

POLITICIAN No, I'm saying–

BUSINESSMAN Your, and I find this an insidious and, okay, offensive in your terms, argument, that, given what happened to us, given the horrible events from the past of my people, that, somehow, now, I am supposed to support an untenable argument, because, because what, because–

POLITICIAN Because you must understand our position, our feelings, our–

BUSINESSMAN I understand only, I... look, you can't sway me with appeals to my emotion, you can't, I'm a businessman, you see, I'm in this business because, first, I love the entertainment of it, and second, and equally, I am an entrepreneur. I want to bring entertainment to people, and the people have spoken, they have said, we want to see this musical, they have purchased ducats, they have spoken, they have voted, and I want to tell you, I want to say because this must be said, you cannot take from my history an issue, out of context, graft it onto your, onto your perspective, and expect me to capitulate, you cannot borrow our sufferings and use them for your own.

POLITICIAN I don't want your sufferings.

BUSINESSMAN What then? What is it you want?

POLITICIAN Change, I want things to change, and I want these things to change.

BUSINESSMAN Which things?

POLITICIAN Words, these words, this book and these lyrics.

BUSINESSMAN You want...

POLITICIAN Yes.

BUSINESSMAN ...to censor...

POLITICIAN No, to change, to...

BUSINESSMAN You want me to alter a work of art, a work–

POLITICIAN You look at these changes and you tell me if you think–

BUSINESSMAN I won't.

POLITICIAN Tell me if–

BUSINESSMAN I won't look at them.

POLITICIAN If they're unreasonable.

BUSINESSMAN I will not alter a work of–

POLITICIAN I have people.

BUSINESSMAN You have people.

POLITICIAN I have an army waiting, an army of people waiting, waiting to advance.

BUSINESSMAN What are you talk...

POLITICIAN I'm talking about something you can understand something about. I'm talking about pickets outside your theatre every day and every night, an army of a thousand people, and I have them, all ready, all ready to go, to hold up signs and shout out words, an army of a thousand people who want to see things change, an army of people who will, do you understand now, who will jam up your phone lines, your fax lines, who will prevent one more "ducat" from being sold, who will, every night, crowd into the lobby of your theatre, a hundred or two hundred or however many it takes, so that not a single patron of yours gets into the theatre, a thousand people who will move into your theatre and prevent seats from being taken, and more than that, more than even that, *we* will purchase tickets, as many as we can afford for every performance, every day and night performance of this monstrosity you insist is nothing more than a diversion, and at every performance my army will rise from their seats and drown out the prejudices and the hatred emanating from the boards in your theatre, every performance, until your patrons, who only wished a little entertainment, leave their seats, run from your theatre, until your enterprise has collapsed in on itself, and you have lost everything that is valuable to you. Now do you understand, do you understand my perspective, my point of view, my angle?

BUSINESSMAN *(looking at revised script)* You want–

POLITICIAN This is the script you will use.

BUSINESSMAN And you think.

POLITICIAN What?

BUSINESSMAN You think it's that easy, to change, to change a work–

POLITICIAN Yes I do, I think it's easy to change an entertainment, change it to no longer reflect what it is you people think of us.

BUSINESSMAN "You people?"

POLITICIAN You people.

BUSINESSMAN You mean "Jews."

POLITICIAN That's right.

BUSINESSMAN You're talking about Jews.

POLITICIAN I am, because I'm talking to one, and talking about one, the one who wrote those words, and saying, try to understand this, because, yes, we were slaves, and yes, you were slaves, and you have suffered through history as we have suffered, and what you are doing, and can't you see this, is you are taking advantage of us, you are enslaving us in your entertainments so that you can feel superior, so that you can–

BUSINESSMAN That is–

POLITICIAN So that you can feel–

BUSINESSMAN That is absolute–

POLITICIAN You can feel superior to us as your self-appointed masters felt superior to you, and it, yes, it makes you feel good, and superior, to see us, to enslave us on stage, it makes you feel like you have the whip, like you are no longer being whipped, and we will not have it, we will not be whipped, not in the fields, not in your homes, and not in your goddamn theatrical representations of it, we will not be enslaved by you, or your "entertainments." You said before, what did you say, you "protected" me at council, you told council, you told the Jewish congress, what, I was having an emotional moment, well, no, no, I was not having an emotional moment, I was calling for change, and I call for it now, and I know, I can see, you understand exactly "where I'm coming from." Now I want an answer, because I'm a phone call away from shutting you down, from wreaking havoc, from creating change.

BUSINESSMAN I'll need to–

POLITICIAN To what.

BUSINESSMAN To read the script.

POLITICIAN Read it. Read it now.

BUSINESSMAN You have.

POLITICIAN What?

BUSINESSMAN You have to–

POLITICIAN Yes?

BUSINESSMAN You have to understand–

POLITICIAN I do.

BUSINESSMAN You have to understand my position.

POLITICIAN Which is what. What is it. What is your position.

BUSINESSMAN Fuck you.

Karen Hines   *Telemarketing:*
                                          The Musical

1994
Karen Hines: Director
Steven Morel: Troy
Jennifer Parsons: Vera
Greg Morrison and Karen Hines: Score
Greg Morrison: Musical Direction

♮•♮

It is morning. Sunlight streams through the high basement window of the Toronto Star Telemarketing Department, revealing a young man who is making copies at the photocopier, which is centre-office. He's the only one in the place.

TROY Ay, me.

TROY staples his first pile of papers. The photocopier malfunctions.

Oh no.

TROY crouches down behind the machine and begins to fix it.

Oh, God. Please, no. Oh, God, not again. Oh, good God. Oh, Christ. Oh, no. God Christ. Oh, God help me. Oh please God help me through this day.

Music wells. TROY sings.

My heart pounds madly and I sob.
I desperately despise my job.
It's just what I imagine hell to be:
An endless stretch of misery.
I've spent my rent on the lottery-y-y-y-y…!
'Cuz I despise my job.

TROY makes a futile paper-cut suicide attempt with a phone book. He rushes into an office off the main office area, and slams the door behind him. The sign on the door reads "Supervisor."

A door opens at the top of the very steep stairway. Enter VERA, a lithe, young woman in her twenties. She is screaming at people in the street.

VERA STOP LOOKING AT ME LIKE THAT! STOP LOOKING AT ME YOU… PEOPLE! LEAVE ME ALONE! I AM NOT SCUM! I AM NO-O-O-OT SCU-U-U-U-U-UM!!!!!!

She slams the door behind her. She weeps. There are long dark streaks of mascara running down her face as if she has been crying for years. A shaft of sunlight illuminates a long, long desk on which sit a long row of telephones, beside each of which there sits a White Pages, open. VERA drifts toward the middle phone, then ascends the desk via a small pile of phone books, and a chair: it is as though she is ascending a staircase. She stands, centre-desk. She sings.

My heart beats wildly and I weep
My hatred of my life runs deep
My life is endless misery
Completely void aesthetically
And I've been robbed of my dignity
The stress of it is killing me
Oh, I despise my job.

VERA hurls herself down from the desk, onto the floor. When she realises she is not dead, she wails uncontrollably.

Oh, Christ! Oh, dear God. Christ! Aaaah!

TROY pops out from his office, and runs to VERA's side.

TROY Are… are you okay?!

VERA *(gasp!)* Oh! I didn't… I thought I wa…. Excuse me. I didn't realise anyone else was in yet. I didn't realise anyone else would come in early to this goddamned hell hole – oh. I'm sorry.

TROY Oh, that's okay. Are you okay?

VERA *(getting up)* Yes, of course.

She bursts into tears, and throws herself across the photocopier. It resumes making copies.

TROY Thank you.

VERA moves around into her telephoning position at the middle of the desk. She picks up her receiver.

VERA No. Thank *you*. I'll be fi-i… I'm just …

VERA wails, and claws at her own face. She tears out bits of hair. TROY grabs her wrists to stop her from hurting herself. Their lips are very close to each other.

TROY STOP!!! Please, tell me what's wrong. I'd like to help… Vera.

VERA H-h-how did you know my name? You're so big and important around here, and I'm… not.

TROY I've been watching you, Vera.

VERA *(horrified)* Listening in?

TROY They make me.

VERA Oh, God. *(She tries to run. He blocks the stairs.)*

TROY Wait! You don't understand!

VERA backs up onto the desk, clutching at phonebook pages.

VERA I know! I didn't stick to the lines! I tried but… I can't help it…

She picks up a phone as though to throw it at him.

I'm sick… this job… I…

She sees the phone in her hands and smashes it onto the desk, and knocks other things onto the ground.

I… it's making me… I'm SI-I-I-I-I-I-ICK!!!

TROY Vera, stop! Look at me!

He rushes to the desk where she crouches, contorted. He puts his face close to hers.

Don't you see? I'm just like you.

VERA What do you mean?

TROY Well… when I was a telemarketer…

VERA You?

TROY Yes. When I was a telemarketer, I couldn't say the opening line either.

VERA It's a LIE!

TROY Yes, it is.

VERA We're COLD CALLING! To say "Hello, my name is Vera. I'm calling from the *Toronto Star*, just to find out how has your service been?" IT'S A LIE! IT'S A STINKING LIE!!!!

TROY Yes, Vera. It's despicable. It's a disgusting manipulation designed to lure unsuspecting dopes into a pitch.

BOTH And they hate us for it!!!

Pause.

VERA I thought I was the only… the only.

TROY One?

VERA Yes! Yes! The only one who… who…

TROY Felt that way?

VERA YES! And I can feel everyone in the entire department shunning me… as if they can sense that I'm falling… I'm falling…

TROY Apart?

VERA *(She nods, fervently.)* Oh, I have been sliced through with the pain of doing what I do every day… and it's as if they can smell smell smell smell the–

TROY Blood?

VERA Yes!!!! They can smell the blood… and they are…

TROY *(too quietly)* …drooling…

VERA Hey! H-How do you know what I'm going to say even before I–

TROY Say it? Because, Vera…. We're the same, you and me.

VERA Oh, Troy, I'm feeling something… something good!

> *Music wells. They sing. Each time TROY completes VERA's sentence, she thrills and is amazed. She slowly descends from the desk.*

VERA Under every rock there is a…

TROY Ladybug.

VERA Inside every can of worms there lies a…

TROY Pearl.

VERA In the midst of any mess there is a…

TROY Shi-i-iny ball…

BOTH I'm so glad that you're the same as me.

VERA Deep inside every kettle of fish there is a…

TROY Pie.

VERA In the midst of any nasty jam there's…

TROY Kittens!

VERA Purrrrr…

BOTH In the midst of any mess there is a shi-i-iny ball…

TROY I'm so glad that you're the same as…

VERA I'm less mad that they all hate us…

BOTH I'm so glad that you're the same as me-e-e-e-e…

> *The song ends, and their lips are very close together.*

VERA Oh, Troy…. Let's get out of here!!!

TROY You mean… quit?

VERA That's EXACTLY what I mean!

TROY And get a different job?

VERA Yes. Yes! YES!!! A better job! We could work in a BAKERY!

TROY Yes! And only sell stuff to people who are actually hungry!

VERA We could work in a bakery where they have really long line-ups!

TROY So that then they would really WANT the stuff!

VERA Then they would NEED us!

TROY Then they would LOVE us!

VERA Because they would be so happy that we had FOOD for them!

TROY GOOD food!

VERA HAPPY food!

BOTH MUFFINS!!!

Their lips are very, very close together.

TROY I can't.

VERA What?

TROY *(backing up toward his office)* I have some photocopying to do.

VERA But Troy…

TROY And I have absolutely no desire for you.

VERA But Troy… you couldn't possibly have no desire…. Why, just a moment ago…

TROY Pphhht! When?!

VERA A moment ago. When we were…

TROY Lying?

VERA No…. No, Troy! We weren't lying! We were…

TROY stares blankly.

We were…

TROY Setting each other up for a big fall?

VERA No, Troy! A moment ago when we were… EXALTING… I felt something, and I know you did too! I could see it in your eyes! I could hear it in your voice! I could FEEL it in your…

TROY TUB?!!?!

VERA gasps.

VERA Oh, Troy, we have to get out of here. *(She rushes to him.)* Let's go now.

TROY NOOOOOOO! Get away from me, WITCH GIRL! GET OUT OF MY AREA! YOU'RE EXACTLY WHAT THEY THINK YOU ARE – YOU'RE AN INTRUSION you TELEMARKETER GIRL! You're the LOWEST OF THE LOW! YOU'RE STUPID! AND YOU'RE RU-U-U-UDE!

VERA Troy…

TROY OW! YOUR VOICE HURTS MY EARS! NO WONDER YOU CAN'T MAKE A SALE!

VERA I'm quitting, Troy. I have to.

TROY GOOD! Because you have a BAD VOICE!

VERA Goodbye, Troy… *(She begins to exit, then stops.)* Maybe you'll… *(She takes a deep breath.)* Maybe you'll call me…?

TROY Ha! Ha! Ha!

VERA Oh, Troy, don't you see? I want you to call. I'm INVITING you to call. Please call. I won't… I won't hang–

TROY NOOOOOOOOOOOOOOOOO!!!!!! *(He crumbles.)*

VERA Oh, God, Troy…. How long did you telemarket? How many times did they hang up on you?

TROY *(too calm)* Too many, Vera. I'm dead inside.

TROY picks up one of the telephones and wraps the cord around his neck.

VERA Troy! NO!

She tries to wrest the phone from him. They struggle. He dies.

Oh, GOD! *(She picks up a phone book.)* When will they learn? *(She holds the book up to the heavens.)* WHEN WILL THEY LEARN?

She cradles TROY, dead, with his eyes open and staring into the audience, in her arms.

There, there. There, there. Everything's all right now, Troy. It's better this way.

Music plays under, softly.

Fly away from here my poor sweet telemarketer man.
Take your troubled soul and fly away with two free hands.

She untangles his wrists from the phone cord, and lays him down across the desk.

I will cleanse your dial finger with my merciful tears.
I will whisper soft sweet nothings, and sanctify your ears.

She whispers in his ears, and kisses him all over.

Oh oh oh, oh oh oh, oh oh oh, o-o-o-o-o-h-h-h-h……

Music swells, tempo quickens: urgent.

I long to fly with you; we'd be what dreams are made of.
Let me lie with you, and I'll receive *(She grabs the phone.)* your love.

She wraps the cord around her neck.

I'm calling to you.
I'll climb this cord to heav'n above.

Just call me back
And I swear I'll never
Hang *(She pulls the cord tight.)*

VERA U-u-u-u-u-u-up...
    (She falls into his arms.)

    (as ghost) Dials spiral by...

    I swear that I...

TROY *(as ghost)* O-O-O-O-OH-H-H
    Fly away with me
    My poor sweet telemarketer girl
    Fly away with me where life's a dream
    Every word a pearl.
    I will heal your dial finger
    With my merciful tears.
    I will whisper soft sweet nothings
    In your precious ears.

They rise together. And start flying, as though ghosts or angels, through the air.

Let me fly with you
My poor sweet telemarketer.
Dials spiral by...
We'll be what dreams are ma-a-ade of.

I'm calling you

Come fly with me
We'll be what dreams are ma-a-ade of.
Come lie with me,
I'm calling to you.
We'll be what dreams are made of.

I'm calling you.

BOTH I'm calling to you.
    We'll climb the wires to heav'n above.
    Just call me back,
    And I swear I'll never hang

VERA
U-u-u-u-u-u-u-u-u-u-up!
I'm less mad that they all hate us...

TROY
I'm so glad that you're the same as...

BOTH I'm so glad that you're the same as
    Me-e-e-e-e-e-e-e...

They embrace. They move down into dead telemarketer positions: sprawled awkwardly across the long desk. A semi-final chord lingers, sustained. A phone falls to the floor. The chord resolves. VERA and TROY, dead, stare into the eyes of the audience. There is the sound of a telephone off the hook. It is quite loud. The audience exits past the bodies.

Jason Sherman

Equity Rules

1994
Ian Prinsloo: Director
Melinda Little: Jane
Murray Farrow: Bill

¤ • ¤

A room. BILL, a director, about forty. JANE, an actor, about thirty, script in hand.

JANE "Is this what you want? Just this? It's only flesh, isn't it? Oh yes, you say you love me but I don't think so. You say you care for me but I think you only see this, my body, not my mind, not my needs, my desires. Is this what you want? Is it? Sometimes... I just want you to hold onto me.... That's all. Is that so much?"

Well that sucked.

BILL No. No, it was good.

JANE Really? Can I do it again? I'm a little nervous.

BILL No, that's good, the nervousness. It's part of the character.

JANE You think so?

BILL Absolutely.

JANE I thought she was a bit more, you know, together.

BILL Could be. In a nervous sort of–. That was good. You memorised the speech.

JANE Well, it was only–.

BILL What do you think?

JANE Sorry?

BILL Of the script. It's just a first draft.

JANE Oh. No, yes, it's good.

BILL It's my first play.

JANE Is it? It's, that's funny, it doesn't uhh–

BILL It's just a rough draft.

JANE No, I like it.

BILL Rough?

JANE Pardon me?

BILL Nothing. Little director joke. Are you available?

JANE Sorry?

BILL I'm doing it in May.

JANE May.

BILL That's right. We'll rehearse through April. It's a full Equity production. It's fully professional. Are you available in that time?

JANE April and May? Yeah. I. All I was thinking was I might take the voice intensive in Vancouver, but. Yeah. I'm available.

BILL Good.

JANE When are the call backs?

BILL I'm not doing call backs.

JANE Oh.

BILL I want to cast it today.

JANE Okay.

BILL This is the last role. I've already cast Ouimette.

JANE Ouimette?

BILL I've asked him to do "John." Would you like to work with Ouimette?

JANE Sure.

BILL He'd play "John." And R.H. would play "Snake."

JANE Really?

BILL Have you worked with R.H.?

JANE I took a class with him. Audition technique.

BILL *(looking at resumé)* You've worked with some good people.

JANE Oh yeah.

BILL Richard Monette.

JANE He was wonderful.

BILL Martha Henry.

JANE Just walk-ons, really.

BILL "There are no small parts."

JANE I guess.

BILL This is a big part. This is the lead.

JANE I know.

BILL Do you think you can handle it?

JANE …Uh…

BILL Can you handle the lead?

JANE …Are you–?

BILL What?

JANE Are you offering – *me* – or–?

BILL I'm saying: do you think you can handle the role?

JANE Well. Yes. I – wow, oh.

BILL I mean. Oh, don't misunder – I'm not *offer*–

JANE Oh.

BILL I'm not offering the–

JANE Oh, I thought you–

BILL I'm saying: Do you think you can *handle* the role?

JANE I don't think I understand.

BILL Do the speech again. Would you?

JANE Yeah, I'd love to, I mean–

BILL The way it's written there. Would you?

JANE The way it's–?

BILL With the stage directions. Would you do it with the stage directions?

JANE The–?

BILL Yes.

JANE I'm sorry, I don't usually read the–. "As she speaks, she removes her"–.

BILL "Her blouse."

JANE "Her blouse… drapes it around his neck."

BILL Yes, go on. Just read them. That's all, just read them.

JANE "She kicks off her shoes, one at a time, slips off her nylons, wraps them around his neck." Ha.

BILL There's more.

JANE Yeah. Um. "Wriggles out of her skirt. Removes her bra, twirls it like a…"

BILL You seem nervous.

JANE It's just…

BILL This is good. This is the character. Use that. Go on. Read.

JANE Uhhh, "…twirls it like a stripper. She takes off her panties. She is naked."

BILL Good. Can you do the whole speech, then?

JANE Uh.

BILL With the stage directions. Would you?

JANE You want me to, to–.

BILL I need to *know*, you see. To *know*, if you would do it.

JANE Look. I don't have a problem, all right, with nudity.

BILL Good, neither do I. Ha. Little director joke.

JANE Yeah, uh. The thing is. The audition notice. There are rules. The audition notice didn't say that nudity would be–

BILL It didn't?

JANE No. It's an Equity rule. I mean, you know that, don't you?

BILL Of course I do. Yes. I've done shows with nudity. I've *done* nudity. It's no big deal, not really.

JANE I'm not questioning the, the nudity.

BILL Good.

JANE It's just – if I'd had some notice…

BILL Look. Here's a story I often tell. I did a show once, a snow with nudity required of the actors. This woman, this one woman. I auditioned her. This was many years ago. She's no longer in the theatre. I think she does *tee-vee* now. Anyway. I asked of her, if she would, as I have asked of you, I said: *could* you do this scene nude? She said she *could*. And when it came time to perform, to re*hearse*, she re*fused*, you see, claimed I was "exploiting" her. And yet, in the audition, to get the role, she told me she could. She lied. So who was exploiting who? Therefore, *now*, I must ask, *would* you, *now*, because I have to *know*, in order to make you an *offer*, to see if you would be *willing*.

JANE I just – would have liked some notice, that's all, to prepare. It's not that easy, and, well, I have to say, there's no one here.

BILL Let me ask you. Since you have brought up the subject, of "Equity rules," okay? Let me ask you: do you consider yourself a professional?

JANE Of course.

BILL Good. And so do I. Consider myself.

JANE This isn't about–

BILL The point is this. We are professionals, removed, detached. This role calls for nudity. The woman is a stripper. Strippers take off their clothes. It is integral to the telling of her story, that we see her naked, because that's the source of her *power*, you see?

JANE No. I don't think I do.

BILL We are being forced to believe certain things which aren't true, about our bodies, our language, our *motives*. Everything is under attack, everything that permits us to be free, to live free. And we, as artists, as professional artists, must resist, resist these restrictions. Are we going to live by a set of dictates, of rules and regulations, or are we going to live up to our responsibility as artists and *challenge* those rules? Look. It's up to you. In the end. I'm sorry about the audition notice. The girl who typed up the notice, she must have forgotten.

JANE It's just – if I *knew* – if I could have pre*pared*–

BILL "All you need to be prepared for is the unexpected."

JANE I'm supposed to have a monitor.

BILL I have one.

JANE A monitor?

BILL In my bag. I brought one. To watch – to–

JANE Oh God.

BILL What is it? What is it?

JANE You want to *film* me naked?

BILL I – only if you – *no*. You *said*.

JANE A *monitor*. A *friend*. Someone I *trust*, to be in the room.

BILL Don't get upset. Please. I tape all my auditions. I taped R.H. Would you like to see it? He's reading "John." Look. I've upset you. This isn't going to, clearly, to work. You have your rules, your limitations, I under–

JANE What?

BILL You have your limitations.

JANE I do not have "limitations."

BILL Well. I'm sorry. You know, what are you, 30? You gonna take "classes" all your life, "voice intensives"? You gonna play it safe? Small roles? Walk-ons? *Tee-vee*? Or do you want to be an artist? To take chances? To risk everything? To free yourself? It's up to you. I need to cast this show today. I'm seeing three more girls after you. Look. You said you like the play. You said you like the part. You said you have no trouble with nudity. I ask you. Would you do the scene with the stage directions? Would you?

JANE I'll.

BILL It's up to you.

JANE Can I–?

BILL Yes?

JANE Do them not exactly…

BILL Not exactly?

JANE Can I do it – just, work through it, work my way up to the…

BILL Sure, we can do it whichever way you like.

JANE All right. Can I have a second?

BILL Yes. Please. Whenever you're ready. And I'll be Snake, so play it to me, all right?

JANE "Is this what you want?" *(She kicks off one shoe.)* "Just this?" *(kicks off the other shoe)* "It's only flesh, isn't it? Oh yes, you say you love me…" *(as she takes off her nylons)* "but I don't think so. You say you care for me but I think you only see this, my body… not my mind, not my needs, my desires. Is this what you want? Is it?" *(unbuttons her blouse)* "Sometimes – I just want you to hold onto me – that's all. Is that so much?"

BILL "Is that what you do? Take off your clothes for anyone who asks? Huh? Answer me! For *money*? You whore! Whore! Put your clothes on and get the hell outta here! Go! Put em on! Put em on! Get out! Get out!"

Blackout. End of Act One.

JANE I'm sorry. I only got down to my – to my…

BILL That's all right. That's a good start. We can try it again if you… all right? Would you try it again? Would you?

Andrew Akman

The Nose Job

1995
Jim Warren: Director
Andrew Akman: Andrew
Diane Flacks: Others

¤•¤

DIANE enters the office, wheeling in a TV and VCR.

CASTING DIRECTOR Okay, are we here? Are we sitting? Good. Okay. Okay? Good, okay. The nail-biting search for the sexy new lead on our sexy new medical series might finally be over. We just auditioned our final choices and here's the tape. So let's see what we got, Okay? Okay, good. Helen, can you get me another latte?

She turns on the VCR. The image is ANDREW reading off a page of "sides."

ANDREW *(on screen)* Hi there, Mrs. Popadopolous. So you're having trouble breathing. Let me just undo your button here. Maybe one more. How's that?

CASTING DIRECTOR Cute. Very cute. Cute is good.

ANDREW *(on screen)* I'm not just any doctor. I'm a street doctor. I save lives on the dirty streets of this throbbing metropolis. It's repulsive yet attractive at the same time. I guess that makes it "repulctive."

CASTING DIRECTOR I think we found our man. What is that… is that real?

ANDREW has turned profile. The camera slowly zooms in on his nose. It fills the screen.

ANDREW *(on screen)* I'm your street surgeon.

CASTING DIRECTOR Honey, you could *use* a surgeon.

She turns the TV off. The real-life ANDREW enters.

ANDREW My name is Andrew Akman. This is my story. It all began when I auditioned for the lead role on a new series for our national television network. After the audition my agent called me.

ROBYN Hi, kiddo. They loved your audition, but you're not quite what they want. They also said that if they'd made you an offer it would have been contingent on you getting a nose job.

ANDREW What's wrong with my nose?

ROBYN They said it's large. I think they found it too… Jewish.

ANDREW What's too Jewish? I *am* Jewish. The part I auditioned for is a Jew. It was written by a Jew. The show is produced by a Jew. Who'd they hire?

ROBYN Albert Schultz.

ANDREW For a Jewish character? He's got light hair, blue eyes, little button-nose.

ROBYN So he's a little WASPy.

ANDREW Schultz is not WASPy. Schultz is Aryan. Doesn't that strike you as ironic?

ROBYN I think you're over-reacting. They thought you were really talented and really good-looking but they said you'd be even better-looking with less nose.

He hangs up the phone.

ANDREW The exact words they used. "Better-looking with less nose." That night I got drunk with an actress friend who had a nose job.

ACTRESS Honey!

ANDREW What is it about my nose?

ACTRESS Well Akman… it's really big. And this business is nuts. I go into this audition, I've got them crying, then laughing. They love me.

ANDREW Did you get the part?

ACTRESS No. They hired somebody with big tits.

ANDREW You should get yours fixed.

ACTRESS You never told me I had small tits.

ANDREW You never told me I had a big nose.

ACTRESS You get your tits done and you lose sensitivity in your nipples. My nipples are very sensitive. And sex is more important than my career.

ANDREW Absolutely. My nose is just like your nipples.

ACTRESS If you want to work in film or TV, you need the face of a leading man.

ANDREW What does that mean?

ACTRESS Like mine. Smooth straight lines. Symmetry.

ANDREW People aren't like that. It's a lie.

ACTRESS It's TV!

ANDREW My nose isn't too big. It just has too much integrity for the medium!

ACTRESS Akman, tits or no tits, I work more now than before I had surgery. If you want to work in TV, this is what you have to do. Period.

ANDREW So that was it. I made an appointment with a cosmetic surgeon. He had worked on a lot of actors. Prominent actors. Actors with leading roles on our national network. I walked into his office and was greeted by his receptionist Carol.

    CAROL has a nose like a pig.

CAROL Oh my God... hello! You're the one in that show about the Jews that get typhoid and die in the Holocaust.

ANDREW Yes.

CAROL You were really cute with that little yarmulke. Except, I gotta tell ya, I kept thinking that boy has too much nose for his face.

ANDREW A direct quote. "Too much nose for his face."

CAROL You'll never regret your decision. I haven't. Oink. Snort. The doctor does three hundred noses a year. He'll give you a nose to match the real you. Oink. Squeeaal!

ANDREW I sat on the doctor's examination table.

DOCTOR Now, what is it you don't like about your nose?

ANDREW Nothing. I like my nose.

DOCTOR Of course you do.

    The DOCTOR pulls, yanks, pinches and measures the nose.

It's very strong. Very masculine. But the nostrils are offensive.

ANDREW *(aside)* That's what he told me. "Offensive nostrils."

DOCTOR You could probably fit a looney up there.

ANDREW Never tried.

    The DOCTOR shoves a looney up ANDREW's nose.

DOCTOR Now that's offensive.

ANDREW I see what you mean.

DOCTOR To narrow the nostrils, I implant cartilage taken from behind your ears. Then I'll chisel down the bump and snip a bit off the tip. We'll save the cuttings and make a soup.

ANDREW I needed a second opinion. I saw Dr. Neville Hoy; the most renowned cosmetic surgeon in the city. He charges $6000 for a nose job. His office is all marble and fountains and original Rodin sculptures. His skin is porcelain. Expression serene. A vampire in Armani.

HOY What do you dislike about your nose, Mr. Akman?

ANDREW I like my nose very much...

HOY Of course you do.

ANDREW But they want me to fit a mould. You know, "All-American Apple Pie."

HOY In your career, you must always try to please and somehow retain your integrity. They ask you for your soul, your individuality, yet would force you into a homogeneous mould. I do not envy your position.

ANDREW (*aside*) Hoy understands me. He is the Zen Master of nose jobs. If I'm going to have the operation, Hoy's my man. Nothing can upset his balance.

HOY Let me have a closer look. Wow!

ANDREW What is it doctor?

HOY That is what you have up your nose. A WOW!

ANDREW (*aside*) Whatever that means, it's a direct quote.

HOY You have a deviated septum blocking two-thirds of your right nostril. It is a mess and must be scraped out. But the truth is, Mr. Akman, I do not wish to operate on your nose.

ANDREW But that's what you do. That's your job.

HOY Mr. Akman, I do not need your money. And I do not believe there is anything I can do to your face that will satisfy both you and these industry people. They want apple pie. But I am not a baker.

ANDREW I resolved not to have the operation. I call my agent to tell her so.

ROBYN (*voice*) Before you make that decision, kiddo, just so you know another casting director told me you should get your nose fixed. Whatever makes you "more marketable," she says.

ANDREW I went to tell my actress friend about my decision, but she had news for me.

The ACTRESS reappears. She has had her breasts enlarged.

ACTRESS I got the part!

ANDREW I called my mom in Montreal.

MOM You always had such a cute nose. Such a nice nose.

ANDREW Thank you. That's what I thought.

MOM But then you hit puberty and it went all long and bumpy and now it's your father's nose. It's the damn Akman Nose. You should do what those casting people say.

ANDREW Mom, I can't believe this. It's *your* father's nose. It's the Stein Nose.

MOM You never had it broken? If you had it broken then it's nobody's nose and you can do what you want with it. There's a lot of money in film and TV.

ANDREW Hang on, I got another call coming in. Hello?

DAD Andrew?

ANDREW Dad? Hi! Mom and I are just talking about a nose job. I'll put us on conference so we can all talk.

MOM He's got the Akman bump!

DAD He's got the Stein nostrils!

MOM He's got the Akman hook!

ANDREW I got another call coming in. Hello?

ROBYN *(voice)* Kiddo, it's your agent. Your nose is up to you. Just think about your future.

ANDREW I don't want to change my face. And I will work in television because I don't believe every casting agent and every producer and every director in this city thinks that I need a nose job.

DIANE But Andrew, what if they do?

> *ANDREW and DIANE watch ANDREW's audition tape on television. "TV ANDREW" turns profile. Nose fills the screen. Fade to black.*

Jason Sherman *The Poetics*

1995
Ian Prinsloo: Director
Ric Waugh: Arts Reporter
Sarah Orenstein: Arts Editor
Ron White: Editor-in-Chief

♮ • ♮

Big city newspaper. Office of the EDITOR-IN-CHIEF. With him, the ARTS EDITOR. The ARTS REPORTER, outside the office, addresses the audience.

ARTS REPORTER There I was, stringer in the Arts section of a Very Important Newspaper. We had a Dance Critic, a Book Critic, a Movie Critic, a Drama Critic. And when these men were sick, I was called to fill in, to "string." It was a Tuesday morning in late fall. A handful of leaves threw themselves against my window. I looked up just in time to see the sun race behind a cloud, and this snowy owl sittin on my windowsill, turning his head like they do. You don't see owls in the city real regular, and though I'm not a religious man, I took it for like an omen. I had a two p.m. deadline, 500 words on this experimental piece of – theatre. Phil, the drama critic, he'd asked me to cover for him. The piece had something to do with a pig. What did I know about it? A buncha skinny kids in black boots kicking this dead pig around the stage. I think it was real. The pig I mean. I didn't know what to say, what to write, so I was glad when the editor-in-chief called, asked me to take a meeting with him, him and the arts editor. I hit the save key and walked the length of the newsroom to the ed's office.

EDITOR-IN-CHIEF Come in.

ARTS EDITOR Come in.

EDITOR-IN-CHIEF Have a seat.

ARTS EDITOR Sit down. We're all sitting down, see.

EDITOR-IN-CHIEF How's it going?

ARTS REPORTER How's what going?

EDITOR-IN-CHIEF The work, dummy, how's the work going. What are you, getting cute?

ARTS REPORTER Nah.

EDITOR-IN-CHIEF I think you are. I think you're gettin cute with me.

ARTS REPORTER Honest, I ain't being cute.

EDITOR-IN-CHIEF Then answer the question, Cutey.

ARTS EDITOR Yeah, answer the question.

ARTS REPORTER What question?

EDITOR-IN-CHIEF There you go again. What is it you're doing, Cutey, the work, today, what is it that occupies your precious time today?

ARTS REPORTER Oh. I'm doing a theatre piece.

EDITOR-IN-CHIEF Theatre piece.

ARTS REPORTER That's right.

EDITOR-IN-CHIEF Like "Les Miz"-like?

ARTS REPORTER Nope.

EDITOR-IN-CHIEF What then?

ARTS REPORTER It's this experimental theatre piece, see?

EDITOR-IN-CHIEF "Experimental."

ARTS REPORTER That's right.

ARTS EDITOR They do this thing with a pig, ain't that it?

EDITOR-IN-CHIEF A pig.

ARTS REPORTER That's right. They do this thing which, with a pig.

ARTS EDITOR The carcass of a pig.

ARTS REPORTER They do this thing.

EDITOR-IN-CHIEF With the carcass of a–.

ARTS REPORTER I don't pretend to get it myself. Phil asked me to do it.

EDITOR-IN-CHIEF Phil did.

ARTS REPORTER That's right.

ARTS EDITOR That explains it. That explains a lot.

EDITOR-IN-CHIEF Here we are, supposed to be running a Very Important Newspaper, and we're running stories about the carcass of a pig which is implicated in an experiment. I find that amusing. Don't you find that amusing, Cutey?

ARTS REPORTER Sure, sure, real amusing.

EDITOR-IN-CHIEF You like writing about such things, Cutey?

ARTS REPORTER Sure I do. It's okay, you know what I mean?

EDITOR-IN-CHIEF Sure, Cutey, I know what you mean. All right. Let's get down to it. Make with the door, Cutey.

ARTS REPORTER Sure.

ARTS EDITOR Shut it tight.

EDITOR-IN-CHIEF Now listen. We got some news to share with you.

ARTS EDITOR Some news about Phil.

ARTS REPORTER Phil?

EDITOR-IN-CHIEF Phil's leaving.

ARTS REPORTER Phil–?

EDITOR-IN-CHIEF Phil is leaving.

ARTS EDITOR Phil is going to Kweebek.

EDITOR-IN-CHIEF Been brushing up on his French, see.

ARTS REPORTER Phil is leaving?

ARTS EDITOR Phil's burnt out.

EDITOR-IN-CHIEF Been here—what—ten–?

ARTS EDITOR Almost eleven.

EDITOR-IN-CHIEF I'd be tired, too.

ARTS EDITOR I'd be dead.

ARTS REPORTER Phil's leaving?

EDITOR-IN-CHIEF He's going to cover Kweebek. All of it. Theatre, film – the arts.

ARTS EDITOR He's going to do all of it.

EDITOR-IN-CHIEF This leaves an opening.

ARTS EDITOR A vacancy.

EDITOR-IN-CHIEF A void, which we must fill, in the area of drama critic.

ARTS EDITOR It's an exciting time.

EDITOR-IN-CHIEF In the theatre.

ARTS EDITOR Things are looking up. In the theatre.

EDITOR-IN-CHIEF Big things are happening. You know who just called me, Cutey?

ARTS EDITOR You know who we just spoke to?

EDITOR-IN-CHIEF Johnny K just called me.

ARTS REPORTER Johnny K?

EDITOR-IN-CHIEF That's right. Called me right here on my private line.

ARTS EDITOR Things are happening. Listen to this.

EDITOR-IN-CHIEF Johnny's bringing in a Big Show. Big, Big Show.
ARTS EDITOR The Biggest.
EDITOR-IN-CHIEF A Musical, yet.
ARTS EDITOR Lotsa singin and dancin.
EDITOR-IN-CHIEF Lotsa coloured folks.
ARTS EDITOR With this like boat on the stage.
EDITOR-IN-CHIEF But here's the best part. Go on, tell him.
ARTS EDITOR Two-page ads.
EDITOR-IN-CHIEF Four-colour.
ARTS EDITOR Front page banner.
EDITOR-IN-CHIEF Inserts even.
ARTS EDITOR It's very exciting.
EDITOR-IN-CHIEF Then there's Shep.
ARTS EDITOR Shep called.
ARTS REPORTER Big Shep?
ARTS EDITOR Big Shep and Little Shep.
EDITOR-IN-CHIEF It was like a conference call.
ARTS EDITOR Listen to this.
EDITOR-IN-CHIEF Big Shep's building a theatre.
ARTS EDITOR A new theatre.
EDITOR-IN-CHIEF For a big new show.
ARTS EDITOR A musical.
EDITOR-IN-CHIEF With lots of parking.
ARTS EDITOR You know what this is?
EDITOR-IN-CHIEF Eh, Cutey, you know what this is?
ARTS REPORTER …This is Big.
ARTS EDITOR Very Big.
EDITOR-IN-CHIEF How big, Cutey?
ARTS REPORTER …Two-page ads?
EDITOR-IN-CHIEF That's right. Cutey's gettin smart. Too bad for Phil he's leaving, just when things are looking up.
ARTS EDITOR Bad for Phil.

EDITOR-IN-CHIEF Good for you.

ARTS EDITOR If you want it.

EDITOR-IN-CHIEF If you want to be part of it.

ARTS EDITOR The explosion.

EDITOR-IN-CHIEF The beginning of something Big.

ARTS EDITOR Real theatre.

EDITOR-IN-CHIEF World-class theatre. No more self-indulgent crap in one-hundred-seat closets, with no cushions on the lousy seats and no backrests, and half the time you don't know what the hell you're listening to, and the other half the time you know exactly what you're listening to, and it makes ya sick, cause it's all whining and therapy, all the crummy little artists spouting off bout things they don't know nothing about, see?

ARTS EDITOR Come on, come on, we're not here to—

EDITOR-IN-CHIEF Burn me up is all.

ARTS EDITOR We don't want to influence the way you think.

EDITOR-IN-CHIEF Can't a guy get something off his chest? You know what I mean, don't you, Cutey? Theatre for the people. Lots of people.

ARTS EDITOR You could be part of it. You could be at the forefront. Helping to light the explosion.

EDITOR-IN-CHIEF Your reviews will be quoted.

ARTS EDITOR Right across the top of them two-page ads.

EDITOR-IN-CHIEF Your words.

ARTS EDITOR Helping to make things Big.

EDITOR-IN-CHIEF Your words.

ARTS EDITOR If you want it.

EDITOR-IN-CHIEF No more things with pigs.

ARTS EDITOR Think about it.

EDITOR-IN-CHIEF Don't give us an answer..

ARTS EDITOR Think it through.

ARTS REPORTER …Boy…

ARTS EDITOR So you're interested?

ARTS REPORTER …Sure…

ARTS EDITOR It's just that you hesitated is all.

EDITOR-IN-CHIEF To hell with Phil. Forget about it, he's nowhere, get me? You remember what he said last time Johnny K tried to bring in a Big Show? Said he didn't like it, got all uppity, all lippy, said the show was lousy, said it wasn't good art. Johnny K got all mad, started pullin out ads. It was a no good time for the buncha us, all on account of that lousy Phil with his lousy ideas bout art. Well let me tell you something, that lousy no-good show is still going, and Phil is packing a laptop for Kweebek.

ARTS EDITOR And he ain't coming back.

EDITOR-IN-CHIEF Ain't never coming back.

ARTS EDITOR Johnny K'll make sure of that.

ARTS REPORTER What's that s'posed ta mean?

ARTS EDITOR Nevermind, you.

ARTS REPORTER I mean that stuff about Johnny K makin sure of...

ARTS EDITOR Shut your lip why don't ya? You want the job or doncha?

ARTS REPORTER Sure I do, sure.

ARTS EDITOR All right then, shut your trap before you fall right through it.

ARTS REPORTER I'm shuttin it, I'm shuttin it.

EDITOR-IN-CHIEF The point is we need someone to step in.

ARTS EDITOR Someone who wants it.

EDITOR-IN-CHIEF Do you like it? Theatre, I mean.

ARTS REPORTER It's okay, I guess. I mean, yeah, yeah, I like it fine.

ARTS EDITOR This for example musical. You like it?

ARTS REPORTER The Shep thing?

ARTS EDITOR For example.

ARTS REPORTER Sure. With the parking, you mean?

EDITOR-IN-CHIEF That's it.

ARTS REPORTER Yeah!

ARTS EDITOR Good.

EDITOR-IN-CHIEF What about the other one?

ARTS REPORTER Uh...

ARTS EDITOR With the coloured folks singin and dancin...

ARTS REPORTER Right. Sure. I like that old time stuff.

EDITOR-IN-CHIEF Exactly. Only it never goes outta fashion, see, cause it's rich with like plots, and characters.

ARTS EDITOR Tell us something.

EDITOR-IN-CHIEF We need to know something.

ARTS EDITOR What do you like?

EDITOR-IN-CHIEF In theatre.

ARTS EDITOR In general.

EDITOR-IN-CHIEF In theatre.

ARTS EDITOR What kind of theatre do you like?

ARTS REPORTER You mean…?

EDITOR-IN-CHIEF What grabs you?

ARTS REPORTER Well.

ARTS EDITOR Take you time.

EDITOR-IN-CHIEF Off the top of your head.

ARTS EDITOR First thing pops into your mind.

ARTS REPORTER Gee. I like a good story. Like that you mean?

ARTS EDITOR Exactly.

ARTS REPORTER I like a good story with… a good beginning, a good middle and… uh… a good ending point.

EDITOR-IN-CHIEF Yes.

ARTS REPORTER And I like good direction.

ARTS EDITOR Good direction?

ARTS REPORTER Yeah.

EDITOR-IN-CHIEF What does a director do, you figure?

ARTS REPORTER What does he do? Well. I guess he… he tells a guy where to stand, is he sayin the words right, that kinda thing. If he's good, he makes a play what flows… he makes it flow, see, and that's what I like, flowing direction.

EDITOR-IN-CHIEF Flowing direction, okay.

ARTS REPORTER And strong acting. That's very important. The acting has to be – be strong. And there has to be plum roles. And, and, and oh! I like a hoot.

EDITOR-IN-CHIEF A "hoot."

ARTS REPORTER Yeah. I like a play that's a hoot. You know – lots of laughs.

EDITOR-IN-CHIEF "Lots of laughs."

ARTS REPORTER Lots of laughs.

EDITOR-IN-CHIEF Good.

ARTS EDITOR And sets?

ARTS REPORTER Sets?

ARTS EDITOR And costumes. Do you like sets and costumes?

ARTS REPORTER Oh yeah. Didn't I mention–?

EDITOR-IN-CHIEF No.

ARTS EDITOR No, you didn't.

EDITOR-IN-CHIEF You left that bit out.

ARTS EDITOR Ignoramus.

EDITOR-IN-CHIEF Fucking idiot.

ARTS EDITOR What do you know about theatre?

EDITOR-IN-CHIEF Dick.

ARTS EDITOR Nothing.

EDITOR-IN-CHIEF You're stupid.

ARTS EDITOR You've got no business.

EDITOR-IN-CHIEF No business.

ARTS EDITOR You're a joke.

EDITOR-IN-CHIEF A sham.

ARTS REPORTER I… I…

ARTS EDITOR Come on.

EDITOR-IN-CHIEF Give it back. You're gonna get it.

ARTS EDITOR You're gonna be hurt.

EDITOR-IN-CHIEF They're gonna tear you apart.

ARTS EDITOR Fucking artists.

EDITOR-IN-CHIEF They'll hate you. Every time you write a review, it won't be good enough. They always want more. You'll say it's good, they'll say what about great? You'll say it's great, they'll say what about brilliant? You give em two stars, they say, what about three? Give em three, they want…. See what I'm getting at? Then there's the shows you won't like, and there's gonna be a lot of those, get me, and you'll say so, and they'll call you names, they'll make fun of you, maybe they'll put on plays about you for some two-bit theatre company wants to produce art, it doesn't matter, the point is they'll come after you.

ARTS EDITOR Think you owe them a living. They're all a buncha welfare bums anyway. They ain't artists, they don't even get paid most the time they're workin, and when they do, it ain't hardly enough to pay the rent, let alone the drugs and booze what keeps them goin. So they're gonna let you have it, brother. So come on. Fight back.

EDITOR-IN-CHIEF Faggot.

ARTS EDITOR Turd burglar.

EDITOR-IN-CHIEF Mama's boy.

ARTS EDITOR Scaredy-cat.

ARTS REPORTER Am not! Am not! Am not! Shut up! I like good sets and costumes. Big, Big sets that let the actors move around a lot and costumes that, that, go with the set like.

EDITOR-IN-CHIEF ...Good.

ARTS EDITOR Good.

EDITOR-IN-CHIEF Very good.

ARTS EDITOR Okay.

EDITOR-IN-CHIEF I like it.

ARTS EDITOR That's good.

ARTS REPORTER That's good?

ARTS EDITOR Very good.

EDITOR-IN-CHIEF Okay.

ARTS EDITOR Okay.

ARTS REPORTER Okay?

EDITOR-IN-CHIEF Now: what doncha like?

ARTS REPORTER What don't I like?

EDITOR-IN-CHIEF Exactly. What in a play which when you see it causes you not to like it?

ARTS REPORTER Well... okay... here's a biggee... I don't like talky plays.

EDITOR-IN-CHIEF Talky.

ARTS REPORTER You know, lotsa words.

ARTS EDITOR I understand exactly.

ARTS REPORTER I especially don't like it when the words are like supposed to be real. Like when they do them plays which when people speak it's supposed to be like real speak which who cares which it is or not? Like they do these plays where people... uh... they... like... they lose their train of... uh... thought... or–

ARTS EDITOR Uh huh.

EDITOR-IN-CHIEF We under–

ARTS REPORTER Hold on–

ARTS EDITOR No, no we understand exac–

ARTS REPORTER Like when they–

EDITOR-IN-CHIEF We said we heard you, so why doncha–

ARTS REPORTER Like when they keep gettin interrupted. I hate that. Or when a character takes a long......... drag off a cigarette. I hate that too.

ARTS EDITOR Good.

EDITOR-IN-CHIEF Well, that pretty much covers it.

ARTS EDITOR That's good. A beginning, middle and ending point, flowing direction, plum roles, a hoot, sets and costumes, no smoking and no funny talking.

EDITOR-IN-CHIEF What else do you need?

ARTS EDITOR That's all you need.

EDITOR-IN-CHIEF Not like Phil.

ARTS EDITOR No.

EDITOR-IN-CHIEF Phil was so...

ARTS EDITOR So... what was Phil?

ARTS REPORTER ...Critical?

ARTS EDITOR So critical.

EDITOR-IN-CHIEF Very critical.

ARTS EDITOR Very unfair. His standards...

EDITOR-IN-CHIEF Very high.

ARTS REPORTER He was so unfair.

EDITOR-IN-CHIEF Didn't like the chandelier thing.

ARTS EDITOR You're not going to be unfair, are you?

EDITOR-IN-CHIEF Uh uh.

ARTS EDITOR To the musicals?

ARTS REPORTER Not me, boy.

ARTS EDITOR And the rest? The self-indulgent, theatre-as-therapy crap? What about that?

ARTS REPORTER ...Well.... Gee...

ARTS EDITOR Don't worry about it.

EDITOR-IN-CHIEF Trick question. We're cutting back.

ARTS EDITOR Cutting way back.

EDITOR-IN-CHIEF Nobody goes to these crummy little shows in crummy hundred-seat church basements, and even if they do, who cares, it's only a hundred people a night, which multiplied by a typical run of maybe sixteen performances is what not even two thousand individuals which would be seeing this particular piece of therapy crap, which is not even what you would find in Big Shep's new theatre on any given weekend evening.

ARTS EDITOR See what we're getting at?

EDITOR-IN-CHIEF Waste of space.

ARTS EDITOR Hardly worth the effort.

EDITOR-IN-CHIEF Fuck em. We'll give em a paragraph once in a while, keep the dogs at bay.

ARTS EDITOR Rename the section.

EDITOR-IN-CHIEF Arts for the People. Television, film, a couple books now and again, and, of course, big four-star reviews for the big shows.

ARTS REPORTER Eh?

EDITOR-IN-CHIEF Which part didn't you hear, Cutey?

ARTS REPORTER About the four stars… you mean all the musicals get four stars no matter what?

EDITOR-IN-CHIEF Listen, Cutey… you know they got a very exciting arts scene in the Yukon… you know about this?… Oh yeah, it's big…. We're lookin to send someone to be our reporter in the Yukon, cover all of it, theatre, movies, the whole thing.

ARTS REPORTER I could do four-star reviews.

EDITOR-IN-CHIEF And every once in a while, you can go see one of these pukey little nothing shows, say some nice things, or not-so-nice things, I won't lose sleep neither way, and we'll run em when we can. Okay?

ARTS EDITOR Don't worry about it.

EDITOR-IN-CHIEF Just think Big.

ARTS EDITOR Think Big.

EDITOR-IN-CHIEF Are you thinking?

ARTS REPORTER Oh yes.

ARTS EDITOR Good.

EDITOR-IN-CHIEF Good.

ARTS EDITOR Okay.

EDITOR-IN-CHIEF Okay, Cutey. Get out. Go on.

ARTS EDITOR Back go work. Go finish the pig story.

ARTS REPORTER Thank you. Yeah, I could get to like it. Thank you.

He addresses the audience.

Well. That was it. My big break. Sure, I felt bad for Phil. He deserved a better ending point. Oh well. I finished the pig story. Got a real good hook into it. I wrote, "What do pigs really want? This is going to sound strange. I saw a piece of absurdist theatre in the rich vein of Louis Pirandello, which had as its main attraction a pig. But hold on. It was a hoot. The direction flowed, and the costumes went really good with the set. Also, there was no funny talkin. I would highly recommend this evening of experimental theatre to anyone what likes experimental art." I don't know. I felt inspired. I wrote and wrote and wrote, and as my hands glided over the keyboard, the wind picked up outside, and more leaves hurled themselves at my window, and that snowy owl what I saw before, sittin there, turning his head, like he had a kink what he couldn't work out. The sun played hide-and-go-seek, so the office was like lighting up and getting dark, lighting up and getting dark. And I thought, that's exactly what life is like, a little light, and a little dark. And right now, I'm standing in the light. The day my first theatre review went in, I saw my name there, my by-line, and right underneath it, the words: Drama Critic. My name. Drama Critic. What a hoot. What an absolute hoot.

Morwyn Brebner   *Coupe de Ville*

1997
Jackie Maxwell: Director
Randy Hughson: Chick – late thirties, early forties
Michelle Giroux: Teenie – younger than Chick

¤ • ¤

A small grubby office. Faint Muzak in the background. A prominent No Smoking sign on one wall. Two closed doors, one beside a window that gives onto the indoor showroom of a Cadillac dealership. Faint rustling sounds from a room, off. The telephone on the desk begins to ring. It rings and rings.

CHICK *(off)* Coming!

CHICK Alluma enters sweatily through the non-showroom door. He looks exerted. One hand holds a tightly rolled magazine. He tucks in a stray shirt-end, straightens his tie, groans with unbearable weariness, picks up the phone.

CHICK Chick Alluma. What? Yeah I'm here. What? No I was in the back, uh, makin' copies. Yeah yeah, send her in.

CHICK hangs up, sighs, lights a cigarette, arranges his tie, unrolls the magazine – a Playboy. *He opens it away from us to the centrefold, shakes his head in awe and wonder. A knock from the showroom door.*

CHICK Yeah.

TEENIE enters. She wears a huge rosary around her neck, carries a clipboard. CHICK shoves the magazine into a desk drawer.

TEENIE You wanted to see me.

CHICK Yeah, uh, siddown. You want a cigarette?

TEENIE You can get fined now.

CHICK Suit yourself.

TEENIE Well, if…

TEENIE takes a cigarette, CHICK goes to light it.

TEENIE No, I quit. I'll just hold it.

A beat.

CHICK I'm going to have to fire you, Teenie.

TEENIE (*firmly*) No.

CHICK Oh yes.

TEENIE No.

CHICK Mm hm. I asked you to take it off. I told you you could wear it inside your blouse. I suggested you, ah, take it across the street and fondle it on your coffee break if you had to. And you nodded, Teenie, which where I come from means yes. Yes I will take it off, yes I understand. So why are you still wearing it? (*beat*) Okay. Help me out here. Explain to me your, what is this, fashion statement? You on a Madonna kick? Because that thing is not in the dress-code book under acceptable accessories.

TEENIE It's a rosary, not a thing.

CHICK I know what it is.

TEENIE I'm Catholic.

CHICK So am I. You don't see me wearing a Cossack.

TEENIE A nun gave it to me.

CHICK A nun. What…?

> *CHICK narrows his eyes, grabs the clipboard from TEENIE, flips through the pages.*

She was in yesterday, am I right?

TEENIE Mm hm.

CHICK Why isn't she on the sheet?

TEENIE She was a nun.

CHICK She was an up. Any single person—nun, whore, president—who walks through that door, is an up. Any single person steps into the showroom, to ask for directions, to use the can, to spit in the fucking ashtray, is an up. You get them to a salesman. That's your job. You don't bring them a brochure, you don't show them the way to the bathroom, you don't accept unsolicited gifts of magical religious jewellery – you get them to a salesman and you write them up on the fucking sheet!

TEENIE Come on, Chick…

CHICK No exceptions.

TEENIE What about the wackos from the welfare hotel who try to cash their cheques at reception?

CHICK Ups. They're ups.

TEENIE They don't have any money, Chick.

CHICK So we get them onto a SmartLease.

> *CHICK wrenches open a desk drawer, pulls out the* Playboy.

CHICK See this magazine? *(Beat. Puts it back in the drawer, pulls out an Economist.)* See this magazine? Car Crash. That's the headline. The death of the automobile dealership. You think I usually read this piece of shit? Nuh-uh. My ex-wife sent it to me. Car Crash. Think about it. This *(gestures towards the rosary)* is the kind of, of flaky inefficiency that is, that is doing us in, Teenie. Do you have any idea how stupid you make me, us, the dealership, look? How fucking totally incompetent? How unclassy? I've got you out on the floor, lurching around like, like Mary-fucking-Magdalene – and Peanut Head, wearing the same fucking shirt every day because his commission's been zero so long he owes *us* money, "chatting" with you instead of, of – I really don't think this is the best way to sell cars. Do you?

TEENIE If your sales department can't sell cars, I don't think it's my fault.

CHICK Excuse me?

TEENIE Frank's selling plenty. Maybe you should ask him for advice.

A beat.

CHICK You're twenty minutes late from lunch, Teenie. Wha'd you eat?

TEENIE Salad.

CHICK Mm. Salad. Where'd you get this salad?

TEENIE Out.

CHICK Really. Let me guess. Howard Johnson.

TEENIE Can I go now?

CHICK You don't feel sick, do you? Salad can't make you sick. How was lunch with Frank?

TEENIE None of your business.

CHICK He your hero now, Teenie? Did he ah, give you some big talk, pay for lunch with that wad he hauls around instead of a wallet? Let you use his cell phone? Impress you with his, ah, virility?

TEENIE It wasn't like that.

CHICK No, I bet not. You want, um… you wanna learn something about Frank? *(looks out in the showroom)* He's good, eh? He's a pusher, the pusherman. Look at that. Frank Armada is a pusher the same as if he was selling crack to schoolgirls. You think those two kids there can afford that GT? Not in a million years can they afford that car. See how he reels them in? See? They GOT to buy it – it's a car, a Pontiac, oh man, better, it's a Cadillac! A motherfucking Coupe de Ville! Those kids live at home, work some fuck-ass job while they fail out of school and drive around in that: ninety percent of their goddamn monthly income. You see Frank on TV? "Come to Frank Armada!" He's got seventy-two-year-old janitors taking out third mortgages to lease new-model Sevilles. Old ladies liquidating their husband's funeral savings so they can spend their last golden years together in a Catera. Loans, leases, mortgages, loans. Jesus. We get any kinda serious hyperinflation in this country, half the working-class immigrants in Toronto are gonna be living in the backs a their luxury cars. Sad but true. *(beat)* No Car Crash for Frank Armada.

TEENIE You should admire him.

CHICK Did he ask you to take off the rosary? *(beat)* Okay. You're a smart girl. Actually, I don't know that. Are you a smart girl? No, don't answer yet. First, let me ask you: when Mr. Young gets back from Nassau, and he finds out—don't pretend you don't know this—that my department has effectively tanked in his absence, that two months worth of leasing paperwork was accidentally recycled, and that I am so out of control of my own people that I can't even make the greeter, the greeter!, take off her rosary… what do you think will happen?

TEENIE He'll fire you.

CHICK See, that's where you're wrong. Do you know who I fired in leasing today?

TEENIE No.

CHICK Dave, can you believe it? I fired Dave. He was fucking up. Do you know who I fired at noon?

TEENIE No.

CHICK The dyke in licensing. Incompetent. Can you guess who's next?

TEENIE The temp at reception?

CHICK No, I like her. She's smart, she can spell.

TEENIE Oh.

CHICK Take off the rosary, Teenie. And be thankful I'm not Frank, who if he had my job would have fired you this morning at nine o'clock sharp then made you trade in your UI for a fuckin' minivan.

>*CHICK holds out his hand for the rosary. TEENIE does not give it. The phone rings.*

CHICK Chick Alluma. *(listens)* What? Oh, come on… I don't, I don't… yeah okay…. Well, have whatserface in licensing – oh fuck, damn! Okay, call the temp agency. *(hangs up)* The receptionist went for coffee and neglected to return. Did you know about this?

TEENIE Frank would never have your job.

CHICK Excuse me?

TEENIE Frank can sell. He would never be a manager.

>*CHICK leaps across the desk, grabs for the rosary. TEENIE shrieks and jumps back.*

CHICK Give it to me!

TEENIE Never! Since I put it on I haven't had my ass grabbed once. That's right! The mechanics, they grab my ass, they don't even ask. I have to wear dark skirts or I get all, all smudgy. I need protection!

CHICK Oh for fuck's–

TEENIE And you ignore my memos, Chick.

CHICK Nobody sends memos here!

TEENIE You don't even read them I'll bet. My request for string? Hmm? Two months ago, a piece of string? Where is it? Where is my string!

CHICK Jesus.

TEENIE *(pulls a crumpled paper from her pocket)* To Chick, from Teenie, double space: things I need to make my job more efficient. I need a chair, because the grate beside the window is hot and, I think, looks unprofessional. I need business cards, also to be professional. Hi, my name is Teenie. *(She proffers an imaginary business card.)* See? AND, I could use a medium or medium long length of string so that I could attach my pen to my clipboard, *(waves around her clipboard, demonstrating the absence of a pen)* a string which I would buy if you would reimburse me or maybe there's some extra string that someone could give me so that the guys wouldn't steal my pen and write me obscene notes like Teenie I love you can I grab your ass! *(no longer reading)* How can I be productive when Peanut Head is promising his customers I'll go out with them if they buy a car? I guess it doesn't work anyway, but it's humiliating. I am not a duck decoy. You know, for a while I was getting very irreligious, you know, very unsure of hell. Actually, I was pretty sure this was hell. Then I got this meditation pamphlet at the Y and for a while I thought I was developing a sort of Zen inner calm but I was just hungover, Chick. And I know what you think but Frank's the only one who treats me like a gentleman because he's the only person who works here who isn't more of a loser than I am. Even you. Especially you! I know you still live at home.

A beat. CHICK's face contorts.

CHICK What the fuck does that mean? What's that, "home?" Everybody lives at "home." That's what the word means, "home." I'm going "home," where I live, where I fucking live! Everybody lives at home! That's what it means!

TEENIE *(calmly)* You don't respect me. You won't give me my string. But it's you who are in trouble. Did you get your invitation to the big sales dinner yet? I didn't think so. Mr. Young isn't sending you one. Frank told me. *(beat)* That's right, Chick. Somebody is being fired.

A beat. CHICK mops his face with his hand. Opens his desk drawer, closes it. Starts to say something, can't. TEENIE takes a small delicate rosary from her pocket, hands it to CHICK.

TEENIE Here. Take it. It's my old one.

CHICK Fuck you.

TEENIE Suit yourself.

TEENIE leaves the small rosary on the desk, exits. CHICK picks it up, holds it, puts it on over his head like a necklace. He lights a cigarette, pulls the Playboy *out of the drawer. He smokes, sighs, loosens his tie, then exits with* Playboy *and rosary through the door he came in.*

Shirley Barrie — *Audience*

1998
Tanja Jacobs: Director
Karen Woolridge: Jenna
Alex Fallis: John

¤ • ¤

> *JOHN and JENNA are a couple. This is a personal fight in a very public place. The performers should experiment with when the characters think they are having a private struggle and when they are aware of, or perhaps even play to, the audience.*

JOHN *(sticks his head in the door)* Hey – In here looks good.

JENNA *(off)* You said we'd leave after the last one.

JOHN *(entering)* But there's an audience in here.

JENNA *(off)* John…

JOHN It won't be long. Come on.

JENNA *(just inside the room)* This is not what we…

JOHN There's space here.

JENNA I want to stay by the door.

JOHN We're on the stage.

JENNA But we can—you know—slip away if it's not any good.

JOHN O, ye of little faith! Where's your sense of discovery, Jenna?

> *He teases her into the room and settles her down. (JOHN has been carrying two small camp stools in a bag which he set up.)*

JENNA I thought we were going to "discover" an antique lamp for the hall table.

JOHN If it's antique, it'll be there tomorrow.

JENNA You have to work tomorrow.

JOHN All the more reason to enjoy myself today.

> *He settles in.*

JENNA Yourself! *(She can barely contain her frustration.)* We agreed. *(pause)* We agreed what we were going... *(pause)* I thought we'd agreed that it was important to spend today together.

JOHN We're together.

JENNA We decided what we were going to do.

JOHN There'll be time to get to the store after this. We'll take a cab.

JENNA I don't care about the damned store!

JOHN Oh. Good.

JENNA I care about us. We were going to talk. About the house.... The future?

JOHN Not now, Jenna. It's going to start any minute.

He waits expectantly for the beginning. Perhaps consults his programme.

JENNA *(pause)* Do you realise you spend more time in pokey, drafty theatres than you do with me?

JOHN That is not true.

JENNA Waking, sentient time, I'm talking here, John. Not snoring through the late news and then falling...

JOHN Gimme a break, Jen. I spend ten hours a day with boring number crunchers who think they've experienced culture when they fall asleep at the opera.

JENNA Opera would be a nice change.

JOHN It's old. Like that lamp you want so much.

JENNA It's stood the test of time. Not here today, gone tomorrow.

JOHN Oh no. This is tomorrow. *(She scoffs.)* Sometimes it is. And you never know when it's going to happen – that moment when what's happening on stage—so close you can smell the perspiration—reaches out and collides with something that's coming from us and a spark shoots up that lifts you right out of your seat.

JENNA And you can brag to all the guys at work that you were there when.

JOHN So? *(pause)* What is the matter with you, Jenna? You're an artist.

JENNA Used to be.

JOHN You could go back to it any time. I've told you. You don't have to work in that grubby law office.

JENNA I happen to like helping real people with real problems.

JOHN Yeah, but don't you miss the freedom? The lifestyle?

JENNA The poverty. The rejection.

JOHN I liked what you did.

JENNA And I thought that you liked me.

JOHN I did.

JENNA Did?

JOHN I do. Why do you always have to twist things?

JENNA You're the pretzel, sweetheart.

JOHN No. I think, I think that deep down you're so upset at what you think of as your failure that you want to deprive others of an audience.

JENNA That is such bull.

JOHN You hardly ever come with me any more.

JENNA I'm tired of being bored.

JOHN You… philistine!

JENNA In what sense are you using that word, John?

JOHN You know.

JENNA Do you see me as the enemy into whose hands you've fallen? Is that what you mean?

JOHN Don't get philological on me. You know what I mean.

JENNA And what about you. Putting down twenty bucks at a pay-what-you-can performance.

JOHN So? I can.

JEENA You can afford to go Saturday night, but you want to rub shoulders with the poor artists.

JOHN That does not make me a philistine.

JENNA *(She relents.)* Look. I'm more than willing for my tax dollars, now that I'm paying some, to fund new work. I just don't want to sit through self-indulgent hunks of coal waiting for the occasional diamond.

JOHN Even coal gives off heat.

JENNA Oh God!

JOHN You used to like my enthusiasm.

JENNA The ideal audience. The fan who can pay.

JOHN I bought your painting.

JENNA Only one I ever sold.

JOHN Are you saying I have bad taste?

JENNA *(beat)* You have better taste in theatre.

JOHN So why don't you come with me.

JEENA No thanks. You can tell me if there's something really special I have to see.

JOHN So everything's okay then.

> *He kisses her on the cheek. Hums "There's no business, like show business…"*

JENNA *(back into the fray)* John, you go five times a week.

JOHN It isn't always five.

JENNA Not if you're working late – no. But you go to the theatre more often than we have sex.

JOHN *(shocked)* Jenna! How can you say that?

JENNA It's true?

JOHN I mean here. Geez!

JENNA It got your attention.

JOHN Is that what this is all about? Sex?

JENNA No. Attention. Theatre isn't life, you know.

JOHN Sometimes it's better than life.

JENNA That's what I was afraid of.

> *She starts off.*

JOHN Where are you going?

JENNA There's nothing happening here, John.

JOHN But there could be.

JENNA Could there? I really don't know anymore. I'm leaving. And if you don't come…

> *She bows.*

JOHN Jenn…

> *She turns. Leaves.*

Wait. Jen…. Oh God.

> *He quickly and awkwardly collects his things and follows her.*

Michael Healey — ***The Button Stories***

1998
Brian Quirt: Director
John Jarvis: Ed
Kristen Thomson: Marni

¤ • ¤

An office. A man enters with his eight-year-old daughter. He rushes to a desk and looks for pen and paper.

ED   762-8904. 762-8904. 762-8904.

MARNI   Dad?

ED   No. 762-8904. 762-8904.

MARNI   Dad?

ED   No! Wait. 762-8904. I'm trying to… 762-8904. 762-8904.

MARNI   Dad? Your office is creepy with no one in it.

ED   Yes. 762-8904.

MARNI   On a weekend. All alone. Dad? Dad? Edward? Dad?

ED   No! Wait! Just–

He finds a pen, now searches for something to write on.

Hang on a sec, Marni. And don't call me that. It creeps me out. 762-8904. *(He can't find anything.)* 762-8904. Jesus.

MARNI   What!?

ED   Nothing, just–

MARNI   *What*??

ED   762-8904. Nothing.

MARNI   I am so *telling*.

ED   Fine. 762-8904.

MARNI   Dad?

ED   One sec.

MARNI   Can you poo here?

ED Hang on, Marni.

> *He gives up, writes the number on his hand.*

MARNI Hey! *(She holds out her arm.)* Me next.

ED *(writing on his hand)* 762-9804. Okay. Yes, Marni. What, Marni.

MARNI *(She's looking at something.)* No.

ED "Can I poo here?"

MARNI Never mind.

ED Do you need to go?

> *Pause.*

To the bathroom?

MARNI No, thank you.

ED Then why the pooing question? If you don't need to go.

MARNI I was asking for you. Not me.

ED Uh huh?

MARNI I can pee anywhere at school. But not poo. From worry. Can you? At work?

ED I see. Well, no. I don't poo here. I usually poo at home before I get here.

MARNI Don't be gross.

ED I need to do one thing here, and then we can go.

> *He switches on the computer.*

MARNI How does he escape?

ED Who.

MARNI Angelo.

> *Pause.*

Dad? How does he escape?

> *ED is looking at the computer.*

Dad? Finish.

ED How does Angelo escape. I… don't know.

MARNI Don't make me laugh. Finish it.

ED You finish it.

MARNI You started. You said he's trapped by the dog.

ED You finish.

MARNI But I don't know. I'm the kid.

ED Well, where is he?

MARNI Trapped by the dog on the ground. Off his nose.

ED How'd he get there?

MARNI When.

ED Way back. At the start.

MARNI He fell off the girl's sweater.

ED How.

MARNI Another jealous button.

ED Jealous Rita.

MARNI Jealous Rita.

ED So?

MARNI So?

ED So then…

MARNI Yes…

ED Go ahead…

MARNI No. You! I'm the kid.

ED But we did this. This is the part we know. Angelo went down the sewer, right? Into the dirty water, and he sank. He fell to the bottom of the sewer and lay there for a thousand days.

MARNI Without breathing. Alone.

ED He got hungry. And thin. And thinner, and thinner, and thinner, and… thinner.

MARNI And then he turned sideways and disappeared.

ED Right. Then he was just a thought. An idea of a button.

MARNI I was a thought.

ED Yes, you were. And thoughts float, and Angelo floated up out of the sewer. It was summer. And he lay on the grass and rested. And then a gust of wind picked him up and put him on the roof of the house.

MARNI On the roof of the house where he lived. He was still alone.

ED The roof was old. It was nearly ruined, and there was moss growing.

MARNI I know: and he ate a bit of moss, moss is button food, and then he got heavier every day, and got pulled harder and harder down. He got to be a button again and then as soon as that happened, he got pulled off the roof and fell. Then the coincidence.

ED The coincidence of the futon extraction. And Angelo bounced.

MARNI Onto the dog's nose. And???

ED Wait.

> *She tries.*

MARNI I'm going to count to five.

ED Be my guest.

MARNI Okay. One. TWO. THREE.

ED But, softly.

MARNI Three. Four.

ED Much Better.

MARNI Five. Hey.

ED Yes?

MARNI What was the very first lie you ever told?

ED Can't recall.

MARNI How old were you?

ED About your age. And you know what? I've told one every day since.

MARNI Really?

ED Yes. Once you start, you never stop.

MARNI I know.

ED So, you know, don't.

MARNI I know. And?

ED You're a dog. You have a button on your nose. You flick your head and it goes up and comes down and you corner it at a rose bush. Or sorry, a lilac bush. Then what do you do?

MARNI Sniff it?

ED Yes. And?

MARNI I don't know.

ED You're the dog.

MARNI I don't know.

ED You're the dog.

MARNI No.

ED Yes.

MARNI No!

ED Sure!

MARNI Eat it?

ED Sure.

MARNI No!!

ED No. Okay. He goes to eat Angelo, and Angelo gritted his teeth. The dog looked in Angelo's mouth and saw green moss stuck between his teeth and was grossed out.

MARNI And runs off.

ED And runs off.

MARNI And throws up.

ED And Angelo sat there, in the grass, Hidden and safe.

MARNI And alone.

ED And it snowed. I'm almost done.

Pause.

MARNI How do I wake up and be the same person from yesterday? When I go to sleep I could wake up anybody.

ED What do you mean?

MARNI There, in my bed. I'm there, I'm by myself and I fall. And I sleep and then when I come back… I could come back anyone. And not me. It's a worry. I could wake up anybody. You wouldn't know.

He looks at her.

ED I say you do not. I say you wake up you. I say. Okay?

MARNI But, who are *you*.

ED Who am I. Hmmm.

MARNI I'm alone. When it happens. I'm by myself in my bed. In my skin. You're not there to see it. You could be anyone anywhere. You know? You could.

ED But no. That's not how it works.

MARNI It's how it works in my head. It could. You know, we all die alone.

ED Marni?

MARNI Yes?

ED Who have you been talking to?

MARNI Get serious. I'm an only child.

ED Yes. Okay. The button stories. You remember the button stories every day. When you wake up.

MARNI Of course.

ED And where did they come from?

MARNI From you.

ED No, they came from us. We made them. You and me. We are tied up together that way. So you can't just wake up someone else. You wake up you because you are tied to things. Me. And Mummy. You are not alone. Okay? Okay?

MARNI Do you say it for you, too?

ED Mummy does for me.

MARNI *(to herself)* For each other.

ED *(shutting off the computer)* Let's go.

MARNI He was buried?

ED Angelo was buried for a time.

MARNI Have you said today's yet?

ED Sorry?

MARNI Have you said today's lie yet?

ED I, yes I have.

MARNI When?

ED …No. I haven't yet.

MARNI Okay. Let me know.

ED Okay.

They leave.

Kate Lynch — *The Newcomer*

1998
Sarah Stanley: Director
Kate Lynch: Woman – Probably around forty. Or fifty.
Sarah Manninen: Young Woman – Probably around twenty. Could be dazzlingly beautiful, but then, who isn't at that age?

⌑•⌑

An office. A WOMAN sits at the desk, perhaps writing on a sheet of paper. She's not doing much, because she's waiting for a knock on the door, so that the other actress can enter and the scene can start. But nothing happens. So she stalls and tries to make up things to do, which is difficult because there are no props other than the paper and pen. This goes on for awhile, and it's likely that she tries not to, but can't avoid the occasional nervous glance towards the door from which the knock should come. Finally, instead of a knock, the door opens very slightly. We can't see who is behind the door.

WOMAN *(looking towards door)* Come in.

No one enters. There is a bit of a stand-off. She tries again.

Please come in. You're... uh... right on time.

Nothing. She perhaps glances nervously towards the audience and back to the person behind the door. Said person whispers something that we cannot hear.

What? Oh, yes... your... coat. You can just put it in the closet. Here, let me do it for you.

She goes into the offstage room, with the unseen actor – or actress, as it happens. There is a muffled conversation which we cannot hear. She re-enters and sits at her desk.

Fine. Good. Please come in.

Again, no one enters. She looks towards the door and the actress behind it. It's likely that there is an edge in her voice now.

Please. We have to begin. I... um... I have another client in... you know... ten minutes.

No one enters. Again we hear the actress behind the door whisper. The WOMAN goes to her. This time she yanks the door open, which reveals the YOUNG WOMAN, who stares out at the audience like a rabbit caught in the headlights. She tries to grab the door and close it, but the WOMAN is too fast for her and grabs her arm. Small scuffle as the WOMAN tries to pull her into the room and the YOUNG WOMAN resists.

(*rather aggressively*) Sit down!

The YOUNG WOMAN jumps slightly and then sits, still not taking her eyes off the audience.

(*rustling papers, or something else of a businesslike nature*) Now then, I see here by your file that you have been in the country for six months, is that right?

YOUNG WOMAN (*just about inaudible*) Yes.

WOMAN Very good. And how are you finding things? Any difficulties?

Nothing.

Any difficulties? Anything you'd like to talk over?

Nothing.

(*fishing*) Perhaps we might discuss your reasons for making this appointment?

The YOUNG WOMAN has begun to cry.

Oh God. Are you… I mean… oh. Um. I guess this is all… I can understand, of course, it's all so new. Shall I… would you like a glass of water?

Nothing.

Well, certainly. There's some just out here. Let's go get you some, shall we? Don't worry. This happens all the time. I'm sure it's all just so new and strange.

The WOMAN gets up and brings the YOUNG WOMAN to her feet. She is still crying and staring at the audience. The WOMAN leads her into the other room and closes the door. We can hear them talking. After a few moments the WOMAN comes out. She address the audience.

Sorry. Um… I'd like… we'd like to start again, if you don't mind. Sorry. She asked me to explain, and I think its reasonable. This is her first real job, she's just out of theatre school, and we wanted someone young, you know, and she read really well. But, she's never really, you know, this is her… first real audience. So. Anyway, we're going to start again, she thinks she feels okay now that she's actually seen you, and we're going to have to go through the first part a bit fast, because the whole piece is only allowed to be ten minutes and we were told we have to keep to schedule. So. Thanks. Okay. Here we go. Ready?

YOUNG WOMAN (*offstage*) I'm fine now. You can start.

WOMAN Good. Okay. (*sitting, to YOUNG WOMAN offstage*) Okay. I'm sitting. Just knock and come in.

Very loud knocking.

Come in.

She enters. She turns to the audience and gives us a dazzling, sheepish smile, then goes and sits.

YOUNG WOMAN *(in a broad Irish accent)* Good morning. It's so kind of you to take the time. Sure 'tis.

The WOMAN stares at her, stunned.

WOMAN Yes. Yes, good morning... Ms Koslovovitch. Uh, I see from your file–

YOUNG WOMAN O'Malley.

WOMAN What?

YOUNG WOMAN O'Malley. Miss O'Malley.

WOMAN Nnno. No, I believe your name is Koslovovitch.

YOUNG WOMAN No, really. O'Malley. *(sotto voce)* Trust me.

WOMAN I...

YOUNG WOMAN Honestly. Go on.

WOMAN I... uh... read in your file that you are a... Muslim.

YOUNG WOMAN Roman Catholic.

WOMAN Muslim. Your name is Koslovovitch and you are a Muslim. I know you've been under a lot of strain, so it's natural you're a bit confused. You've had a terrible time, and had to flee your country to escape the ethnic cleansing and that's why you are here today, to discuss your being a newcomer to Canada–

YOUNG WOMAN *(still Irish)* Sure, and it's a grand country too.

WOMAN No! I... uh... no. I think... this is not...

She stands and addresses the audience.

Excuse us, please, we're... we... *(to YOUNG WOMAN)* Please come with me.

She exits. The YOUNG WOMAN rises, gives the audience a warm, martyred smile, and follows the WOMAN to the other room. The door is closed. A fight ensues and this time the voices, or at least the WOMAN's voice, is less muffled. We hear "This is not the time!" "but you said!" "you were hired to do my script, the way I wrote it!" "I just thought!", etc. Eventually the door opens. The WOMAN re-enters, looking quite cranky, and sits at the desk.

(aggressively) Come in!

The YOUNG WOMAN walks in the room, looking glum, trying to put a good face on it.

Hello, Miss Koslovovitch. Welcome. Please sit down. Now I see by your file that you have been in the country for six months. How are you making out? We have to hurry, because... so, please just tell me the main thing that's on your mind.

YOUNG WOMAN *(in a not-so-good Muslim Serb accent)* Is very difficult. In my country women must work very hard, there is no time for school...

WOMAN *(sotto voce)* Yes but, what about Canada? Go to the part about... uh... tell me about Canada.

YOUNG WOMAN Oh. Okay. Um. But here is hard too. At first it seems so good, so free. So much opportunity. But I think maybe it is the same. For women. It is true we can wear nice clothes, but I think maybe there is no real respect for us here. Like today, when I come here on the bus, and I feel the men's eyes, undressing me. I just don't think she'd say that.

WOMAN *(past patience)* She does say that! You do say that. I mean.... You're obviously still very upset. Okay. Lets get some more water. Please step out here.

Pushes YOUNG WOMAN out the door.

YOUNG WOMAN *(exiting; to the audience)* I just don't think she would say that. *(in the outer room)* I just don't think she'd be so... so...

They are both offstage.

WOMAN So what?!

YOUNG WOMAN Well, it's like she's a victim. You know. She's so full of self-pity.

WOMAN Not if you don't play her like that.

Popping her head out to speak to the audience.

I'm sorry. I don't think she's a victim. Well, she is a victim, but of circumstances way outside her control, and then she comes to Canada, finally safe, she thinks, and then she runs into our version of patriarchy, in our bureaucracy, and in our institutions, and on the streets and she finds a friend at the immigration department, me, who guides her through and teaches her. And they become friends.

Back inside, to YOUNG WOMAN.

And that's what I wrote. Which I wish you would fucking play. You did it in rehearsals. You agreed.

YOUNG WOMAN I know, and I meant to. I really did. But then I came out and I saw the audience, and it suddenly just seemed so dishonest. *(She is starting to cry. She speaks to the audience.)* I just can't find the truth in it. I really can't.

WOMAN *(grabbing her head and turning it back)* Stop that. That's not fair. Don't you dare cry.

YOUNG WOMAN You hired me because I could cry. You said... you said that was what distinguished my audition, that the material moved me to tears.

WOMAN The material! My material. You're just crying now because you can't get your own way. It's cheap. It's a cheap female trick.

YOUNG WOMAN Maybe that's why Miss Koslovovitch cries. To get her way.

WOMAN She cries because she's had a horrible life! She's seen her family killed, she's been raped. She's left behind everything she knows.

YOUNG WOMAN You could do all that with Irish you know.

WOMAN She's not Irish! She's a Muslim Serb!

YOUNG WOMAN I know, but it's funnier with Irish.

WOMAN For Christ sake, it's a serious piece about war and patriarchy and woman, and female friendship and…

YOUNG WOMAN I know, but it's just a little ten-minute piece, it would be better if it was funny.

WOMAN Look, goddammit. This is my first piece of writing. By myself. I'm very new to all this. And I wrote it. It's mine. Why can't you just read what I wrote?

YOUNG WOMAN Well, it's all very new to me too. It's my first professional job. I just don't want to look like an idiot. I mean, what do either one of us know about war, and Muslims and rape.

WOMAN We're women! We can relate on that level! Women reaching out and helping each other in a male world of war and aggression. Just fucking play that!

YOUNG WOMAN But that's part of the problem, it would be better if it was a bit funny. I mean, I think your writing is really good, I do. It's just that, you know, its only ten minutes and it's a bit… well a bit…

WOMAN A bit what?

YOUNG WOMAN Sort of, um, serious. You know, earnest. For ten minutes.

WOMAN Jesus, you've been out of theatre school for ten minutes and you're telling me how to write. I think I know a little bit more about this sort of thing than you do.

YOUNG WOMAN Well, after all, you're new to writing. I mean, you've had about as much writing experience as I have acting. And all I'm saying is its hard to get really heavy in ten minutes. Urjo said he told you it should be funny–

WOMAN Whoa! Urjo? Urjo said? When did Urjo tell you that my script should be funny?

YOUNG WOMAN The other day. We were discussing the season, and writers, you know, and he said he thought–

WOMAN And Andy? Did Andy have anything to share with you about my script?

YOUNG WOMAN Well it got late and he had to go, but he did say–

WOMAN Never mind!

To audience.

Look, I tried to write something a little deeper than the usual bullshit sketch for a few cheap laughs.

YOUNG WOMAN I know, but I just had trouble finding the truth in it.

WOMAN Truth! Oh, God. Look, you're a woman, you must have been badly treated by men at some point in your life?

YOUNG WOMAN Not really. No.

Pause.

WOMAN Did Urjo tell you how the scene should end?

YOUNG WOMAN He said just try to get through it gracefully.

WOMAN Would a bow be graceful?

YOUNG WOMAN Sure.

The WOMAN bows as YOUNG WOMAN says–

And I really want to thank you for this wonderful opportunity.

Michael MacLean   ***The Audition***

1998
David Ferry: Director
Jill Dyck: Officer
Paul Braunstein: Peter

¤•¤

The American Immigration and Naturalization interrogation room in Vancouver airport. It is a bare office: a desk, a telephone, two chairs; also a video camera on a tripod, focused on the second chair. The officer enters carrying PETER's passport (inside it is the declaration form), and turns on the camera.

OFFICER   Step in here please.

PETER   Thank you.

OFFICER   Have a seat.

PETER   Thank you.

The OFFICER sits down. Pause. PETER clears his throat. Pause.

OFFICER   So… *(checks passport)* Peter: you want to visit America.

PETER   Yes, that's right.

OFFICER   Ever been there before?

PETER   No. No, I haven't.

OFFICER   Well, it's a wonderful place, Peter. Land of opportunity, you know – I don't know if you know that; that's what we call it: the Land of Opportunity. What are your plans?

PETER   Oh, you know, I thought I'd just, you know, take a look around. I've got a, uh, friend in Los Angeles, she said she'd, you know, show me around.

OFFICER   Oh, well that's good. Good to have a friend.

PETER   Yes.

OFFICER   Los Angeles.

PETER   Yes.

OFFICER   Nice town, L.A.

PETER Yes.

OFFICER Centre of the entertainment industry, if I'm not mistaken.

PETER Yes. I've heard that.

OFFICER Never been there myself; and no desire to. Planning on staying long?

PETER No, no. A week. Maybe two. Three max. I have to get back to work.

OFFICER *(looks at the form inside the passport)* You're a waiter, Peter. That's what it says.

PETER Yes.

OFFICER *(picks up phone, dials)* Clement. You go on ahead without me, Clement, I may be a while. *(hangs up)*

PETER There's no problem, is there? I mean I'm not going to have to take my clothes off, am I? *(laughs nervously)*

OFFICER *(beat)* Tough profession, waiting.

PETER Yes. No. Oh, you know, it's not that bad. You're not cracking down on waiters all of a sudden, are you?

OFFICER What have I seen you in?

PETER Pardon?

OFFICER I've seen you in something, haven't I?

PETER I don't–

OFFICER I have. On TV. Right? Or a movie…? No. "X-Files?" "Nikita?" "Outer Limits?"

PETER *(beat)* Oh! You thought I was – you thought I was an *actor*, didn't you?

OFFICER Did I?

PETER Didn't you?

OFFICER You know what? I did.

PETER Oh God. No no no. No no no. Huh uh. I'm just a waiter. I wait on tables, that's what I do.

OFFICER Ah.

PETER I *know* actors. Of course. How could I not? But God, I'd never *be* one; who'd want to be – oh God, of course: *Los Angeles! Hollywood*! You thought I was – off to Hollywood or something, off to be a movie star!

OFFICER Which you're not.

PETER Just like every other Canadian actor. *Waiter. Actor.* No, God – are you kidding? No. No: just a waiter here, that's all, just a regular tourist.

OFFICER Because, you know, I see "waiter"–

PETER You don't think "waiter," you think "actor." Right? Of course. No, that's okay: that's the stereotype, right? Hey, listen, I don't blame you at all. Don't worry about it.

OFFICER Well, I wasn't.

>   *Beat.*

PETER No reason you should. Well. Can I go? My plane's leaving in…

>   *Beat.*

OFFICER An hour.

PETER Yeah. No rush, I guess. *(beat)* I was hoping I'd maybe get a magazine, or something.

>   *Pause.*

Do you get lots of, uh, actors? Trying to…

OFFICER Oh yeah. This time of year; it's pilot season, you know.

PETER Right, of course. *(beat)* Lots?

>   *The OFFICER nods.*

How many? About. Any idea?

OFFICER Thousands.

PETER Thousands. Huh.

OFFICER Thing is, of course, it's illegal, you know. Looking for work without a permit. Just like any other job.

PETER Is it? Really. I didn't know.

OFFICER Oh yeah. Also, it's illegal to try and lie to an INS officer.

PETER INS?

OFFICER Me.

PETER Oh.

OFFICER I'm *sure* I've seen you in something.

PETER No no. No. I don't think so.

OFFICER You're sure.

PETER No. I mean, yes. I mean, look: I'm not an actor, so you couldn't have seen me in anything. I mean, unless you were at my grade three Christmas pageant. I was Joseph.

OFFICER *(beat, staring)* No. Something else.

PETER *(beat)* Look–

OFFICER "X-Files!"

PETER What?

OFFICER Wasn't it!

PETER What?

OFFICER "X-Files!" Yes! That's what it was!

PETER No!

OFFICER Yes!

PETER No!

OFFICER Yes! Come on, admit it: you were that guy.

PETER No! It wasn't me!

OFFICER Oh please, Peter, give it a rest.

PETER But–

OFFICER You were very good. In my humble opinion. If you'd come through a couple of years ago I would've remembered your name, too, but the credits just whiz by now, you know? And they do those promos now; they squeeze the credits into one side of the screen so they can tell you what's coming up next. I hate that. It makes my job tougher, and I think it's disrespectful to the artists.

PETER But I'm a waiter!

OFFICER You are an actor.

PETER I'm a waiter!

OFFICER I don't think so.

PETER But I am! I'm a waiter! I'm a poor little Canadian waiter; please, *please*, you've got to believe me. Don't send me back. *Please*, officer: I worked all year, I took double shifts, I saved my tips. Listen. My girlfriend, my ex – oh God, my *ex*-girlfriend – she's the most beautiful woman I ever met, she's so right for me, we're so good together, but she doesn't know it, she won't admit it – she moved to L.A., she's got dual citizenship, she says that's where the action is; L.A.! the action! My God! *I'm* the action; *Red Deer's* the action! She phoned me last month after a year and a half, she said – she said – she said she misses me. She said she thinks maybe she made a mistake. But she said she's not sure. She said she needs to see me again. She wants to see if we can work it out. She wants to *see me again*. I was hoping for it, waiting for it, praying for it. My God! I lit candles! I'm not even Catholic! And finally she calls and I take all my savings and I buy a non-refundable ticket and you're not going to stop me, are you? Please don't, Officer. I'm not an actor. I swear it.

Long pause.

OFFICER That was *good*.

PETER But it's true!

OFFICER Yeah. Right. Or it's true. *(thinks, turns off camera, takes out a sheet of paper)* Those are the two possibilities, all right: it's good, or it's true. Sign this.

PETER What is it?

OFFICER Just sign it.

PETER It's blank.

OFFICER You're right. Sign it.

>   *PETER hesitates.*

What, you never signed an autograph before?

PETER No.

OFFICER Yeah, well, that's one of the possibilities. *(beat)* You going to do it, or are you going to go back to Red Deer?

PETER *(starts to sign)* Do you want me to make it "to" anybody?

OFFICER *(beat)* "Clement." C-L-E-M-E-N-T. He's a friend.

>   *PETER writes, signs, puts the paper on the desk.*

Okay. Go. Have a nice flight.

>   *PETER exits. OFFICER puts the paper in the drawer.*

Kate Lynch   ***Ten-Minute Play!***
(The Musical)

1999
Leah Cherniak: Director
Mark Christmann: Alex
Allegra Fulton: Tamara

¤•¤

ALEX and TAMARA are lovely and lithe and in love. There's lots of singing and dancing.

SCENE ONE

As the lights come up, our two lovebirds have their backs to us, facing into Tim's office, just finishing a song and a dance. They embrace.

ALEX   Oh Tamara, you're wonderful!

TAMARA   Oh Alex, I love you. I need you. Take me away from all this. *(gestures expansively into Tim's office)*

ALEX   *(holding TAMARA's hands)* And I love you darling. But you know I'm penniless. How can I take you away from this house, this huge house. You need huge houses, and lovely things. Why, this room alone – it's the size of… of…

TAMARA   A football stadium?

ALEX   Exactly.

TAMARA   Actually, its bigger. It was modelled after the throne room of the Taj Mahal.

ALEX   It's so big it echoes whenever we burst into song. Listen– *(He is about to burst into song.)*

TAMARA   *(putting her hands over his lips in some kind of adorable fashion)* No, Alex. I want you to use those lips for something other than bursting into song.

ALEX   Then dance around the room with me!

He grabs her by the waist and is about to do something physically large with her.

TAMARA   No! I want you to use those arms for something other than lifting me into the air and spinning me gaily about the room.

ALEX   But–

TAMARA Yes, darling. Please! Please take me away from all this! I can't bear these huge houses anymore. Don't you know what it's like for me? Why, if I happen to forget my reading glasses in my bedroom when I come down in the morning, it's nearly lunchtime by the time I get back.

ALEX My poor darling.

TAMARA This place makes Xanadu look like Andy McKim's office. At breakfast this morning I read in the *papers* that the east wing burned down last night. I knew nothing about it. Oh, Alex, it's a living hell.

ALEX My love.

TAMARA I know what I'd be giving up. We met in this room. Remember?

ALEX How could I forget? When I walked through the door and saw you standing – down there at the other end – *(He points to a vast distance.)* I thought – what a tiny woman. Then, in the twenty minutes it took you to skip across the room to greet me, I lost my heart to you forever. But, Tamara, I'm so poor, how could I take you away from all this *(gestures expansively)* to my tiny little house? Would you ever burst into song in such squalor?

TAMARA But Alex, don't you see? It's our love that needs to be big, not the rooms we sing and dance in. We can sing and dance anywhere – in a… factory, or… or a lab. In a room without walls–

ALEX …beyond walls.

TAMARA Yes. With our friends, our… our…

ALEX Buddies.

TAMARA Yes! As long as I'm with you, every house, no matter how small, is the theatre centre for me.

ALEX Oh Tamara, are you saying…?

TAMARA I'm saying it doesn't matter that you're poor, Alex. I don't need space, I could even work *without* a space. Our own space isn't necessary, angel. I need you. I want to play with you at *your* house.

ALEX Oh my love!

> *Music swells. Big light change. Or not. TAMARA and ALEX turn around and face the house.*

TAMARA *(looking about in fascinated horror)* Well! So. This is your… little… house.

ALEX My darling. Is it all right?

TAMARA Yes! Of course! It's… intimate. Warm. No doubt.

ALEX *(hideously downcast)* Oh Tamara. I knew it. You hate it here.

TAMARA No! no, you big dope. I love you all the more, knowing that this is the world, well, the place, that you sing and dance in. Oh how I admire you. Oh how it makes me want to burst into song.

She is about to do so, but ALEX quickly covers her mouth.

ALEX Um, better not. I mean, not just now. Maybe later.

TAMARA What do you mean? Why shouldn't I burst into song? Isn't that what we came here to do?

ALEX Yes, yes, but, well, you see, the… our… neighbours.

TAMARA You mean… those people on the other side of the wall?

She flings the door into the lobby open and stares at whoever happens to be in there.

Do you mean to say they can hear us?

ALEX Well, yes. I mean, they're right there.

She slams the door.

TAMARA But, but, that's inhuman. *(stage whisper)* How can anyone work under these circumstances?

ALEX It's not always easy. You're used to big houses. Of course this all must come as a shock to you.

TAMARA Well, oh. But, we can dance, can't we?

ALEX My love! Of course we can dance. Come to me.

TAMARA Yes, first let's just roll up this carpet.

ALEX No, no, I'm sorry, it doesn't come up.

TAMARA It doesn't… but how can you…?

ALEX Well, it does take a little extra creativity.

TAMARA But Alex, I can't do it! I can't work in these conditions! There must be somewhere else…

ALEX Well, there is a fairly large room downstairs, but–

TAMARA Downstairs? You mean, that nice little place we passed on the way up here? Yes, I think I know it! It's not too bad, really. In a pinch. Lets go there and dance!

ALEX But we can't, Tamara, that is… I've never been invited there…

TAMARA Oh, poor dear. *I* have.

ALEX I don't think they'd let me. They never have before.

TAMARA How awful for you.

ALEX Yes. But, surely you can work here, too. You just need to get used to it.

TAMARA No, no I don't think I can, Alex. This house is just too small. I mean, look at it. It's silly to even call it a house. No one could create in here, no one. I mean, not anything of any real importance. Oh, a little sketch perhaps, something that might please the undiscerning, but why waste time with that sort of thing. It's pathetic.

ALEX *(aside)* Darling please.

TAMARA What?

ALEX *(whispering)* Not in front of the house.

TAMARA I suppose you're going to tell me the walls have ears.

ALEX Well…

TAMARA What am I saying? The walls have ears?! Listen to me. I've completely switched metaphors now. It's this place. This house. It's having a very bad effect on my creativity. We're meandering. Where is the ending?

ALEX The what?

TAMARA The ending? Where is the ending?

ALEX *(looking around)* Well, it's–

TAMARA You don't know, do you? You don't even know where the ending is. That sort of thing always happens with these little houses. You become complacent. Any sort of thing will do. Well, go on then.

ALEX What do you mean, go on.

TAMARA Create an ending. We have to have one, even here.

•

Hi Andy! This is sad eh? I just can't quite get to the ending. I figure they both have two more lines each and we're outta here. But what are those two lines? I just don't know yet. Think of it as a serial. It's quite the little cliffhanger eh?

Kate

Ivana Shein *A Doctor, A Secretary and a Bag of Apples*

1999
Chris Abraham: Director
Nola Auguston: Jane
Ted Atherton: Doctor

⌑•⌑

The setting is a veterinarian's office. The design of the office is open: there is an operating area with various instruments, and an office space, with an old typewriter and small desk. The mood the room should evoke is that of veterinarian's office in a 1950s sitcom. Very clean, very black-and-white. JANE is a woman in her forties who has maintained her girlish charm and has an energetic verve, which she brings to her job. The DOCTOR is also in his forties. He is a very nervous man who comes to work to see JANE and rarely operates on animals. He is always inventing different experiments for JANE to partake in. This has been going on every day for twenty years.

JANE enters carrying her purse and a pile of papers. The DOCTOR is busying himself at his operating station examining different medical objects, stethoscopes, etc.

JANE Well, hallo doctor.

DOCTOR Hallo Jane. You're looking quite fresh today.

JANE Well thank you. You're looking quite burnt.

DOCTOR Burnt?

JANE I said nice.

DOCTOR Well, thank you.

JANE sits at her desk and begins to type.

Listen Jane I was wondering if you would mind doing me a favour.

JANE Yes?

DOCTOR Would you mind biting into this apple for me? It's for a health experiment.

JANE I would love to.

DOCTOR It's such a silly expression, a doctor a day keeps the apple away.

JANE You mean an apple a day keeps the doctor away.

DOCTOR That's what I said.

> *He hands her the apple. She takes a bite.*

Very good. Thank you, Jane.

JANE You're welcome. What's the health experiment for?

DOCTOR It's for a case of dying cows in New Mexico. Have you heard of it?

JANE No, not at all. I didn't know that they had cows in New Mexico.

DOCTOR Well they do. They are purple. Well the dying ones are. It's quite tragic.

JANE I'm so sorry. I'm glad I was able to help.

> *She smiles at him, returns to typewriter.*

DOCTOR Well yes. Perhaps you could take a few more bites. For purposes of the experiment. You can never collect too much data.

JANE All right then. *(She finishes eating the apple.)*

DOCTOR I need you to eat another one. I've mistaken the procedure. Just have one more bite and then spit out the apple into this tissue.

> *She takes another bite and spits it at the DOCTOR. He looks at her astonished.*

DOCTOR But Jane, why did you do that?

JANE I'm so sorry. Something must've come over me. Some sort of demon entered my body. It was incredible. One moment I was myself, about to bite into your apple and then poof.

DOCTOR Poof?

JANE Poof. Evil. Darkness and Sin entered me. First in my tonsils and then in my very mouth. And the evil forced me to spit this apple at you.

> *They look at each other. The DOCTOR smiles.*

DOCTOR Do it again.

JANE You want me to do it again?

DOCTOR Please. *(He is very excited.)* Conjure up this demon of yours…. What is her name? What does she look like?

> *He hands her another apple.*

JANE Oh doctor. I don't think I could.

> *She takes the apple in her hand. She bites into the apple, then spits apple bits at him fiercely*

Doctor, I hate you! You are a pig!

DOCTOR Jane!

JANE *(mocking him)* Doctor!

DOCTOR That was it! That was the demon, you conjured her. Wonderful.

JANE That was the truth.

DOCTOR *(He stares at her blankly.)* The truth?

> Pause.

I'll take a bite of one side and then spit it at you and then you can take the other side and spit it at me.

> *They do this and both let out a squeal of delight. They continue to spit bits of apple at each other.*

JANE Can all this biting and spitting really be for your experiment?

DOCTOR Yes. The effect spitting has – on cows. Purple cows have been known to die spitting. It's quite tragic. I finally feel like I'm at a point in my career, where I can venture out of the office and do something noteworthy. In the world, field work, they call it, do you know what I mean?

JANE Would you lie to me doctor?

DOCTOR Of course not. I don't believe in lying.

JANE What about bending?

DOCTOR No. I don't even bend.

JANE Omit?

DOCTOR Omit what?

JANE The truth. It's another form of lying, you know. Not saying something.

DOCTOR No, I don't even omit.

> Pause.

I curve.

JANE Curve?

DOCTOR *(avoiding eye contact)* In certain very very specific and unique situations I will curve the truth. Placing a curve in the truth is different then a bend. A bend suggests that you will eventually break the truth, a curve simply suggests that you are mildly avoiding it, and perhaps in some accidental way touching it briefly.

JANE There are cows in New Mexico.

DOCTOR Yes there are.

JANE They are blue.

DOCTOR Purple.

JANE That's a curve.

DOCTOR Precisely.

JANE I'm sensing a bend. Are you lying to me, doctor?

DOCTOR Please Jane, there is work to be done. Cats to be neutered, dogs with terrible breath that need special mints. I can't stand around talking about the parameters of truth with you. It's much too painful.

JANE Very well. Just answer me one thing. Was there a health experiment?

DOCTOR Yes.

JANE That's all I needed to know. *(She turns away to do typing.)*

DOCTOR *(whispers)* No. No health experiment.

JANE *(She turns around hearing him and smiles.)* I didn't think so.

DOCTOR So then why did you do it?

JANE I was testing you.

DOCTOR Curve!

JANE I am not curving!

DOCTOR Bend!

JANE I am one hundred percent honest. I wake up in the morning, I wash my face, brush my teeth, I give money to the homeless, I work earnestly for you and throughout my day I am honest. To everyone!

DOCTOR Except for who?

JANE Myself! But that is allowed in the rules of honesty.

DOCTOR If you are not honestly in love with yourself, how can you be honest to everyone?

JANE You said in love.

DOCTOR I did not.

JANE Oh, you curver. You are the curviest of all curvers. As a matter of fact you are worse than curvy. Even worse than a bender. You are a breaker. I heard you say the words IN LOVE. And I know doctor, that you are in love with me.

DOCTOR Oh. Oh. OH. OH. Well well. There are dogs to be neutered and cats to be spayed. So. So.

JANE *(walking towards him)* That's not bending now. That's pretending. Pretending that you just didn't say the word love. And that I didn't just say the word love. It's out there. The animal has left the cage. Do you get it? Roaming free.

DOCTOR Well I suppose it has.

JANE Doctor, are you honest with yourself?

DOCTOR Yes. Well it's quite impossible to be honest all the time. There must always be a compromise. The world would never accept an honest veterinarian.

JANE What with the dying cows and all.

DOCTOR When you die they ask you if you have received the one thing you came for. I've seen it happen with the animals. And I have received being spat at by you. That is all that has ever mattered to me. You are my life apple. What is yours? Please tell me what you want and I will give it to you.

JANE *(eyeing the bag of apples)* I have, always wanted you to be honest with me.

DOCTOR I am honest with you. Me and the dying cows are gratefully indebted to you.

JANE *(looking up and smiling)* Well doctor, it's five o'clock so I'll be leaving.

DOCTOR Leaving so soon Jane?

JANE Well, that depends.

DOCTOR On what?

JANE Goodbye, doctor.

DOCTOR I want to tell you–

She turns.

I love you.

JANE Oh?

DOCTOR No bend or curve there.

JANE I see.

DOCTOR I had to tell you. It's just too tiring hiding behind all these layers. It's just that as you get older there are all these layers. These rejections and disappointments that pile on top of each other and it becomes much more difficult to be the kind of honest man you may want from someone – you may want from me.

JANE Yes, I know.

DOCTOR And I have sat across from you every day for twenty years and looked at you, and longed for you and have never had the words to tell you.

JANE Well.

DOCTOR It's really the only thing we have left. Just the truth. It's the only thing that can safely see us through.

JANE Yes.

DOCTOR We have to be true to ourselves. To each other.

JANE Quite right.

DOCTOR I suppose I am a better man for saying it. Finally. So you may go home. Tomorrow we will resume as usual.

JANE Of course doctor. Well then see you tomorrow.

DOCTOR Yes. See you t-t-tomorrow.

JANE There is just one thing.

DOCTOR What is it, Jane?

JANE I have this bag of apples and I was wondering if you would mind spitting them at me. For a science experiment.

DOCTOR An experiment?

JANE Yes. An experiment.

> *She hands him an apple, he bites into it.*

Good, now hold the apple in your mouth and I am going to bite into the other side.

> *The DOCTOR nods. JANE bites into the other side, the apple falls. They are left staring at each other. Lights down.*

Chris Earle   *Runneymede*

2000
Chris Earle: Director
Robert Smith: Mark
Shari Hollett: Carolyn

¤•¤

A park. A woman sits on a bench. A man stands a few feet away. They are staring at each other.

CAROLYN Hi.

MARK Hello. God. Oh… um… this is very…. Shit. Hi. Oh, this is so weird.

CAROLYN How are you?

MARK Fine… uh…

CAROLYN Good.

MARK I'm sorry–

CAROLYN Why?

MARK Nothing. Are you just…?

CAROLYN What?

MARK Just… enjoying the day?

CAROLYN Yeah.

MARK Okay. You don't still work for…

CAROLYN No.

MARK No. I guess I knew that…. So you still live here?

CAROLYN Where?

MARK Here. Toronto.

CAROLYN Yes.

MARK I thought I heard you moved out west…

CAROLYN No.

MARK Okay.

CAROLYN Where did you hear that?

MARK Uh, I don't know… I think maybe it was a friend of yours from the store… Jamie… Joanne…

CAROLYN Oh.

MARK This was a while ago.

CAROLYN No. I've been here.

MARK Okay.

CAROLYN New glasses.

MARK What? Oh, yeah. Well, not really. A year.

CAROLYN They're good.

MARK Thanks. They're supposed to, you know, suit the shape of my face more, or something.

CAROLYN They do.

MARK Yeah, well, just… a change.

CAROLYN Right.

MARK So–

CAROLYN Are you okay?

MARK No… I'm just… it's so strange…

CAROLYN Why is that?

MARK Just… seeing you.

CAROLYN Oh…

MARK Um…. Do you have to be somewhere?

CAROLYN Not really.

MARK Do you… would you like to go for a coffee, or something?

CAROLYN Why?

MARK I don't know… just to talk…

CAROLYN About what?

MARK I don't know… about us, I guess… about what happened…

CAROLYN What happened…

MARK Yeah.

CAROLYN I don't think so.

MARK Okay. Fair enough. How are things going?

CAROLYN Great.

MARK I'm sorry I haven't kept in touch. *(CAROLYN laughs.)* I'm not saying that you care. You probably couldn't give a shit, but I'm just saying that I'm sorry. I… don't think I handled things very well.

CAROLYN I'm not sure what you mean.

MARK At the end…

CAROLYN What was there to handle?

MARK I don't know.

CAROLYN You didn't skip town. You didn't do it on my birthday or Christmas Eve. You didn't do it over the phone, or in a crowded restaurant. You weren't cruel about it. You sat me down face-to-face, alone, in my apartment. I was home. It was a Friday night. I didn't have to go anywhere after you did it. I didn't have to go into work the next day. You obviously put some thought into it, right? Unless that was all just a coincidence. But I don't think so. I think you took some care with it. You planned ahead, with some consideration for what I might be going through.

MARK I guess.

CAROLYN It seems to me that whatever there was to *handle,* you handled very well. Even before the fact, you were careful to give me some clues as to what might be coming. Weeks before. Little clues. Simple things, like putting off our summer holiday plans, and refusing to have sex with me. Little clues that might make a person wonder: "Hm, maybe there's something wrong here. Maybe this isn't just a phase or a bumpy patch. Maybe this is a sign." Not that I necessarily interpreted IT that way. I didn't. I was still the sort of person that hoped for the best. But then when you sat me down, that night, in my apartment. And you looked down at the floor, well then, all those clues, they were right there, stored in the back of my brain, in the base of my spine, and they just sprang—they leapt—right up to the front, right before my eyes, I was momentarily blinded by them. And I think that was part of the plan too. That look down at the floor. It was a warning: "Prepare yourself, Carolyn." And there is the one regret, my only regret about the way I *handled things,* because in hindsight I should have stood up and gone to the front door and opened it and made you leave right then. But I couldn't. I couldn't move. And so you began to talk… and I only remember the first thing you said. Do you remember the first thing you said?

MARK Not really.

CAROLYN I do. How long has it been? Five – six years?

MARK Five.

CAROLYN But I remember. It's all I remember, of everything you said that night. You looked down at the floor and you said this: "I'm not… happy." Just like that. With a little pause just before the "happy." "I'm not… happy." It was like getting hit by a freight train going one mile an hour. Just inching along, and you're standing in it's way and it just nudges you, almost gently, but there are tons and tons of cold dark metal behind that nudge, and for an instant you feel the force of all that weight, all that mass, directed at you, speaking to you, saying to you: "You do not exist. You thought you did but you were mistaken. The universe has just revealed itself to be of such a scale as to render you statistically insignificant. You have no mass. You exert no gravitational pull. You are not... there."

"I'm not... happy." Boom.

It was a year before I could taste food again.

And then you looked at me. That was brave. To look at me. To look into my face. My God, I tried, I tried to keep it from splitting open like that, but, well, it was an involuntary physical response. And the tears – the way they jumped out of my eyes. Squirting, shooting out of my eyes. Hideous. You had to look into my face and see that, and know that you were the cause. Poor you. It must have been awful. Was it awful?

Look at me. *(He does.)*

Was it awful?

MARK Yeah...

CAROLYN Poor you. What were you thinking?

MARK I felt awful.

CAROLYN No, no. I know pretty much what you were feeling. But what were you thinking? The part of you that was not emotionally involved – that wasn't filled with pity and guilt – you know, the part that watches, and calculates and plans and thinks; the part that handles things. What was that part doing?

MARK Nothing.

CAROLYN Mark. Look at me. It was five years ago. I'm fine. I'm over it. You still seem to be holding onto some guilt.

MARK Yeah, of course.

CAROLYN Why?

MARK I don't like causing pain.

CAROLYN Sure. Who does?

MARK So...

CAROLYN My God, you are really fucked up about this. All right, well, you seem to want to say you're sorry. I accept your apology.

MARK Okay.

CAROLYN I'm not bitter. I'm not holding a grudge. I have moved on.

MARK I know.

CAROLYN Good. So I'm curious: what were you thinking? After you dropped the bomb?

MARK I don't really remember.

CAROLYN Sure you do.

MARK Not really.

CAROLYN Come on. Be honest. You're fucked up about it. You remember.

MARK I just wanted it to be over.

CAROLYN Over.

MARK Just to have it be… done.

CAROLYN Done.

MARK To not have to…

CAROLYN –to…

MARK –to… deal with it…

CAROLYN sure…

MARK To just not have to see…

CAROLYN Me.

MARK –the pain.

CAROLYN yeah…

MARK I remember thinking ahead…

CAROLYN Sure.

MARK To the future…

CAROLYN Of course…

MARK the good things…

CAROLYN the good part…

MARK –the good part, when I would be…

CAROLYN I know.

MARK just…

CAROLYN Free.

MARK Free.

CAROLYN Sure.

MARK Just free… and far away.

CAROLYN Gone.

MARK Far away from this… pain, from this moment–

CAROLYN My face.

MARK this moment in time…

CAROLYN sure…

MARK already passing, going by…

CAROLYN Almost behind you…

MARK almost done… won't have to say that again…

CAROLYN I'm not… happy.

MARK Won't have to do that again… never again… just finish this thing, do it right, make it clear, leave no room for doubt…

CAROLYN Yes. Do it right.

MARK And then it's done.

CAROLYN Over.

MARK And then…. Think about the good part…

CAROLYN …so free… so light… so–

MARK So…

MARK …excited.

CAROLYN Of course! Excited and free and ready. Ready for the new thing, the next thing, ready for…

MARK Ready for…

CAROLYN For…

MARK For… her.

CAROLYN Of course, ready for her. *(not an accusation)* You were thinking about her.

MARK I guess…

CAROLYN of course.

MARK I had to. I'm sorry…

CAROLYN Okay.

MARK Otherwise, I couldn't have done it.

CAROLYN She gave you courage…

MARK Yes…

CAROLYN hope…

MARK Yes.

CAROLYN So at that moment, you were thinking of her…

MARK I was.

CAROLYN Of being with her.

MARK Yes.

CAROLYN Understandable.

MARK I guess.

CAROLYN Her face.

MARK Her.

CAROLYN Her face.

MARK …Yes.

CAROLYN Her.

MARK Yes.

CAROLYN *(long pause)* And I was thinking: "I'm so ashamed… I'm so ashamed I want to die."

MARK I know.

CAROLYN Oh well. *(beat)* Are you and she…?

MARK No…

    Silence.

  I –

CAROLYN Please go. *(He doesn't move.)* Please. Go. *(He doesn't move.)*

Diane Flacks   *A Slice of Heaven*

2000
Alisa Palmer: Director
Jordan Pettle: Dennis
James Kidnie: Tommy
Carly Street: Mandi

¤ • ¤

TOMMY walks in. He is a big, swaggering, arrogant man in his early sixties. He has an infectious laugh, a great smile, and a way of making people want him to like them. He's an old Philadelphia-born Italian. He's a bully. He talks as he walks in and sits down. He checks his e-mail as he talks. Following him is DENNIS, a man in his early thirties. Ambitious, a little naive, gung-ho but insecure, and trying to get along and be this guy's buddy. He's a theatre writer turned TV writer. He carries a script.

TOMMY Now don't worry, I'm in your corner.

DENNIS Well, I hope Stuart just – I mean he's the producer but a lot of this *(indicating the script)* was my idea, and I'd hate Stuart to shut me out because of money. I mean, I don't care about the money, I care about the credit–

TOMMY Sure sure, don't worry. You know what your problem is? You're too smart for your own good.

DENNIS *(flattered)* Oh, come on.

TOMMY No seriously, that's your problem. You've got like three or four complete story ideas here. Audiences can't follow that. They need a simple story.

DENNIS Yeah, but what about things like "West Wing" or "Six Feet Under?"

TOMMY Yeah, but audiences don't watch that. What we did on "Three's Company" was we had one simple idea per show. Maybe a little B-story. That was farce, really classic farce. Those guys, they knew how to tell a story. Maybe it's a Canadian thing–

Enter MANDI, TOMMY's beautiful smart young assistant. She hands TOMMY a paper bag with a bottle of Scotch in it (unseen) and some keys.

MANDI Tommy, here're your car keys.

TOMMY Oh, did you get my other stuff?

MANDI It's in the production office.

TOMMY You got the uh…

MANDI The other bottle's in your trunk.

TOMMY Thanks sweetheart. You're the best.

> *MANDI leaves.*

She's great, that kid. I'd be lost without her. Really, she handles everything. She's my script queen. Smart as hell.

DENNIS Yeah, she's great.

TOMMY If I were twenty years younger I'd jump her bones. *(He laughs, a great, infectious warm laugh.)*

DENNIS Oh hahah.

TOMMY *(laughing)* You know, I mean, you know.

DENNIS I guess it's just in theatre, you want to keep the audience in suspense a bit, reveal things slowly, and–

TOMMY *(definitively)* We don't want to do that.

DENNIS Okay, it's just, I guess that's the difference–

TOMMY Just give them the story. So, you're doing a play now?

DENNIS Yeah.

TOMMY What's it about?

DENNIS Well, it's about like this older man, he's been away and he comes back home, and there are motifs of the ocean, and a huge overwhelming urge to sink deeply, like being drawn in–

TOMMY Hang on a second, ooh, I'm not feeling so well, I had some broccoli–

> *He is comedically screwing his face up like he's in pain. He lets out a huge fart. DENNIS is shocked, then TOMMY pulls out a fart toy. They both laugh, DENNIS uncomfortably.*

Oh, that's better. Ha ha. I got this from Sergio – he gave it–

DENNIS The director?

TOMMY Yeah, he gave it to me. His father's an inventor, he invents these things. He's a real butt-kisser.

DENNIS Sergio?

TOMMY He'll be kissing your butt soon enough. Ooh, God, I have cramps. *(He does it again.)*

DENNIS Let me try that. *(He does it.)* Ah, Jeez, too much Indian food.

> *He lets out a fart and TOMMY laughs. They seem to be bonding.*

TOMMY So, look, I have no idea what Stuart's gonna say. I mean, who knows what he wants, right? He may like what we've given him, he may want totally new ideas, I don't know. I don't think he knows.

DENNIS Yeah, I know, God, it's annoying.

TOMMY Well, what are we gonna do, kid? He's calling the shots. So we just gotta listen and try and do our best. And not to mention what the network, uh, whosername – Eve, is gonna say.

DENNIS *(correcting him)* Eva. Right.

TOMMY It's not how I'm used to doing things. We always gotta wait for their notes. I'd just get the formula together and pump out the scripts myself. I could just pump out like ten scripts myself, and with your three that's thirteen, I mean, all this waiting around, and dickin' around – scotch?

DENNIS Oh, uh, no thanks.

TOMMY You sure?

DENNIS Aw, what the hell. Fillerup. Just a little.

TOMMY Let's celebrate.

DENNIS Sure, I mean, we could do some really sophisticated stuff here–

TOMMY Right, but remember, kid, keep the story simple.

DENNIS Oh sure, the story will be simple, but really it's the characters–

TOMMY Comedy is about story. All this crap about it's the characters and the relationships. Comedy is not about relationships.

DENNIS It's not about relationships?

TOMMY Not at all.

DENNIS I thought it was all about relationships. That's been my–

TOMMY Well, it's not. Are you feeling a little gassy?

DENNIS Oh. *(He reluctantly makes the toy do a little pathetic fart sound.)* Well, I mean, it's about story but also about relationships, as long as the relationships serve the story–

TOMMY No, it's about story. Audiences follow action. *(very charming)* What's that one with the couple who sits around and talks – bored the hell out of me – they have a dog–

DENNIS "Mad About You?"

TOMMY Whatever the hell it is.

DENNIS Right, but what about "Absolutely Fabulous?"

TOMMY That freakin show. You know what that's doing? That's killing us.

DENNIS What do you mean?

TOMMY What the hell is funny about that show? Those women are disgusting! I mean, who can watch that? And who can understand a word they say? And now they want us to be like that?! That's what Eve wants.

DENNIS Eva–

TOMMY They can get someone else to do that.

DENNIS Well, we can't *try* and be derivative–

TOMMY Classic. Not derivative. And why not? You want a hit don't you? Have some more.

DENNIS Oh, you know, I can't. One scotch and I'm flyin'.

TOMMY All right, sure, well I will then.

>   *MANDI comes in.*

MANDI Tommy, I couldn't get your Giants tickets.

TOMMY *(He throws his pen violently across the room. MANDI doesn't flinch.)* DAMMIT! Those putzes! *(suddenly fatherly)* It's all right, kid, you tried. Thanks babe.

>   *MANDI leaves.*

She's the best.

DENNIS I know.

TOMMY She has terrible luck with men.

DENNIS I bet.

TOMMY Look at her, she's smart, she's gorgeous, I mean, that rack, whoa! *(He laughs.)* You know, I mean, you know–

DENNIS It's hard for women like that, I bet.

TOMMY Men are pigs. Really, we're scum. No one's coming near my daughter until they get through me. I'll say, "Look, you little creep. I know what you're thinking. Forget it!" Ha ha.

DENNIS Ha ha. She'll die a virgin, your daughter.

TOMMY Damn right.

DENNIS You keep her locked in the attic, right?

TOMMY Right, like Anne Frank. *(bad German accent)* I just follow orders. Hey that'd be a great episode. How about the lead woman, Darlene, it turns out she's really a man.

DENNIS Darlene? Our female lead? What do you mean?

TOMMY Like she goes on a date, and they start to go to bed, and the guy realises, holy hell! She's got a dick! *(laughing infectiously)* I mean, that's hilarious. That's a great joke. *(He starts to write it down.)*

DENNIS *(caught up in the infectious laugh)* But our lead actress, I mean, would you recast her part as a man now?

TOMMY No, no, she plays it, but like a man. I mean, her character has a lot of balls anyway.

DENNIS But, she's like five foot two, and I mean, I wrote it for a woman – I guess I could think about changing it…

TOMMY No, the idea is it's a woman.

DENNIS Who's a man–

TOMMY –playing a woman! THAT'S not derivative.

DENNIS *(knowing it is)* Yup.

TOMMY Well, you know, just a thought. It's funny though, huh? *(infectious laugh)* "Hey! You're a guy!" *(writing)* That's great.

DENNIS Yeah, maybe it could be one episode or something where she has to play a guy.

TOMMY No, she IS a guy. That's the joke, kid.

DENNIS Right. Right. So in this meeting, should we tell Stuart we want to have a really good roundtable meeting with all the other writers, like not just you and me–

TOMMY I don't know, kid, I just don't know. I can't figure the guy out, honestly. Oh, and I wanna change her name.

DENNIS Whose?

TOMMY Darlene. I don't like it. And we already have a 'd' named character in the series. I get confused when I type it. I like "Sandra."

DENNIS But that's her name, I mean, that's the name I gave her. It's perfect. "Darlene."

TOMMY Okay kid, it's your show, but I think we should change it. It's confusing. No big deal.

DENNIS No, well, it's not a big deal, anyway.

TOMMY If it doesn't work, we change it back.

DENNIS Well, let's see what he thinks.

TOMMY He said he doesn't care.

DENNIS Oh. Well, I don't wanna make an issue of it.

TOMMY Listen, whatever, kid, it's your show. Think about "Sandra" though.

MANDI pops her head in again.

MANDI Tommy, Lily's on line two. She's calling from the theatre.

TOMMY Oh, great, oh fantastic, you are the best, babe. *(to DENNIS)* I gotta take this. Hey Lily, you remember me, Tommy Mollina? I worked on your variety special for ABC. Yeah, Tommy Mollina. Yeah! *(He laughs.)* That's right, that Tommy. Oh yeah, oh that's so sweet, Lily. Well, I was hoping to come see your show tonight. You could? Well, that's great Lily. Yeah I'm working on this thing here, this Canadian sitcom here. Yeah, well, you know how it is now in L.A., if you're over 30 they don't wanna hire you. Yeah some executive producer's 33 years old telling me what comedy is, screw him. Yeah, so anyway that and a few other things, *(He drinks his scotch.)* that's why I left L.A., yeah, so that's why I've been here for a while. But I'm doin' comedy again so that's great. I might. I might go back. It always draws me back. L.A,'s got that pull, it's like the ocean, yeah right, it sucks you in. Right. So yeah tonight and – oh, I'd love to, Lily, I'd love to come backstage. Sure. Oh, you're a doll. See you then.

DENNIS has been bursting through all this.

DENNIS Was that Lily Tomlin?!

TOMMY Oh yeah, from the old days. Yeah, she's a real class-act.

DENNIS *(impressed)* Yeah.

MANDI pops her head in again.

TOMMY Oh, hey, Mandi, here's one. I got one for ya. *(He's a great joke-teller.)* This actor goes out for an audition. When he comes home, his house is surrounded by ambulances, fire trucks, you name it, and his house is burned to the ground! His neighbour comes up to him and says, "Listen, I hate to be the one to tell you what happened, but, you went out this morning, and a few minutes later, your wife comes back home. A couple minutes later, your agent comes to your house. Your wife lets him in, and I hate to say it, but I think they were having an affair. A few minutes later the house goes on fire, something with the gas line, and I'm sorry, but there were no survivors. Your wife and your agent are dead." The actor waits a beat and says to the neighbour, *(incredulously)* "My agent came to my house?"

TOMMY laughs first, they all laugh, infected by his laugh and trying to be buddies. They laugh hysterically.

TOMMY Isn't that great?! "My agent came to my house?"

DENNIS *(killing himself laughing)* "My agent came to my house!"

They are all laughing, TOMMY the most. MANDI tries to break in a few times. Finally it dies down.

MANDI He's here.

TOMMY Oh.

MANDI He's in the production office.

TOMMY Okay, great. Tell him we'll be a second, would you Mandi?

MANDI leaves. TOMMY watches her and gives a "whew" about her body. They both laugh.

What a great kid she is. Listen, Dennis, one thing, in this meeting, one of us has to run it. One of us has to be in charge here. And I think it should be me.

DENNIS Oh, okay, um, well–

TOMMY Don't worry, I'll protect you, but you can't have two voices in there.

DENNIS All right.

TOMMY All right, so I'll just lead the thing. Okay, let's go get him! I'm just gonna go to the can, and then we'll go.

TOMMY leaves, making the fart noise as he does. DENNIS laughs until he's gone and then his smile instantly fades. He is troubled. MANDI comes in and starts cleaning stuff up.

DENNIS Hey, Mandi. You like working with Tommy?

MANDI He's the greatest. Really you're lucky to be working with him. He's so funny.

DENNIS Yeah. And he really appreciates you. You should hear how he talks about you.

MANDI Oh, you too. You should hear what he says about you.

They look at each other for a beat.

BOTH Yeah.

TOMMY comes back in.

TOMMY Let's go! Get me my notebook, would you?

BOTH Okay.

DENNIS Oh, sorry, I guess he means you.

TOMMY *(popping his head back in)* Dennis, you coming with that notebook?

MANDI I guess he meant you.

DENNIS Right.

TOMMY *(offstage)* I wanna show Stuart the idea that Sandra's really a guy.

DENNIS *(to himself)* "Darlene."

MANDI Good luck in there.

She exits.

DENNIS I think I'll need it.

DENNIS reaches for his script which is on the desk. On the way to it, he smells TOMMY's coffee cup which reeks of booze.

TOMMY *(offstage)* Dennis!!

DENNIS seems at a loss.

DENNIS *(calling)* Coming! *(small panic)* Don't start without me!

DENNIS looks around. He speaks more to himself than anything.

It's going to be okay. I can handle this!

He leaves, takes a spectacular tripping fall, and exits.

Michael MacLean — *You May Already Be a Winner*

2000
Tanja Jacobs: Director
Jan Derbyshire: Amy
Peter Smith: Eric

⌑•⌑

The door opens, a woman enters carrying takeout Coffee Time coffee and a honey-dip doughnut. She shuts the door without looking. She doesn't see that it's prevented from closing all the way. She sits at the desk, opens the coffee lid, sips.

AMY   Ew.

Sees the door's slightly ajar, gets up and closes it. As she crosses back to desk it opens again. She looks at a sheet of paper. Dials. Line picks up

Hello. This is– *(stalling while looking for another piece of paper)* –uh… the Fraud Squad… *(finds it)* Sgt. Amy Drennan, Fraud Squad, here. Could I speak with Mrs. Janet Trevail, please.

Beat.

You did? Huh. Listen, honey, is your mommy there? Could you – uh huh. Uh huh. Could you – Hey, that's great. Listen, honey – Listen, honey – Listen – Kid! Shut up! Put your mother on. Right now…. Well, wake her up. Tell her it's the Fraud Squad…. No, *Fraud* Squad, not *frog*…. *Fraud*, it means – *(beat)* That was great. It was like I was right there in the pond. Now could you – No, I don't think so…. No, I'd rather not…. No, kid, listen to me: I'm not going to – All right all *right*. But you have to promise to go wake up your mom, okay?

Ribbits like a frog.

Okay?… Now go wake up your Mom. Tell her it's the – tell her it's the police; tell her it's about the lottery. Okay? Good boy.

Kid drops phone, AMY flinches. Enter ERIC.

ERIC   Hello "Sergeant."

Beat.

AMY   Can I help you?

ERIC   Nice frog.

AMY   Thanks. Can I help you?

ERIC Why am I not surprised you do animal impersonations, too?

AMY Do we know each other?

ERIC I think we do, "Sergeant."

> *Beat.*

AMY Agh!

> *Drops receiver like a hot potato. Picks it back up gingerly.*

Hello? Kid?... What's your name, kid?... Okay Teddy, I'm going to tell you something *very important*, okay?... Ted, don't *ever* do that to me again. Okay? *Ever.* Got it? Because if you do – It was fine, sure, it was grand, that's not the p–…Well, I don't know. A collie? A beagle? I don't know…. Oh. *Oh!* Well, that's exactly what it sounded like. Ted, hang on for a second.

(to ERIC, while covering phone) Listen, sir, I'm in the middle of a fraud investigation here.

ERIC Somebody else has been told they won the lottery? "You've already won! Just send us a finder's fee!" Was that the line?

AMY That's right, sir, that's the line they used. *(beat)* My God, you too?

ERIC Yep.

AMY When?

ERIC Couple of months ago.

AMY Okay. Listen, uh, I need to speak to you, but…. Could you come back in… an hour or so?

ERIC Nope. Sorry. I'm not going anywhere.

AMY Sir, I can't…

> *Stops, exasperated. Holds up a finger to signal "wait" and goes back to the phone.*

Ted. You still there?... What? No, Ted…. Because, because I only do frogs, that's why; you want barking, you have to talk to the Dog Squad. Listen, is your mommy up yet, Ted?... Well, remember you said you'd go wake her up?... So could you do that for me now?... Good boy.

(to ERIC) Look, sir, not to brush you off, but time is of the essence here. This woman *just* sent her cheque in, just the other day: the trail is still warm, as it were. Now you – how long ago was it?

ERIC Two months.

AMY Two months. Well, look, I'll lay it out. There's likely not much we can do in your case, in terms of recovery of any moneys you may have…. On the other hand, if we act fast, it's just possible we can get Mrs. Trevail's money back for her. *If* we act fast. You see what I mean? Now, I'd like to take a statement from you, for sure, but later, okay? Because – right now? – right now I really need to focus on Mrs. Trevail, okay?

>   *Beat.*

ERIC "Time is of the essence."

AMY That's right sir.

ERIC I remember that phrase: "time is of the essence." But it's the voice that really does it. Urgent. But official. "We must act now!" "Time is of the essence!" Where's the rest of the squad, Sergeant?

AMY Uh – Downtown.

ERIC Ah.

AMY I'm part of a… special unit here.

ERIC Ah.

AMY Flying squad.

ERIC Ah. Flying *frog* squad.

AMY Yeah, right.

>   *They laugh.*

AMY Mrs. Trevail!… Oh. Hello, Ted. Where's your – Oh for God's sake. Yes, sure you can. When you're older. Listen, Ted, where's your mother?… No Ted…. Because I'm not *on* the Dog Squad…. Listen Ted, I'm not going to, that's all there is to it, now go wake up your – *What?* What did you say?

>   *Beat.*

Little extortionist.

>   *She howls, a little embarrassedly, like a dog.*

All right? Now go…. Yes. Yes, there is one, you *know* there is.

>   *Beat. She neighs like a horse.*

All right? Are we happy now, Ted? Good.

(*to* ERIC) Sir, I'm going to have to ask you to leave.

ERIC Oh no! Just when I found you again. *(sees her paper)* What's this? Is this what they call a sucker list?

AMY Sir, this is highly confidential work we're pursuing here, as you may have surmised. And even if–

ERIC "Surmised." Whoa: *dat's* a big woid.

>   *Beat.*

AMY Have you got a problem?

ERIC Not any more. Things are looking up. And what are the odds? You walk into some Coffee Time, just any old Coffee Time, nothing special about it, you're just standing there, you know, trying to decide if you can afford a cream *and* a jelly, because things have been a little tight lately, you know, just in the last couple of months, you know, ever since your entire savings account went south in the aid of what you *thought* was a fraud investigation into a national lottery scam and you're standing there in front of the doughnut counter lost in fantasies of revenge and mutilation and suddenly: suddenly: you hear the voice.

AMY The voice.

ERIC Right there beside you. Ordering coffee. Large. Milk. Two sugars. And without turning to look, you don't trust your luck, so you close your eyes tight but – the voice comes again: it says, "Thanks. And also, I'll take a honey dip." And you say to yourself, "But I *do* know that voice. Yes, that's the voice of my friend Fran."

AMY Fran.

ERIC Fran of the Mounted.

AMY *Fran.*

ERIC Constable Fran Stanford, RCMP Fraud Unit.

AMY I don't know a Constable Fran–

ERIC Neither does the RCMP Fraud Unit, it turns out. I called them a week after I sent you the cheque. *(beat)* Despite my intense embarrassment.

> *Beat.*

AMY *(into phone) What?*... No. No, Ted. That's one squad we *don't* have.... How would I know – *No. Ted–*

> *Catches herself.*

Just a second, Ted.

(to ERIC) What sound do aardvarks make?

ERIC Aardvarks?

AMY Yeah.

ERIC Aardvarks?

AMY Yeah. *You* know. Those animals.

ERIC You mean like anteaters?

AMY Yeah! Yeah! What sound do they make?

> *Beat.*

They're mute, right?

ERIC I don't–

AMY Sure they are. There's a saying even: "mute as an aardvark." You've heard that, right?

(*into the phone*) Ted, they're mute, all right? I just consulted my colleague here, he's an expert in animal noises, he says aardvarks are mute…. It means they don't make any sound.

> *Beat. Covers mouthpiece.*

(*to ERIC*) But if they *did* make a sound, what kind sound do you think they would make?

ERIC I don't know!

AMY *What kind of sound do you think they would make?*

> *Beat.*

ERIC Maybe, kind of a… lowing sound, maybe?

AMY A *lowing* sound?

ERIC Like a cow?

AMY I know what "lowing" means! This is an *aardvark*!

> *ERIC shrugs helplessly. AMY turns back to the phone, takes a deep breath and moos into it. Beat.*

What do you think, Ted?… Yes… I know! That's what *I* said!

(*to ERIC*) You're cuckoo.

ERIC What?

AMY He said it, not me.

ERIC Don't be ridiculous.

AMY (*into phone*) Don't be ridiculous, Ted.

ERIC Don't say that!

AMY (*to ERIC, quoting Ted*) It's not ridiculous. That was a cow.

ERIC Don't be stupid. We're making it up anyway.

AMY (*into phone*) Don't be stupid, we're–

ERIC Don't say that!

AMY (*to ERIC*) Oh, for God's sake, now he's crying. Thanks a lot.

ERIC I didn't – Here, give me that.

> *Through the following, he reaches for phone. AMY keeps it away from him.*

AMY (*quoting Ted, maybe even tearfully*) That's a cow! That's not an aardvark!

ERIC We're making it up anyway! We don't know!

AMY (*quoting him to Ted*) We're making it up, anyway! We don't–

ERIC Don't say that! Give me that!

AMY *(quoting Ted)* It's a COW! It's not an AARDVARK!

ERIC All right all right all right! I'm sorry! You're right!

AMY *(quoting Ted)* You're an ASS!

ERIC I beg your pardon!

AMY *(quoting Ted)* ASS ASS ASS ASS ASS!

ERIC *(the voice of authority)* Give me that phone!

Cowed, she hands it over.

AMY Got to go, Ted.

ERIC Go to your room!

AMY But–

ERIC Go!

Exit AMY. He waits until she's good and gone.

ERIC *(into phone)* Okay Ted, now just calm down, all right? Ted? Hello?

Beat.

The penny drops. He drops the phone, goes to door, looks out, then comes back, a defeated man, but picks it up again anyway.

Ted?

Beat. He hangs up the phone.

Eric Weinthal   *On the Door*

2000
Eric Weinthal: Director
Joel Keller: Volunteer
Nicky Guadagni: Actor

⌑ • ⌑

A VOLUNTEER is at the main door. Although the audience is sitting inside the room, it's as if they are outside the room, the office supposedly just beyond the door.

The ACTOR arrives from the other door, a little out of breath, and goes to the volunteer.

ACTOR Hi. Excuse me.

He goes for the door.

VOLUNTEER You can't go in.

ACTOR Sure I can.

VOLUNTEER It's sold out.

ACTOR Very funny. Excuse me.

VOLUNTEER I'm sorry, you can't go in.

ACTOR I *have* to go in.

VOLUNTEER You have to.

ACTOR I have to.

VOLUNTEER Let me guess – you're a friend of an actor in the show; you're an artistic director just in town for the day and you must see this gem; you're on the board of–

ACTOR Look–

VOLUNTEER I've heard them all, okay?

ACTOR I'm in the show.

A beat.

Haven't heard that one, have you?

VOLUNTEER You still can't go in.

ACTOR What are you talking about?

VOLUNTEER It's sold out.

ACTOR Okay, I get it. Look, I appreciate what you're doing, I'm sorry, I wasn't very friendly there but I'm a little late, a little rushed, it's not easy doing this kind of–

VOLUNTEER You think it's easy what I do?

ACTOR No, certainly not. Well, you don't have to learn lines.

VOLUNTEER How about this line: "It's sold out."

ACTOR My point is I'm not one of those actors who thinks they're above the volunteers. It's just a little hectic, I could've been nicer, okay, point taken, but now I have to get in and do my show.

VOLUNTEER *Your* show?

ACTOR Are you going to get out of the way?

VOLUNTEER Did you write it? How is it *your* show?

ACTOR Okay, so that's my point, you're a little miffed. Again, I'm sorry.

VOLUNTEER You're not sorry.

ACTOR Excuse me?

VOLUNTEER An actor? Sorry?

ACTOR Look, you and your issues stay out here, I'm going in.

VOLUNTEER You can't go in. It's sold out.

ACTOR Sold out. Well I'll take that as a compliment, I don't see how else to take it, that'll just have to do for a warm-up, feeling that compliment of a sold-out show since my warm-up is *shot* from talking to you. *Shot*. They came to see *me*, you know. Sold out. Now I'm going in there to do my job. I came here to do my job and I'm going to–

VOLUNTEER I have a job to do too.

ACTOR And you're doing it wondrously, if a tad on the rigorous side.

VOLUNTEER You don't think this *is* a job, do you?

ACTOR I don't have time to discuss this.

VOLUNTEER Sure you do. The show's about to start and as long as you keep your voice down, you can stand right here till it's over.

ACTOR That's it. Excuse me.

> *The ACTOR goes for the door.*

VOLUNTEER You can't.

ACTOR I can.

But before the ACTOR can open the door, the VOLUNTEER does, peeking in and then closing the door.

VOLUNTEER No you can't. They've started.

ACTOR What? They *can't*.

VOLUNTEER They did.

ACTOR They cannot start this show without me!

VOLUNTEER They did.

ACTOR I'm in the show!

VOLUNTEER Apparently you're not missed.

ACTOR It's a monologue!

A beat.

VOLUNTEER Well, *that* isn't much of a compliment, is it?

ACTOR They *can't* have started.

The volunteer peeks in the door.

VOLUNTEER *(whispering)* Yeah, it's going. Pretty well, too.

ACTOR It is not *going*! That is impossible.

VOLUNTEER *(whispering)* Could you keep your voice down?

ACTOR No, I couldn't. I trained to keep it up.

VOLUNTEER Well that's working against you right now.

ACTOR Get out of my way before I'm really late!

VOLUNTEER It won't be long.

ACTOR What won't?

VOLUNTEER It's only ten minutes.

ACTOR Shut up! I'm in the show! It has *not* started, it *couldn't*, this is *not* Pirandello, at least not the way we rehearsed it, not that we had much *time* to – Excuse me.

The ACTOR opens the door. Closes it. Pretty freaked out.

It *has* started.

VOLUNTEER You're not supposed to open that door. We have rules, you know.

ACTOR WHAT ABOUT THE RULE OF A MONOLOGUE NEEDING AN *ACTOR*?

VOLUNTEER That's not one of our rules.

The ACTOR doesn't know what to say.

VOLUNTEER Well, it's blissfully quiet out here now.

The VOLUNTEER sighs contentedly.

ACTOR You don't like me, do you?

VOLUNTEER No.

ACTOR You don't like actors.

VOLUNTEER No.

ACTOR You couldn't be happier that the show is going on without me.

VOLUNTEER No, I couldn't.

ACTOR Admit it, you did this. You somehow made the show go without anyone in it.

VOLUNTEER Yes I did.

ACTOR What kind of sick–

VOLUNTEER Never thought you'd see that happen, did you?

ACTOR No…

VOLUNTEER Aren't actors supposed to love new discoveries like that? Aren't you supposed to love spontaneity and just *go* with it?

ACTOR Where am I supposed to go?

VOLUNTEER How long have you been at this anyway?

ACTOR Who are you?

VOLUNTEER Please keep your voice down, just a few more minutes.

ACTOR WHO THE HELL ARE–

VOLUNTEER Do you see how polite I am, and how polite you are not? I keep asking you to keep your voice down, do you have any concern for the audience's enjoyment of the show? Where were you trained anyway?

ACTOR What show?!

VOLUNTEER I'm going to have to ask you to leave.

ACTOR What??

VOLUNTEER I'm pretty sure in the history of this theatre no one has been forcibly ejected from the building, but we do have a plan for that, just in case. I guess we're finally going to have to use it.

ACTOR You miserable little–

VOLUNTEER Yeah, we're definitely going to have to use it.

The VOLUNTEER whips out a walkie-talkie.

1 Adam-12 to Mother Goose. Over.

No response on the walkie-talkie

Repeat, 1 Adam-12 to Mother Goose. Over.

Nothing.

ACTOR That isn't real, is it?

VOLUNTEER Of course it is.

ACTOR That's a prop.

VOLUNTEER No, we use real things out here.

ACTOR Well, it isn't working.

VOLUNTEER We have a back-up plan.

ACTOR Do not.

VOLUNTEER You'll see.

ACTOR No one ever got anywhere preying on my paranoia.

VOLUNTEER I think they did. I think they got real far.

ACTOR Who did?

VOLUNTEER See?

The VOLUNTEER opens the door a crack.

Almost over.

ACTOR No…

VOLUNTEER There's the back-up plan: small shows equal small problems.

ACTOR I had a lot invested in this, you know.

VOLUNTEER I know.

ACTOR I *needed* this gig.

VOLUNTEER Believe me, I know.

ACTOR It's not easy getting a job at Tarragon. You ruined it for me. I'm going to have to ruin it for you.

VOLUNTEER You can't.

ACTOR You'll never work at this theatre again.

VOLUNTEER Uh-huh.

ACTOR I'm going to ruin the end of the show. They won't be able to hear it. You'll be finished.

VOLUNTEER I don't think you can–

The ACTOR starts to yell, make babbling noises, scream, sing loudly, bang at the door repeatedly, and make pain sounds as if there's a beating going on.

Nice.

ACTOR Was, wasn't it.

VOLUNTEER Best I've seen you.

ACTOR You were good too.

Deep breath, then together, they open the door and with their backs to our audience, they bow to the supposed audience beyond the door.

VOLUNTEER Think they heard everything okay?

ACTOR Are you kidding? You've got the best stage whisper in the biz.

They bow again. When the real audience—the one behind them—applauds, they turn and bow to them.

Carol Anderson   *Jazz at 3 a.m*

2001
Alison Sealy-Smith: Director
Yanna McIntosh: Jazz
Deborah Drakeford: Fiona
Richard Greenblatt: Roger

♮ • ♮

Mac's: a small Scottish bar in East York. JAZZ, a Black woman, early thirties, tends bar. FIONA, mid thirties, and ROGER, early fifties—both white—sit at the bar drinking.

JAZZ You have five minutes to drink up.

ROGER *(drunkenly)* What?

JAZZ Five minutes. I have to take your drinks in five minutes.

FIONA Thanks, honey.

JAZZ *(to ROGER)* Drink up.

ROGER We heard you the first time.

JAZZ Good.

> *JAZZ starts to move away.*

ROGER Hey!

FIONA Roger…

ROGER Come here!

> *JAZZ stops.*

JAZZ What?

ROGER Come here!

JAZZ *(turns around)* What do you want?

ROGER What's your name again?

JAZZ AND FIONA Jazz!

ROGER *(to FIONA)* Very good. *(pause)* She's kinda sexy, isn't she?

FIONA Roger…

ROGER What?! Hey... Jazz. What're you doing after work?

JAZZ It's almost 3 a.m. What do you think I'm doing?

ROGER I don't know. What?

JAZZ I'm going home.

ROGER How boring.

FIONA God, you're an asshole, Roger.

ROGER Oh, c'mon. Don't tell me you weren't thinking the same exact thing.

JAZZ Look, guys. I just want to–

FIONA Just ignore him.

JAZZ I'm trying.

ROGER Fuck you!

JAZZ I beg your pardon?

ROGER Fuck both of you!

FIONA You wish.

JAZZ I don't.

ROGER Ahhhh. I was just joking. Hey! Why don'tcha both come back to my place for a little... drink?

JAZZ Look. Why don't you work on the drink you have in front of you. You only have about two minutes before I have to take it away.

ROGER You're a real charmer... Jazz. Jazz! What kind of a name is that, anyway. Jazz. All of you people give yourself these stupid made-up names. I think I'm gonna make up a name for myself. I think I'm gonna call myself... Bluegrass from now on. Whaddaya think, honey.

FIONA I think it's time we paid up.

FIONA rummages in her purse.

ROGER What do I owe?

FIONA It's on me tonight.

ROGER Goddamn women's libbers!

JAZZ It's forty even.

FIONA hands her a crisp fifty-dollar bill.

FIONA Keep the change. You earned it.

JAZZ Thanks.

JAZZ picks up her cash tray and moves to the end of the bar to cash out.

FIONA So, what do you think?

ROGER About what?

> *FIONA motions towards JAZZ.*

ROGER Her?! You gotta be kidding. I mean, there's no doubt she's a.... But she's hopeless. *(laughs)* Fucking hopeless!

FIONA I don't know... I think she likes me.

ROGER *(rising)* Yeah? Well, good luck.

FIONA Where're you going?

ROGER I gotta take a leak.

> *He exits to the men's room. FIONA drains her glass as JAZZ heads towards her. She smiles at JAZZ seductively as she hands her the glass. JAZZ takes FIONA's empty glass, as well as ROGER's half-full one.*

FIONA I don't know why the hell I stay with him.... Habit I guess. God! Sometimes we women are such masochists, huh?... I'm sorry about–

JAZZ Don't worry about it.

FIONA No. I'm really really sorry... *(sweetly)* Hey Jazz?

JAZZ Yeah?

FIONA I know it's probably none of my business. I mean, I just met ya tonight for the first time, but... well, you just seem like you have things on your mind or something, and if you... well, if you wanna talk about it, I'm–

JAZZ No, I'm fine. I'm just... *(She suddenly looks very tired.)*

FIONA *(kindly)* What?

JAZZ *(sighs)* I moved in with my partner six months ago. And today we broke up. And then I started working here tonight. And now I have to start thinking about moving again, and I... well, I guess I'm pretty bummed out about the whole thing.

FIONA Your partner?

> *JAZZ studies FIONA's face for a beat.*

JAZZ Yeah, it's a woman.

FIONA I have to hand it to Roger. He always guesses right.

JAZZ What?

FIONA Listen. Why don't you take Roger up on his offer, and come back to his place with us? He's really much more bark than bite.

JAZZ Oh, I don't think so. I'm... I'm pretty exhausted.

FIONA *(seductively)* Might help you get your mind off of... things.

JAZZ You mean... you, me and Roger?

FIONA Um hmm.

JAZZ Roger, you and me?

FIONA Why not?

JAZZ The three of us?

FIONA Yeah.

JAZZ Drinking, laughing, getting to know each other. Contemplating people like me, and… and all of our stupid made-up names.

They look at each other for a beat.

I am not into scenes, honey. But if I was, it definitely would not be with – *(laughs)* Look. I just want to cash out, go home, and try to forget this whole day ever happened, all right?

JAZZ starts to move away.

FIONA You think you're too good for us?

JAZZ stops, but doesn't turn around.

JAZZ Excuse me?

FIONA You think we're just white trash, and you're the big black important dyke bartender who can't give us the time of day?

ROGER enters.

Is that what you think? Bitch!

JAZZ turns and looks at FIONA.

ROGER What happened to my drink?

FIONA Bitch here took it.

ROGER I wasn't finished.

JAZZ Look. It's 3 a.m., and the law of this city says that all drinks have to be cleared by–

ROGER Don't you tell me about the laws of my own goddamn country. I've been coming to this bar since before you even got to Canada. Jesus Christ! This is a Scottish bar! I don't know what possessed Mac to hire someone like you to work here.

FIONA Yeah, you don't see us working at some… Jamaican beef jerky joint.

ROGER *(bad Jamaican accent)* Look at me, mon! I'm the Rastaman. But you can call me, Bluegrass.

ROGER and FIONA laugh. JAZZ just glares at them. They stop laughing.

FIONA What're you looking at?

JAZZ doesn't respond.

FIONA Who the hell do you think you are, anyways?

JAZZ Thankfully not you.

FIONA What did you say?

JAZZ I said, thankfully I don't think I'm you.

FIONA *(rising)* You little twat! I could wring your stupid little–

> *FIONA lunges towards the bar. ROGER grabs her just before she flings herself over it. JAZZ doesn't move.*

ROGER Whoa! We're not going to jail over her, baby!

FIONA Let go of me!

ROGER She's not worth it, Fiona!

FIONA Let go of me!!

ROGER She's not worth it!

FIONA Let me go, Roger!!… I said, LET ME GO!!!

> *ROGER slowly lets go of FIONA. She slowly regains her composure.*
>
> *FIONA picks up her purse off the bar. She removes a compact, and prepares to powder her face, but instead just stares at her own reflection in the mirror. She puts the compact back into her purse, and then heads for the door.*

JAZZ My family comes from Barbados.

> *FIONA stops, but doesn't turn around.*

Not Jamaica. Barbados. My great-great-grandmother worked on a sugarcane plantation, where she was raped by the Scottish overseer, and gave birth to a half-Scottish son. My mother came here in 1959. She worked as a domestic for a year, studied nursing and then sent for my father. And then she gave birth to me. Right here in our goddamn country. And that's who the hell I think I am.

FIONA *(without turning around)* So, what do you want from us? A goddamn medal?… C'mon Roger.

> *FIONA heads for the door.*
>
> *JAZZ and ROGER look at each other. ROGER is about to say something.*

Let's go Roger.

> *ROGER turns and follows FIONA out the door.*
>
> *JAZZ stares after them for a long beat, and then slowly walks to the end of the bar to finish cashing out.*

Leah Davidson

Ladies' Room

2001
Ken Gass: Director
Shari Hollett: Dionne
Amy Rutherford: Marie
Jenni Burke: Claire

⌑•⌑

Lights rise on a women's washroom. Upstage centre are three washroom stalls. All three stall doors are shut. Upstage right there is a small sink and mirror. DIONNE barrels in from stage left.

DIONNE Marie! Marie! I know you're in here, Marie! I saw you come in here. Marie, you take the whole thing too damn seriously, you know. It's not that big a deal. You gotta let it roll off your back, like I do. It just rolls off my back like a duck – or somethin'. Whatever. The point is, I don't care. I don't care what they think of me.

MARIE *(from the middle bathroom stall)* You aren't supposed to be in here, Dionne.

DIONNE See what I mean, Marie? What do you care if I'm in here or not? It's not like we're gonna get caught by the guidance counsellor. Not that I ever cared about that, either. Shit, I got detention all the time – like every other day.

MARIE He said I must be stupid.

DIONNE He's the one who's stupid.

MARIE He's a vice president.

DIONNE Yeah, because he's stupid. They gave him that big office way in the corner, hoping he wouldn't find his way out and screw everything up.

MARIE I don't understand what happened. It followed the instructions in the manual to the letter. To the letter, Dionne. "To set up a three-way call, park Party A at extension 400…"

DIONNE Marie, he's an asshole to everyone.

MARIE "Then capture Party B at the extension designated for inter-office transfer. Then connect your parties by using *, # extension 5053." Why didn't it work?

DIONNE I just tell them to use the speaker phone.

MARIE I'm never going to get a real job here.

DIONNE What in the hell would you want that for, anyway?

> *MARIE emerges from the centre bathroom stall wearing a telephone headset. The cord of which dangles in front of her.*

MARIE Look at this thing! Look at it! It's like a leash. It's a leash you would put on an animal to make sure they don't wander off. It's a wonder they don't put an electric fence around the reception desk to make sure I don't go for an unauthorised pee.

DIONNE Did he say you could take a break right now?

MARIE No. I… I just went.

DIONNE How does it feel?

MARIE Good.

DIONNE See? There you go! You just can't take the whole thing so damn serious.

MARIE I don't even have to pee.

DIONNE You know who never pees? Claudia on four. I swear to God, in six years no one has ever actually seen her in the ladies' room. It's creepy.

MARIE I hope he's not too mad.

DIONNE So who did you connect him with?

MARIE The coffee lady. She gave him an espresso order for next week.

> *CLAIRE enters stage left. She stares at them, almost in horror, and then scurries into the furthest bathroom stall.*

MARIE I really need to get off that desk, Dionne. I'm serious. I don't know if I can take it.

DIONNE You've only just started. I been here ten years.

MARIE But don't you want to do more? We could do so much more.

DIONNE Marie, you're in by nine, you're out by five and if you manage get the fax pages in the right order, everyone thinks you're a genius. The joke's on them as far as I'm concerned.

MARIE I want more.

DIONNE Calm down, Melanie Griffith.

MARIE I've thought of a campaign, you know. I was sitting there yesterday, counting the stucco bumps in the ceiling and it just came to me.

DIONNE You're taking this all too seriously. It's just a job. It's a means to an end. That's it. Why do you want to go further in? Just skate around the edge, I say.

MARIE You know they're pitching True Satin Ultras tomorrow. And they are really stuck. Martin is so freaked out, they've taken away his neckties.

DIONNE That's not out of the ordinary.

MARIE But I've got it. I've got the perfect idea. We center the spot around this woman.

DIONNE See, already you're down the wrong path. They're looking at animated butterflies and spring meadows with bunnies. That's what they want.

MARIE We open on this woman in the pouring rain. She's having a really bad day. Her umbrella's turned inside out. Her hair is plastered to her face. She's just had it, right? And she's walking home with her groceries along this stone seawall. All of a sudden, she comes across a group of townspeople. They are hysterical and they're shouting, "There is a leak in the seawall! We are all doomed!" Cut to this dapper looking man who gallantly whips out his handkerchief and stuffs it in the hole. The water leaks through. Cut to a second burly looking man. He rips off his shirt and again, the water leaks through. Well now the townspeople are just freaking out completely, when up steps… our woman. She reaches deep into her grocery bag, pulls out a True Satin Ultra and deftly stuffs it in the hole. The leak is stopped, the townspeople are saved and the tag reads, "True Satin Ultras with greater leak protection. Tougher than you think."

DIONNE That's good, Marie.

MARIE Thank you.

DIONNE And they want to hear good ideas. But Marie, they don't want to hear them from you. Not yet. Just forget about all that for now and don't be in such a hurry. And don't try so hard. You're setting a bad standard for the rest of us. Bide your time, lie low and stop taking the whole thing so seriously.

Flush. The stall door opens with a bang and CLAIRE leaps out as if something has bitten her. She stares at them for a moment.

CLAIRE The photocopier on the 11th floor works without a key card. You can copy anything you want and they will never know. I'm copying all the *Reader's Digests* in the Library. One by one. I'm up to October 1997. They'll never know.

She turns to the sink and starts washing her hands.

DIONNE And on that note…

MARIE Dionne, I just hate going back out there. I hate it. I can't…

DIONNE The caged bird still sings Marie. Just let it slide…

DIONNE exits. CLAIRE has finished washing her hands and walks toward MARIE on her way out.

CLAIRE October 1997.

She exits. MARIE shuts her eyes, exhales slowly and pinches her cheeks.

MARIE Right.

She exits. Lights fade to black.

Melody Johnson and Bob Martin   *Shoe Store*

2001
Bob Martin: Clerk
Melody Johnson: Woman

¤•¤

A distraught WOMAN enters a shoe store and approaches the waiting clerk.

CLERK *(surprised to see her)* Back so soon?

WOMAN Yes. I'm having a problem with the shoes.

CLERK The brown pumps?

WOMAN Yes.

CLERK *(taking the box from her)* Are they too tight? The leather will stretch–

WOMAN No. It's not the fit. It's me. It's just that, ah, I'm always buying brown pumps. I'm so predictable. Every seven months like clockwork. Time to get another pair of brown pumps, Linda. God forbid I should try something new. Why can't I be more impulsive, unpredictable, irresponsible, spontaneous? I'm so conservative, conventional, unimaginative, Milquetoast, goody-two-shoes – it's all about rules for me. Don't take the car downtown, Linda – get the GO pass. Organise from the inside out, Linda. Remember to take your Paxil, Linda. Don't smoke. Don't drink. Don't get a life, you can't handle it. Where's Linda? We're out of toner. The postage meter's empty. Where's Linda? She's hiding in her office. She hiding in her office. I hate myself.

CLERK So, it's not the fit?

WOMAN Um, the thing is I spotted a shoe in the window, I think it was a few days ago. I'd like to see it, please.

CLERK In the window?

WOMAN I think it's on the left side. I think it's on an acrylic stand. Beside a champagne bottle. With a photo of Venice behind it. It has a bra draped over it.

CLERK The red stiletto

WOMAN Yes, that's it. I think.

CLERK It's quite a leap from a brown pump.

WOMAN I know. I know. I'm just curious. It caught my eye. Seven and a half.

The CLERK retrieves a box from the rack.

CLERK You're in luck.

He sits on the stool in front of her, and takes a shoe out of the box.

CLERK This is a very special shoe. Very sensual, isn't it? Very feminine.

WOMAN Is it? I hadn't noticed–

CLERK *(caressing the shoe)* It's a Franco Mirabelli. Italian. Four-inch heel. Very narrow. Very sharp. That's why it's called a stiletto heel. Like the knife.

WOMAN Yes. I like the red.

CLERK The colour is unique to this shoe. Mirabelli based it on the colour of the lips of his favourite Parisian whore.

WOMAN What's it called?

CLERK Parisian Whore Red.

WOMAN Oh.

CLERK The upper is calf skin. Feel it. Go on. It's soft. Like flesh. You know how they get that texture?

WOMAN How?

CLERK Old Italian women sit in the hot sun and work the leather with their thick thumbs until it is soft, like the skin of a wanton school girl.

WOMAN Really?

CLERK That's what it says in the literature. *(points out features of the shoe)* It's a very spare design. An open toe. One thin strip of leather across the ankle is all that holds the shoe on your foot. It could fly off at anytime.

WOMAN It's a very dangerous shoe.

CLERK It's unpredictable.

WOMAN It's a shoe that doesn't consider the consequences.

CLERK It's a shoe completely without morals.

WOMAN I need to try them on.

CLERK You'll have to take off those wool socks, first. You can use one of our courtesy stockings, if you wish.

WOMAN *(She tears off her own shoes and socks and slips on the stockings.)* I've been dreaming of these shoes for weeks. My sister Margaret has a pair of shoes just like this and she always gets whatever she wants. Always. Her hair has a natural wave, and she's never had her teeth bleached although you'd swear she has. She's an extremely happy person. *(She puts on the shoes.)* My feet feel so exotic. So strange.

CLERK Actually. You've got the shoes on the wrong way round. Here, let me.

WOMAN I'm sorry.

He places them on her feet

My God! I don't feel like I'm wearing shoes at all. It's like my feet are sitting in two small red chairs.

CLERK Your feet are lounging in the shoes. Mirabelli based his design on the gondolas of Venice.

WOMAN I've always wanted to go to Italy.

CLERK Well, in a sense, you're there now.

WOMAN I am.

CLERK Look at your nakedness. The calf skin falls across your feet like gauze across the genitals of a Botticelli angel.

WOMAN They're so insubstantial.

CLERK The shoe exposes the toes; the most sensual part of the foot. The shoe says "look!"

WOMAN "Look at my toes!"

CLERK "I'm not afraid to show them to you!" *(looking at her feet)* Where are your toes, Linda?

WOMAN They should be there.

CLERK They're clenched up under the balls of your feet. Let them go.

WOMAN I'm trying.

CLERK Unfurl your toes. Free them!

WOMAN Come on! There they are.

CLERK They're pale, like the roots of a young plant.

WOMAN Well, they don't get out much.

CLERK Display them with pride. They're Linda's toes. You should trim those nails.

WOMAN Sorry.

CLERK Stand up.

WOMAN I'm scared.

CLERK I'm here for you.

WOMAN *(standing)* It's very odd. I feel disoriented.

CLERK You are not vertical. It's a four inch heel. You have to compensate. *(She straightens.)* Do you feel your calves tightening?

WOMAN Yes. They're cramping.

CLERK The heel firms the calf and raises the buttocks.

WOMAN I wondered why my sister's buttocks were so high.

She straightens.

CLERK That's it! Look how you tower over me. Over all men.

WOMAN *(looking through the window of the store)* I can see my car!

CLERK Let's walk to the mirror and back.

WOMAN Spot me.

CLERK I will.

WOMAN *(She walks awkwardly.)* Look at me! I'm Margaret! I'm Margaret!

CLERK Straighten! Straighten, Linda! Compensate for the heel!

WOMAN I'm trying!

CLERK Your arms are flailing. Be careful of the displays.

WOMAN I feel like I'm going to fall!

CLERK I'll catch you.

WOMAN Ow! The pain!

CLERK Unclench your toes!

WOMAN I'm trying to keep them unfurled. They're fighting me! They're shrinking from the light like little moles!

CLERK Your nails are shredding our courtesy stockings.

WOMAN Ow! The pain is excruciating!

CLERK Where? In the arch?

WOMAN Everywhere. My whole body! The cramp in my calf is making me squint. And I don't think my buttocks are rising at all!

CLERK Quite the opposite, in fact.

WOMAN Help me back to chair! Help me back to the chair!

She collapses into the chair

What am I going to do? It's the heel. It's too high. It's just too high.

CLERK It's a very high heel.

WOMAN But my feet look so beautiful. Could I wear them at work? While I'm sitting?

CLERK Well…

WOMAN I only have to get up to go to the photocopy room once every 15 minutes–

CLERK Linda. No.

WOMAN How can I go back to the brown pumps after I've been to Venice?

CLERK There's no shame in a pump. The pump is a fine shoe.

WOMAN I don't want a fine shoe! I want a brash, devil-may-care shoe, that sparkles at parties, and knows what wine is right with lobster, and has a good sense of humour and big breasts. *(She jumps to her feet again and takes a few awkward steps.)* I'm Margaret! I'm Margaret! *(She crashes to the floor.)*

CLERK *(crouching by her side)* Linda. Please. Dignity.

WOMAN I'm sorry.

CLERK You know, we are not the shoes we wear.

WOMAN Yes. I know.

CLERK We cannot let ourselves be defined my material possessions, or the fickle winds of fashion. These things are meaningless. And remember: Jesus wore no shoes at all.

WOMAN He didn't?

CLERK So they say.

She takes off the shoes and stands holding them.

WOMAN Thank you. Thank you for everything.

CLERK Don't mention it.

The CLERK takes the shoes from her.

WOMAN Don't bother bagging them. I'll wear them home.

Blackout.

Eric Weinthal   *Let Me Out of Here*

2001
Eric Weinthal: Director
Dan Warry-Smith: Young Man
Sally Cahill: First woman
Alex Bulmer: Second woman
Scott McCord: Man

¤•¤

A room. Two doors. The main door is upstage, facing the audience. All entrances and exits will be by this door. The other door is stage right. It leads to another room, never seen. A WOMAN comes in the upstage door. She is deaf. From within the stage right door, we hear frantic knocking and a YOUNG MAN's voice.

YOUNG MAN   *(offstage)* Hello! Let me out of here!

    The WOMAN does not react to this.

(offstage) I said let me out of here. The door's stuck. I can't– *(beat)* Hey, I heard you come in, now help me!

    We hear him banging on the door but the WOMAN does not even flinch.

(offstage) What is your problem, do I have to ask nicely? I'm not in a great mood, being as I'm stuck in a room. Not a great room, either. Now let me the hell out of here!

    The WOMAN looks around the room.

(offstage) What are you, not letting me out because you fear my mood? Let me tell you, you should fear my mood! I was in a bad enough one when I got stuck in here, but now I'm really–

    The WOMAN leaves.

(offstage) No! Don't go! I'm sorry. Really. Forget all that stuff about my mood! *(He bangs pathetically on the door.)* Please…

    Another WOMAN enters the room. She has a white cane.

(offstage) Thank you. Thank you for coming back.

WOMAN   Coming back?

YOUNG MAN   *(offstage)* I knew you were a woman. I don't know why. What amazing intuition. Thanks for coming back, now if you could just–

WOMAN I've never been in this room.

YOUNG MAN *(offstage)* Very funny.

WOMAN I wasn't trying to be funny.

YOUNG MAN *(offstage)* Well, lucky you to have the natural gift.

WOMAN Maybe I have been in here and I don't remember.

YOUNG MAN *(offstage)* What, you've got a little memory problem?

WOMAN *(as she feels her way around the room)* Not exactly.

YOUNG MAN *(offstage)* You were in here two minutes ago. I yelled for help and you ignored me.

WOMAN That sounds like a paranoid delusion. *(beat)* Except that I heard the yelling.

YOUNG MAN *(offstage)* So why didn't you do anything!

WOMAN I did. I came in here.

YOUNG MAN *(offstage)* When?

WOMAN Just now. It sounds like *you* have the memory problem.

YOUNG MAN *(offstage)* Yeah, you know it's real nice to take advantage of someone in my situation. I guess you wouldn't know anything about how that feels but let me tell you it isn't a very nice–

WOMAN I don't know how that feels?

The WOMAN leaves in a huff.

YOUNG MAN *(offstage)* NO! NO! Why must I eternally be left!

He fiddles with the door.

(offstage) Please, someone! Anyone. *(beat)* I know there's people out there who can hear me. I know there are. *(beat)* Compassion? *(beat)* Guilt? *(long beat)* Money?

A MAN comes in the room.

(offstage) I heard that. Someone came in. Don't tell me you didn't! Let's not get into a whole thing about whether you were here before. I don't really care. It's funny how sometimes you care about getting those things straight 'cause it's kind of important—*lying*—but interesting, when you need to get OUT OF A VERY SMALL VERY BAD ROOM you find things going by the wayside – truth, honesty, someone's character, the unfair way life has of treating you when you simply don't deserve any of – Please let me out of here. The door is stuck. *(He fiddles from within.)* See? I can't open it. Now help me.

The mute MAN fiddles with the door.

(offstage) Oh my lord, what a lovely sound.

He keeps fiddling.

(offstage) That's it.

Keeps fiddling but he can't open the door.

(offstage) Come on.

He keeps trying.

(offstage) What's wrong?

Keeps trying to open the door.

(offstage) What's the problem? (beat) I said what's the problem?

He keeps trying.

(offstage) Don't tell me it's stuck on your side too!

The MAN writes a note.

(offstage) Hey, "don't tell me" doesn't mean "don't tell me!" TELL ME! There is nothing worse than not knowing what is going on!

The MAN slips the note under the stage right door.

(offstage) What the hell is that? It's dark in here, don't freak me out.

The MAN opens the upstage door.

(offstage) No! No! Stop right there. I know what that is. I've become an expert on the niceties of door sounds since being stuck in here and let me tell you some of the niceties are not very nice. Now that is clearly the sound of you about to leave and I'm going to have to demur and furthermore strongly disagree, please, you can't leave this room, at least not without an explanation.

The MAN looks concerned but leaves.

(offstage) No! Oh my God! The inhumanity! The inhumanity of it all! My faith in my fellow man, shaky at best till this juncture in time, now dashed all to–

As he's talking, the mute MAN comes back in with the deaf WOMAN, gesturing for her to try and open the door. She tries.

(offstage) Oh hello. Thank you.

The mute MAN leaves.

(offstage) Okay look, I'll try to–

The deaf WOMAN and the MAN inside the room both fiddle with the door.

(offstage) Okay, you stop and I'll try to–

The WOMAN keeps fiddling.

(offstage) I SAID, "YOU STOP." IT'S LIKE A CAR DOOR, YOU CAN'T BOTH TRY AT ONCE. Now you stop and I'll try, then I'll stop and you try.

She keeps fiddling.

(offstage) Okay, now my turn.

They both fiddle with the door.

(offstage) I SAID "MY TURN" – WHAT ARE YOU, DEAF?

The blind WOMAN comes back in.

WOMAN   I decided it was rude of me to leave.

YOUNG MAN   *(offstage)* What is there, a party going on out there?

WOMAN   No, actually there's a conference going on in the hotel and many of us have much better things to do than–

YOUNG MAN   *(offstage)* – than care about your fellow man?

WOMAN   I'm back, aren't I?

YOUNG MAN   *(offstage)* Well, some of the others out there have a lot to learn about manners.

WOMAN   Oh, are they the ones I heard yelling?

The deaf WOMAN looks at her watch and then puts the blind WOMAN's hand on it.

Go ahead.

The deaf WOMAN leaves.

WOMAN   Now what seems to be the problem?

YOUNG MAN   *(offstage)* Oh nothing. It's a totally normal door that just happens to make this sound.

He bangs on the door, loudly. The blind WOMAN feels for the door handle and tries to open it.

WOMAN   It's stuck.

YOUNG MAN   *(offstage)* Wow, thanks for clearing that up.

WOMAN   What are you doing in there?

YOUNG MAN   *(offstage)* Well, considering there's pretty much only room in here to FREAK OUT, that's what I'm doing.

WOMAN   You got trapped?

YOUNG MAN   *(offstage)* Thanks, now there's nothing to do but freak out AND see myself as a furry animal.

WOMAN   How did you get stuck? The reason might help you get out.

YOUNG MAN   *(offstage)* Hey, I don't need a philosopher, I need a wrecking ball.

WOMAN   I got trapped in a room once.

YOUNG MAN   *(offstage)* Swell.

WOMAN   I didn't see a sign that said "Locks From Within."

YOUNG MAN *(offstage)* Didn't see the sign? That's pretty stupid.

WOMAN I'm blind. What's your excuse?

    Long beat.

    Cat got your tongue?

YOUNG MAN *(offstage)* Yes.

WOMAN I'll try to find a janitor.

YOUNG MAN *(offstage)* Thank you.

WOMAN You're welcome.

YOUNG MAN *(offstage)* Um… I'm sorry.

WOMAN Hey, you're stuck.

    She turns to go.

YOUNG MAN *(offstage)* Don't go yet.

WOMAN I have to get some–

YOUNG MAN *(offstage)* There's no lights in here. It's kind of scary.

WOMAN Close your eyes.

YOUNG MAN *(offstage)* That won't brighten it.

WOMAN When you're afraid of the dark and your eyes can't help you, don't try to see with them. Is there room in there to lie down?

YOUNG MAN *(offstage)* I don't know.

    He bangs into something.

    (offstage) No.

WOMAN Then sit.

YOUNG MAN *(offstage)* Okay.

WOMAN Close your eyes. Breathe. Relax. Are your eyes closed?

YOUNG MAN *(offstage)* Yes.

WOMAN The room's bigger now, isn't it?

YOUNG MAN *(offstage)* No, I can still touch the walls.

WOMAN Don't.

YOUNG MAN *(offstage)* Oh. Yeah, it's a little bigger.

WOMAN You can fill the darkness with whatever you like.

YOUNG MAN *(offstage)* Really?

WOMAN Well not when you're in traffic, but sometimes… yeah. *(beat)* So what do you see?

YOUNG MAN *(offstage)* I'd rather not say.

WOMAN Come on...

YOUNG MAN *(offstage)* Okay. A puppy.

WOMAN A cute little puppy?

YOUNG MAN *(offstage)* Yeah...

WOMAN The puppy loves you.

YOUNG MAN *(offstage)* Yeah.

WOMAN Breathe. See the puppy.

>   *The YOUNG MAN makes a happy sound.*

Are you better now?

YOUNG MAN *(offstage)* Yeah...

WOMAN Now I'm going to go and get some help.

>   *The YOUNG MAN makes a sleepy sound.*

All right?

>   *The YOUNG MAN makes no sound. The mute MAN comes in the room. The blind WOMAN turns to go and her cane touches him.*

Who's that?

>   *Of course, the mute MAN says nothing.*

Hello?

>   *He stares at her longingly.*

Hey, to you it might be a meaningful pause, but for all I know you've gotten on a bus.

>   *He touches her arm. He is shaking.*

Shy?

>   *He takes her hand, puts it on his face and nods.*

Oh... *(beat)* Well, not so shy – you took my hand.

>   *He nods.*

Do you want to help me get some help?

>   *He nods.*

Good.

>   *They exit the room.*

Teresa Pavlinek *The Weekend*

2001
Layne Coleman: Director
Andrew Moodie: Man
Caroline Gillis: Woman

⌑ • ⌑

An office. A thirty-something WOMAN sits at a desk in front of a computer. She has a Starbucks coffee beside her. She wears a black blazer, fitted blouse, black skirt, and pumps. A Mix 99.9-type radio station plays softly on a radio that sits on top of a filing cabinet. She sits in silence, looking outside. A MAN carrying a worn briefcase and wearing a suit enters.

WOMAN You're late.

MAN *(frazzled)* I know.

    Silence.

WOMAN We have the Dexter and Suckling presentation in ten minutes.

MAN I know.

WOMAN I thought we were going to come in early and go over it.

MAN I'm sorry.

WOMAN What was it this time?

MAN I didn't have any socks.

WOMAN You waited until Monday morning to realise you didn't have clean socks?

MAN No, I didn't have any socks, I… it doesn't matter.

WOMAN Well, luckily, everyone's still at some pre-breakfast meeting on the third floor.

MAN *(preoccupied)* Good.

    Pause. MAN takes papers out of his briefcase. He stares at her.

WOMAN What's wrong?

MAN I – uh – I need to talk to you.

WOMAN How was your weekend?

MAN What?

WOMAN Did you and Helen have a nice dinner?

MAN Yes. It was fine. No, it was bad. The restaurant she picked had horrible service and I–

WOMAN Did she like her present?

MAN I didn't give it to her.

WOMAN Why?

MAN I just didn't. It wasn't appropriate.

WOMAN It was your anniversary.

MAN I know.

WOMAN Did you have a fight?

MAN Yes.

WOMAN *(puzzled)* Did she give *you* something?

MAN Sort of.

WOMAN What do you mean "sort of"?

MAN Well, she gave it to me and then I gave it back.

WOMAN Why?

MAN I didn't want it.

WOMAN You didn't like it.

MAN I didn't even open it.

WOMAN So you didn't give her your gift and she took back hers?

MAN Yes! Is the gift exchange really important?

>   *Pause. WOMAN gives him a look and then continues to work.*

   I'm sorry I ran out on Friday. *(pause)* How was your weekend?

WOMAN Fine. I picked up some groceries, paid my phone bill and… met someone.

MAN What?

WOMAN I met a man.

MAN On the weekend?

WOMAN Friday, on my way home from work.

MAN You're joking.

WOMAN No.

MAN This is one of your "I'm mad at you so I'll screw with your head" joke.

WOMAN I don't need to screw with your head anymore.

MAN We have a fight and you just go out and find someone new–

WOMAN We've gone over this again and again. It's pointless. You said so yourself on Friday. "What do you want me to do? Leave my wife and kids?"

MAN Where did you meet this person?

WOMAN *(enjoying it)* Well, on the way home Friday night, I decided to walk because it was nice out. It starts to pour so I run under the awning of this apartment. I'm standing there soaking wet, my bag, my feet just soaked. This tiny, frail-looking old woman was already there. She was just sort of shuddering, like she'd be swept away to sea if she tried to move. Then this man rides up on his bike and gets off right in front of the building. I thought he lived there but he got off his bike, propped it up against the fence and came and stood beside us. He had beautiful crème-coloured linen pants that were covered in mud and rolled up on one side. He was wearing those really nice brown leather, wing-tip shoes and a pale blue dress-shirt that was soaked right through to his white t-shirt underneath. He had tousled, sandy brown hair, funky glasses and the most stunning blue eyes I've ever seen. Anyway, I guess I was staring at him because he looked at me and sort of said hello in that way where you don't speak you just sort of nod. And then the old woman started to make small talk with me about her arthritis but I wasn't listening. The man and I both sort of glanced at each other and smiled in a "isn't this odd" kind of way.

MAN Did you sleep with him?

WOMAN I'm not finished! So there we were and it was raining and it's me, the cute guy and an old lady, and I started thinking about our fight that day. I thought, what is the point of my stupid life if I don't do what makes me happy? So I turned to him and said, "I bet those are dry-clean only." He turned and looked at me sort of puzzled. I said "I mean your pants, they're probably dry-clean only and now they're all dirty. That sucks." A B.A. in Commerce and that's all I could come up with. He started to laugh. Like really laugh. I thought he was going to just walk away laughing out into the rain. But he didn't. He said, "That's funny" and looking at him smile made me, I don't know, something took over and suddenly I felt confident and sexy again. So I blurted out, "I'm walking to Bloor, do you want to come?" He smiled and said yes. It was that easy. Just act like you aren't afraid of failure and you won't fail. So we walked to Bloor huddling under a piece of cardboard the old woman offered us. And then I said "I'm going further north do you want to walk with me?" And he said yes. It was like a video game, I kept getting more lives. We get to the front door of my apartment and I said "Do you want to come in?" And he said… Yes! I couldn't believe it. And when he was taking off my pantyhose, I still couldn't believe it. An hour later we sat on my couch in the darkness. Then he got up, put on his mud-stained crème-coloured linen pants and pale blue dress-shirt and left.

MAN What the fuck are you doing?

WOMAN Sorry?

MAN Have you lost your mind?

WOMAN No, I made a connection with another human being. You wouldn't understand.

MAN Do you have a fucking clue as to what you've done?

WOMAN Yes, I had the guts to be true to myself.

MAN A one-night stand? You call that being true to yourself? *(mocking)* "The most stunning blue eyes I've ever seen?" You're pathetic.

WOMAN I'm not going to fight about this.

MAN I've destroyed my life for you.

WOMAN What are you talking about?

MAN I've got to call Helen.

WOMAN Great.

MAN I stupidly thought for a moment that maybe you knew what you were talking about and that you were saying all those things because you actually loved me. So I sat there on the GO Train thinking about what you said. "What's the point of my stupid life if I don't do what makes me happy? I should be going home with her. I thought the rest doesn't matter she makes me happy. I missed my stop, so I got off the train and walked all the way home. I felt like a weight had been lifted. I started to notice things. All the people being picked up at the station, so many minivans, the buzzing sound of the stoplights, the waste, the regret. *(pause)* I left Helen and the kids.

WOMAN It's too late. It's finished.

MAN How can you say that? After all your tears and the arguments trying to fight for this relationship.

WOMAN We don't have a relationship. You're married and we sleep together on our lunch breaks. That's it. And now it's finished.

MAN I wish you had said that Friday before I left.

WOMAN I did. You never listened.

MAN So what now?

WOMAN We have to present the green sheets to Dexter & Suckling in five minutes.

MAN What?

WOMAN Our presentation. The one we've been "working overtime" on for months.

   Pause.

MAN "What's the point of your stupid life if you don't do what makes you happy?"

WOMAN You can't bail on me now.

MAN Why? You did.

WOMAN I did what I had to do.

MAN Right. Do you have the files?

WOMAN I've already printed everything and made copies.

MAN I'm just supposed to walk into a room full of people and pretend this never happened

WOMAN You've been doing it for months.

> *The WOMAN grabs a stack of papers and they walk out of the office. The radio plays.*

Susan Coyne   ***Captive Audience***

2002
Eda Holmes: Director
James Kidnie: John
Kate Lynch: Patricia
Julian Richings: Charles

¤ • ¤

An office. Desk, chair, adjustable lamp. A maquette of a stage design.

Enter two men, carrying a chair. In the chair is a woman—Patricia Caller—bound and gagged and struggling valiantly to make a noise.

CHARLES   Yes. I'm awfully sorry. We won't be a moment. I just need to – John, would you please make sure the door is locked?

JOHN   Of course.

JOHN goes over and locks the door.

CHARLES   There. All right, I think we can take the gag off.

JOHN removes the gag.

PATRICIA   Help! Someone!

CHARLES   Oh dear.

PATRICIA   Help! You bastards! Help!

She tries to kick at CHARLES.

CHARLES   *(with a sigh)* Oh, dear. I hate being the bad guy… John.

JOHN makes a move to put the gag back on.

PATRICIA   No! No! Please. Please. I promise – I'll cooperate.

CHARLES   Oh, thank you so much. Really, if I thought there was any other way – I wouldn't be doing this–

PATRICIA   Doing this?

CHARLES   I beg your pardon?

PATRICIA   What is it that are you doing?

CHARLES   Kidnapping you. I'm sorry, was that not clear?

PATRICIA This is a kidnapping?

CHARLES Yes! Oh, God, what a muddle. I'm going to start all over again. Hello. I'm Charles and this is John and we're – yes, kidnapping you.

Pause.

PATRICIA I'm an artistic director.

CHARLES Yes!

PATRICIA I don't have any money.

CHARLES Oh! Money! Money's not what we're after! Good lord, what do you take us for?

PATRICIA Well, kidnappers…

CHARLES Oh, I see where the confusion lies…. No, this is not an ordinary—or um—regular kidnapping…

PATRICIA Oh. Not a regular kidnapping.

CHARLES Yes.

Pause.

CHARLES Oh dear, this is…. I've never done this before. I had it all planned out and now – I've lost my place. It's a bit awkward…

Pause.

PATRICIA What? What? Please…

CHARLES All right. I'll wing it: Patricia. We're here, John and I, as representatives of the community at large, well, because we have a bone to pick with you. An old, old bone…. Got it?

PATRICIA looks blank.

PATRICIA No.

CHARLES Think hard, Patricia.

PATRICIA Oh, God. You're not from Equity are you? That business with the apprentice…? Look, I took the course, I got the certificate, what more do you–

CHARLES No, no, not from Equity.

Pause.

PATRICIA The Canada Council. The travel grant? Listen, I made a ton of contacts in Vegas, I can show you the list of potential corporate sponsors, I've got a deal on a co-pro just about sewn up, a winter tour–

CHARLES No, no we're not from the Canada Council

PATRICIA Oh, thank Christ…

CHARLES Think, Patricia…

PATRICIA I'm stumped.

CHARLES Edward de Vere…?

PATRICIA Is that you?

CHARLES Oh, goodness no…. I'm from the Edward de Vere Society.

PATRICIA What?

CHARLES Don't tell me you haven't read the – oh, my. We've sent you all the material – over thirty packages…

PATRICIA Uh-huh…. Well, you see, boys, I've been kinda busy getting a season ready. As a matter of fact tonight's the opening of *Hamlet* and–

CHARLES Oh, yes we know–

PATRICIA –and actually, I'm supposed to be backstage right now. Rallying the troops, so to speak. So perhaps you could just give me the gist of what it is you want from me, and then I can get back to work.

CHARLES Yes, yes… *(with a sigh)* Well, I'm afraid I can only give you the roughest outline of what we're about…. The Edward de Vere Society is an organization devoted to setting the historical record straight with regard to the authorship of the plays of the man known as Shakespeare.

   Pause.

PATRICIA You think Shakespeare didn't write his own plays.

CHARLES That's correct. We believe they were written by the seventeenth Earl of Oxford.

PATRICIA What does that have to do with me?

CHARLES We need you to tell the world.

PATRICIA You're insane.

   JOHN makes a threatening gesture.

CHARLES Never mind, John…

PATRICIA Only cranks and conspiracy theorists believe that Shakespeare's plays were written by someone else.

CHARLES Unfortunately, you are behind the times. There are many eminent scholars, jurists, senators, and Hollywood celebrities who now agree that the plays of Shakespeare could not possibly have been written by the vulgar and illiterate "Man from Stratford."

PATRICIA Scholars? Don't make me laugh. Nothing but ignorance and intellectual dishonesty, fueled by anti-populist bile.

CHARLES You see. This is why it's necessary to resort to extreme measures. It's so very hard to overcome these kinds of prejudices…. Tell you what, since time is short, why don't I just give you a brief introduction to the life of our hero, the seventeenth earl. Then we'll take a look at some of the orthographical evidence.

I'd also like to show you some of the latest empirical data. Using n-gram statistics we are able to compare the frequency of certain anomalous features in Shakespeare's sonnets with those found in the works of Edward de Vere.

PATRICIA Look, Charles, I have an opening tonight. Do you have any idea of the kind of stress I'm under? *Hamlet.* The most heavily-scrutinized work in the canon. In half an hour the audience will be arriving, ready to eat my actors alive. They need me, holding their hands, calming their fears, fighting their demons.

CHARLES Ah, yes…. Well, we'd love to be able to have you give a speech before the show, but if necessary, it can come after.

PATRICIA A speech?… What kind of speech?

CHARLES A statement. Just something simple, stating your unequivocal support for our organization… I can write it up for you, but it would help if you knew what you were talking about.

PATRICIA You're not serious.

CHARLES Yes. Oh yes.

PATRICIA Why me?

CHARLES I beg your pardon?

PATRICIA Why me? Why not Richard Monette? The Stouffville Shakespeare Festival is – I'm not even sure we'll be here next year.

CHARLES Well, frankly, we thought we might be doing you a favour.

JOHN We've seen what's happened to your subscriber base in the last three years.

CHARLES You know, John, I really do think we need the overhead projector for this. Why don't you stay here, make sure our guest is comfortable and I'll be right back.

JOHN Okay, Mr. A.

CHARLES All right Patricia?

PATRICIA Do I have a choice?

CHARLES No. Won't be a moment.

> *CHARLES exits. Silence. JOHN regards PATRICIA. PATRICIA smiles. JOHN takes out an apple and a knife and starts eating.*

JOHN So, I see you're doing *Merchant* this season.

PATRICIA Yes. If the bank doesn't close us down…

JOHN Who've you got playing Portia?

PATRICIA Umm, Jenny Armour.

JOHN Oh yeah…. She's got a nice rack.

PATRICIA Yes.... She's a board member's daughter, all right?... Are you in the business?

JOHN Call me an aficionado.

PATRICIA And how long have you been a convert?

JOHN A what?

PATRICIA What do you call it? An Oxfordian?

JOHN Oh. Never.

PATRICIA I'm sorry?

JOHN It's a load of crap.

PATRICIA Oh, thank God you're not both crazy.

JOHN No, I'm a Marlowe man, myself.

PATRICIA Christopher Marlowe?

JOHN Yes, I'm convinced he didn't die in that bar brawl but was spirited away by members of Lord Burleighs' secret service.

PATRICIA Good God.... Look, does Charles really think that I'm going to read a prepared speech in front of my opening night audience?

JOHN Why not?

PATRICIA It would seriously damage my credibility in the community.

JOHN Patricia.

PATRICIA What?

JOHN Credibility?

PATRICIA What?

JOHN Those cringing thank you's on opening night?

PATRICIA That's different. That's survival. Without sponsors we wouldn't be here. Anyway, I'm not going to make a fool of myself to promote some crackpot authorship theory.... Look, I'm supposed to be at a corporate function – can't you just untie these–

JOHN I thought you said you were supposed to be seeing the actors.

PATRICIA Well, yes, if I can get away. Which is why I need you to–

JOHN Oh, no, I don't think so. I'd feel badly about betraying Charles.

PATRICIA But you said yourself...

JOHN He's been awfully good to me.

PATRICIA In what way?

JOHN Well, you know, he helped me buy a house. He's got me on a dental plan. He took me and the wife to St. Bart's last year.

Pause.

PATRICIA What exactly does Charles do?

JOHN He's the president of the Edward de Vere Society.

PATRICIA But what's his job?

JOHN He doesn't have to work, if you know what I mean.

PATRICIA Rich?

JOHN Oh. Yes.

PATRICIA I see…

CHARLES bustles back in with the overhead projector.

CHARLES Sorry, sorry, you'd think for 75,000 you'd get a car with a remote access that actually worked…. Do you have an outlet here somewhere?

PATRICIA Don't worry about it. Look, Charlie, I've been talking to John here, and I'm beginning to understand why it's important to get the message out. I'm not all the way there yet, but why don't you just jot down a few speaking points…

CHARLES Really?

PATRICIA Absolutely…. Let's go in the other office.

PATRICIA holds the door open for CHARLES.

PATRICIA I don't know if you're aware of some of our exciting new sponsor benefits…. It's all here in our VIP brochure. You'd be there at all the openings, plus attend rehearsals, vocal warm-ups, fittings, drinks with the actors, anything you want. In addition, your name—or that of the Edward de Vere society—would appear in all promotional material…

Sonja Mills   *Mouse*

2002
Melody Johnson: Director
Janet Van de Graff: Save
Lisa Merchant: Kill
Teresa Pavlinek: Waffle

⌑ • ⌑

Kitchen, early in the morning. SAVE enters with a bluebox, wearing a green robe. As she turns on the light a mouse scampers across the counter.

SAVE   Eeek!

KILL   *(from upstairs)* What is it?

SAVE   Mouse!

KILL   Mouse?

SAVE   Mouse! *(It scampers back across the counter.)* Eeek!

KILL runs down the stairs, into the kitchen, with a bottle of toxic household chemicals, wearing a red robe.

KILL   Where's the mouse?

SAVE   There!

KILL   Here?

SAVE   *(mouse scampers)* Eeek!

KILL searches for something under the counter as WAFFLE enters, in a green and red striped robe.

WAFFLE   I was upstairs, coming downstairs to make breakfast when I heard the screaming. So I came downstairs to see what the screaming was all about. So now I'm here, but am I here for the screaming, or to make breakfast? I'm unclear.

SAVE   *(mouse scamper)* There!

KILL has found a cartoon-sized inflatable hammer (or something) which she now wields over her head as if to bring it down on the mouse, but SAVE grabs her arms to stop her.

SAVE   No! Don't hurt it!

KILL It won't hurt a bit. (*The mouse scampers, she swings at it but misses.*)

SAVE No! Don't kill it!

KILL You said don't hurt, not don't kill.

SAVE We have a no-kill policy in this house.

KILL That policy's been repealed.

SAVE We have to catch it, and then release it outside.

KILL Yes, that's how your last bleeding-heart roommate dealt with mice. That's how you became infested. (*The mouse scampers, she swings and misses.*)

SAVE No! We have rules against killing!

KILL The rules have changed.

SAVE You can't change the rules by yourself.

KILL According to the new rules, I can.

SAVE We have a treaty!

KILL It's been overturned.

SAVE We have an accord!

KILL It's been overruled.

SAVE When did all this happen?

KILL While you were busy "saving the environment."

SAVE (*to WAFFLE*) Can't you do something?

WAFFLE I am 100% prepared, as always, to lend my full support to either side of this debate. I suggest we break off into committees and discuss it over breakfast.

SAVE Compassion!

WAFFLE Absolutely. The lives of the innocent must be spared. Breakfast?

KILL Self-defence!

WAFFLE Definitely. We must destroy them before they destroy us. Breakfast?

KILL (*to WAFFLE*) It's your lax controls at the entry points that's to blame for all this.

SAVE (*also to WAFFLE*) You ratified me out!

WAFFLE I have always made every possible effort to ensure the best of both worlds for all parties concerned, regardless of the options they may choose one way or another. I can't decide – should I have pancakes or french toast?

KILL (*The mouse scampers, she lifts her weapon over her head.*) Kill the mouse!

SAVE (*grabs KILL's arms*) Save the mouse!

WAFFLE (*goes to the freezer*) Waffles!

SAVE Mice were here before us.

KILL And then we conquered them.

SAVE And enslaved them as part of a food chain that ends with us.

KILL Not enslaved, gave them meaningful jobs in fields across the country.

SAVE Save the mouse! Save the mouse!

KILL This is starting to sound like a protest. There's all kinds of rules against that now.

SAVE What rules?

KILL Secret rules, sorry.

SAVE Are you even listening to me?

KILL I'm smiling. I'm nodding. Of course I'm listening.

SAVE *(to WAFFLE)* Aren't you going to say something? Aren't you going to speak up?

WAFFLE *(has been searching in the freezer, fridge, cupboards)* Round waffles or square waffles. Perhaps I should go back to not being able to decide. Or perhaps not.

SAVE Do you believe we have a moral obligation?

WAFFLE In every society, we must be certain to consider all things that might be affected by our considerations of them.

KILL Don't you want more stuff?

WAFFLE Of course, we must not stand in the way of progress, for to do so is to prevent the further advancement we need to proceed forward.

SAVE We should take a poll.

KILL Smiling. Nodding. Yes, a poll.

SAVE A fair vote.

KILL Smiling. Nodding. That sounds democratic.

WAFFLE I fully support democracy.

> *SAVE steps up on a step-stool set on the floor (in lieu of a spotlight). During her speech KILL prepares a ballot box. The mouse which has been scampering across the counter now sits still, listening to SAVE.*

SAVE Why should one species dominate and destroy another? We should live but they must either die or live in a sewer? They have warm blood and suckle their children. We are related. They are not the enemy. We have no enemies. Thank you. *(steps down)*

WAFFLE That was moving, warm, heartfelt and sincere. I feel guilty! So guilty!

KILL *(steps up)* Mice are evil vermin who eat our crackers and leave turds in the sink and spread disease. They must be eliminated at all costs. *(steps down)*

WAFFLE That's good, square-headed thinking. I'm convinced my taxes are lower already.

KILL I'll count the votes. *(prepares to count the ballots, which were never cast)*

WAFFLE My congratulations to both candidates, and I sincerely hope you both win.

KILL *(reads the first vote)* Kill the mouse. *(reads the second vote)* Kill the mouse.

SAVE *(looks to WAFFLE)* What? We had a deal.

WAFFLE I never make deals! Or do I? No, never! Or is it always?

KILL And, *(third vote)* kill the mouse.

SAVE That's not my vote!

KILL Unanimous!

SAVE I demand a recount!

KILL The count is verified. Kill the mouse!

SAVE The vote was rigged!

KILL The vote stands. Kill the mouse!

SAVE The ballots were improper!

KILL Complainer!

SAVE The ballots were confusing!

KILL Moron!

> *The mouse, who has been listening, jumps up and down on the counter.*

SAVE Look! I think he wants to say something!

> *The mouse turns to the audience, takes a breath as if about to speak – then KILL whacks it with the hammer, killing it.*

SAVE He was just about to say something!

KILL Thank God! I prevented even more violence!

SAVE I condemn your actions!

KILL I repudiate your condemnation.

SAVE I denounce your repudiation

KILL I reject your denunciation.

WAFFLE I'm so glad that's settled.

SAVE I think a full inquest of the preceding events would be appropriate.

KILL The inquest is complete. I've been cleared of all charges.

SAVE Appeal!

KILL Denied.

WAFFLE I would like to express my deepest sympathy to the families of the victim, as well as my deepest gratitude to the slayer of the beast. You know, it isn't always easy for those of us who live here to decide what's right and what's wrong, as long as we always choose right over wrong, of course, and not the other way around. But I'm sure if we go to bed together, we'll all come out clean in the end. *(puts her arms around KILL and SAVE's waists)*

KILL Now that you mention it, I feel strangely aroused.

SAVE Please hold me. I'm so frightened.

> Exeunt, *turning off the kitchen light as a string of mice scampers across the counter.*

Paula Wing — Thirty-six C

2002
Stewart Arnott: Director
Dixie Seatle: Marie
Jennifer Gould: Barbara

✳ • ✳

BARBARA Hi. Is this Suite C? The Essential Foundation? I hope you can help me.

MARIE That's what I'm here for, dear.

BARBARA You're Marie? You come very highly recommended. I'm researching supporting data for a study and I wanted to ask you a few questions: general technical questions, about architectural theory and mechanics, of course, and also your basic philosophy and how it's changed over the years.

MARIE It hasn't. New isn't always better and frankly, it's often worse. I've been in this business thirty years and I can tell you this for free: you're under-supported.

BARBARA Studies like this may not be hip any more–

MARIE I'm talking about your bra.

BARBARA –but when you actually study it you see so clearly there are so many unexplored areas! There's almost no scholarly work on the breast, how it's perceived, who's controlling its image.

MARIE Theory doesn't interest me, honey. We've got a new boss, she's always saying it's about optics, Marie. How it looks. I said, yes, looks, of course looks are important. I'm not a nun for God's sake. But how come nobody gives a damn about what you know anymore?

BARBARA My study is exactly about that, the knowledge behind the looks. *(to herself)* That's good, concise, insightful – I'm going to use that! So in your line of work you deal intimately with attitudes about women and sexuality, you're witness to hidden agendas of manipulation and domination. My thesis – The Structural Poetics of the Breast in the Twentieth Century—that's the working title—is going to deal with how–

MARIE Here's what I don't get: how you can wear a bra like that?

BARBARA What? Oh, it's a little old.

MARIE That's the understatement of the year. Don't tell me you're comfortable.

BARBARA What I wanted to focus on with you is how styles have come and gone, and how breast shape has been defined over the generations.

MARIE You have no clue what size you really are, that's your problem.

BARBARA I'm a thirty-six C. Which is one of my questions: has the average bra size changed? In your opinion, are breasts bigger now, smaller, the same?

MARIE You're a thirty-four C or D, max. No wonder you're uncomfortable.

BARBARA I'm not uncomfortable, stop focusing on my personal breasts. I want to look at the larger sociological landscape.

MARIE Go into the dressing room and strip to the waist.

BARBARA No. Thanks. Let's start with an obvious area of change: sports bras. Have they really revolutionised breast perception?

MARIE You're not going to understand anything until you get in there.

BARBARA I'm not here for a fitting.

MARIE You're lucky. You're going to get one anyway. *(She pushes BARBARA into the change room. They speak through the door.)*

BARBARA I'm only doing this in the spirit of research.

MARIE To answer your question, most young women don't have a clue. For starters, and I don't know how many times I've said it: what most stores call bras aren't really bras at all, they're breast coverings.

BARBARA All right, good! That's exactly the kind of thing I'm looking for. Listen, would you mind if I taped our conversation?

MARIE As long as you undress.

BARBARA All right, all right.

MARIE What's changed is time. Nobody has it any more. So you get cutting corners, the death of quality, I've watched it happen. Just because something looks like a bra doesn't mean it's an actual bra. Look beneath the surface. Don't take everything at face value.

BARBARA That is so – what's the difference between a bra and a breast covering?

MARIE Underwire. Underwire, underwire, and underwire.

BARBARA You're not saying I need underwire? My God, I'm barely thirty.

MARIE Your age has nothing to do with it. If you have breasts they need to be held up. They need structure. Are you naked yet? Hand out your old bra. *(BARBARA hands it out.)* I knew it. This thing's got about as much hold as a Kleenex.

BARBARA I belong to a health club. I'm in great shape.

MARIE Dear, you're a woman. You have a mother. You know it's not always going to be this way. You're flirting with chest wallbang here.

BARBARA Chest wallbang?

MARIE A condition brought on by not giving your breasts enough support. You flop around long enough, you do serious damage. As I say, it's typical. You think it can't happen to you. You think you'll never be forty.

BARBARA No, I have historical perspective. I'm a scholar. Would you say the trend toward breast coverings is creating a future health crisis for women?

MARIE Your breasts are going to drop. Suddenly. Bam. Like that. And you won't be prepared.

BARBARA But are breast coverings contributing to the drop or is the drop going to occur regardless, that's the issue.

MARIE Mind you, nothing registers these days if it's not sudden. In my opinion that's how those terrorists did it. They just went along for ages, looking normal, moving fast, acting busy. It was happening all along but we didn't know it. That's what made it seem so abrupt. Just like turning forty or having your breasts drop.

BARBARA On the other hand, maybe it means we're more relaxed about the nature of breasts. We don't need to imprison them in harsh, restrictive garments anymore because we've gone beyond that.

MARIE Nobody gets beyond the laws of gravity, honey. Nobody. *(She opens the door, shoves a few bras through.)* Try the top one on and you'll see what a real brassiere feels like.

BARBARA You mean the white one?

MARIE It's ivory.

BARBARA It looks white.

MARIE Well it's ivory. I'm a professional and I'm telling you.

BARBARA Oh, yes the other one's–

MARIE Cream. We also sell ecru and foam.

BARBARA And flesh-tone.

MARIE Cappuccino.

BARBARA All these frilly names, are you trying to appeal to more socio-economically advantaged women?

MARIE You do know the right way to put on a bra, don't you?

BARBARA There's a wrong way?

MARIE Cover up. Come out. You need a lesson.

BARBARA A lesson?

MARIE Bucking for her Ph.D. and she doesn't even know how to put on a bra. Typical.

BARBARA Can I have my old bra back?

MARIE Really dear, I couldn't stand it. There's a wrapper hanging up in there, put that on. *(as BARBARA emerges in a wrapper)* This job is like a public service. My boss says I should retire but how can I? I'm needed. Now, Rule One, and it's eternal, honey: you bend over when you put on your bra.

BARBARA My mother always bent over.

MARIE She was right and there's no point rebelling against her anymore.

BARBARA I'm not rebelling.

MARIE Do you bend over? Then you're rebelling and it's holding you back. Any professional worth her salt can see it. So can all those men who are out there resisting you right now. You don't have a man, am I right?

BARBARA I have a really full life.

MARIE Yeah, and my car has a really full tank but it's not going anywhere if I don't put the key in the ignition.

BARBARA I'm not interested in a relationship. My research takes up all my time.

MARIE I always tell my customers: bending over is the beginning of the end of your problem.

BARBARA What problem? I don't have a problem. Can we get back to my questions, please?

MARIE After you go back in there and bend over into that ivory bra. Go on. Let your whole breast just fall into the cup. *(BARBARA goes back in.)* I don't blame you, dear. These days everybody's in a big rush. But back to bending over: be sure to place the underwire directly *under* your breast.

BARBARA *(from behind the door)* And then hook it up?

MARIE Yes! What are you going to do, stay bent over all day? *(The dressing room door opens, MARIE pulls it shut.)* Not so fast, where's the fire? You haven't done the critical thing. You have to reach inside your cup, take your breast in your hand and lift it up.

BARBARA What? Why?

MARIE To showcase your nipples. My God this is basic! Nipples don't automatically go to the most flattering position, you have to place them.

BARBARA My mother never did that.

MARIE Yes, she did, you just weren't watching. Have you got your breast? Lift it so the top half of your nipple crests over the centre seam and the bottom half goes below it. Do it to both your breasts and then come out.

BARBARA *(stepping out)* Oh my God, it's way too tight.

MARIE Just a second. Your straps are wrong. *(She adjusts.)*

BARBARA That's even worse. I can hardly breathe.

MARIE Take it easy, dear. You're just having a little identity crisis.

BARBARA This can't be right. It's so oppressive and confining. I'm going to have marks.

MARIE All your adult life you thought you were a thirty-six C. That's your identity. Change that, you have to change everything! You may not have a boyfriend now–

BARBARA I am not trying to find somebody.

MARIE You should be. You're going to be forty much sooner than you think.

BARBARA I just can't date. It's so unfocused. You get all dressed up and nothing happens.

MARIE A couple of these good bras will help. Those boys zero right in, trust me.

BARBARA I'm really not that lonely. I don't think I am.

MARIE You didn't think you needed a good bra either.

BARBARA And anyway, loneliness isn't the worst thing. Is it? Actually, I have no idea what the worst thing is but I think about it a lot. Do you? I wonder what it'll be, how I'll handle it. I guess everybody lives with it – the knowledge that that moment is out there, it'll come, and you just know: this is the worst.

MARIE Yeah. Until the next time.

BARBARA And I think, will knowing it's the worst will be comforting?

MARIE *(finally finished her finessings)* A world of difference. How does it feel?

BARBARA Like a vice-grip with lace.

MARIE Good. How does it look?

BARBARA Who cares? Nobody's going to actually see it. *(MARIE turns BARBARA toward the mirror.)* Oh. Oh my…

MARIE You're not nobody, honey.

BARBARA It's really – I mean, I look–

MARIE Completely gorgeous.

BARBARA I kind of do, don't I?

MARIE This one's on special for eighty-five.

BARBARA Eighty-five dollars for a bra! I can't afford that, I'm a student.

MARIE Try the black one.

BARBARA Mind you, if they're essential to my study, I could get the department to fund them… submit a materials invoice…

MARIE Now all you need is a mesh bag for washing them and bra detergent so you don't corrode the underwire. I'll be right back, dear. *(She exits.)*

BARBARA Well. You know what they say… *(She picks up the black bra and goes back inside the fitting room.)* You have to be a slave to your research.

Richard Greenblatt and Guillermo Verdecchia

My Cigarette Break With Guillermo

2003
Guillermo Verdecchia: Guillermo
Richard Greenblatt: Richard
Andy McKim: Andy
Jordan Pettle: Guest Actor

♯ • ♯

RICHARD comes out onto the loading doors of ANDY's office. He is laughing. He lights a cigarette. He continues to chuckle. GUILLERMO enters onto the fire escape. He screams.

RICHARD Guillermo.

GUILLERMO Richard.

Beat. He screams again

RICHARD How're rehearsals going?

GUILLERMO You got a cigarette?

RICHARD Sure. *(He takes one out and throws it to him.)* I thought you quit.

GUILLERMO We preview in six days.

RICHARD Ah. Third-week syndrome.

GUILLERMO Big time. Gotta light?

RICHARD *(throws him a lighter)* Who's in your cast?

GUILLERMO You ever work with _____? *(name of guest)*

RICHARD Oh, s/he's great.

GUILLERMO Yeah?

RICHARD I love working with him/her. S/he's so open, so willing to try anything, smart, aware…

GUILLERMO *(He looks over his shoulder.)* S/he's driving me crazy.

RICHARD Really?

GUILLERMO Lots of skill. Lots of technique. And sure, smart. But I'm so tired of smart. You know? Smart. What is smart anyway? I want questions. I want uncertainty. I don't want a good, clear performance. I'm so bored with all that.

I want some… it's an old fashioned concept… soul. But when I talk like this to him/her, s/he looks at me like I'm speaking Martian. You know what I mean?

RICHARD *(He looks at him like he's speaking Martian.)* Yeah.

GUILLERMO I mean, sure we can get it up. Make it palatable. Clean. A clean production. I'm so tired of clean. I want something else. I want…

RICHARD Dirty?

GUILLERMO Sure. Dirty. Messy.

RICHARD That takes time. You can't do good messy in four weeks. You can do bad messy in one week, but good messy takes months. Years. You need a lot of shared vocabulary for good messy. *(beat)* You know, I feel like everything I spend an hour on, I want to spend a day on. Everything I spend a day on, I want a week on. And everything I spend a week on, I want… *(Guillermo joins in.)* …to spend a month on.

GUILLERMO I know. It's crazy. The same amount of time to do a Norm Foster as to do the most complex adaptation of… I don't know… *Finnegans Wake*. *(pause)* How's your show going?

RICHARD Great actually. We're laughing a lot. I guess that's a good sign.

GUILLERMO Yeah. *(beat)* Or…

RICHARD Or what?

GUILLERMO Rehearsal hall triumph.

RICHARD Don't say that.

He retreats, turns around three times, spits, swears, and knocks.

GUILLERMO *(rolling his eyes)* Come in. Oh God, Richard. How can an atheist be superstitious?

RICHARD The Theatre Gods are the only deities I recognise. Now I'm worried. Maybe we're having too good a time. Maybe a little misery would be better.

GUILLERMO Misery loves creativity. *(beat)* Or maybe it's the other way around. I'm sure it's fine. Is anyone else laughing or is it just–

RICHARD You think it's not funny.

GUILLERMO No. You never know. I mean how many times have you gone out with something that you thought was a sure thing, can't miss, dead funny, and nobody laughs.

RICHARD Is this supposed to be reassuring?

GUILLERMO No, well, I mean, yes. You know. Like if you think it's not funny then it probably is.

RICHARD We're screwed, in other words.

GUILLERMO No, I just mean, you never know. You never know. It might actually be funny. Anything can happen.

RICHARD *(not too confident)* Yeah.

GUILLERMO What's the time?

    RICHARD tells him the real time.

Five more minutes. Hey, remember that idea we were talking about a long time ago?

RICHARD Which idea?

GUILLERMO You know, adapting Trotsky's *Writings on Aesthetics.*

RICHARD Oh. Yeah.

GUILLERMO Well, I've been thinking a lot about it lately.

RICHARD You have? Gee, we haven't talked about that in… years.

GUILLERMO I know, but it's always stayed in the back of my brain, somehow. I think I have a way in with the adaptation. So I was thinking we could apply for some development money, maybe see who might be willing to produce, or for that matter, produce it ourselves, and…

RICHARD I'm doing it with someone else.

GUILLERMO What? *(pause)* Who?

RICHARD Look, I'm sorry Guillermo, I thought we had moved on. I didn't know you were still interested in it. I talked about it with several other people, and…

GUILLERMO No. That's cool. I understand. Hell, it was your idea in the first place.

RICHARD I guess I should have talked to you before I started talking to other people, but I honestly thought you weren't interested in it any more. You're so busy, and we were working in such different circles, I just thought… I am really sorry, man.

GUILLERMO Hey, it was just an idea. Ideas are a dime a dozen. Nobody owns ideas. *(beat)* Who? You owe me that much, Greenblatt.

RICHARD Ross. He had a Canada Council application in before I finished describing the project to him. And he can read the stuff in the original.

GUILLERMO Ah, yeah, well, he's a smart guy.

RICHARD And John is doing the music.

GUILLERMO Good choice. I went to public school with him. Known him forever. Well… good luck with it. Call me if you need a Trotsky.

RICHARD Yeah, I will. That's a great idea actually. *(beat)* Of course, it's not just up to me…

GUILLERMO It was a joke.

RICHARD Oh. *(beat)* Ha ha.

GUILLERMO How're the kids? Natasha?

RICHARD Great. Anais?

GUILLERMO Will?

RICHARD Theo?

GUILLERMO Luke?

RICHARD Perfect. *(beat)* Tamsin?

GUILLERMO *(He nods.)* Kate?

RICHARD Same. *(pause)* You're not pissed off?

GUILLERMO No. Really. I've got a ton of stuff coming up.

RICHARD Really? Like what?

GUILLERMO Oh, I'm directing two shows back-to-back and I'm doing Daniel's new piece at Necessary Angel.

RICHARD Your doppelganger.

GUILLERMO Well, yours is running this place. And I'm acting in *The Goethe Project*.

RICHARD Really? What are you playing?

GUILLERMO The Guy.

RICHARD Really? I was up for that. I was supposed to hear about it soon, but they never did get back to me. I've been wondering about it for days. Now I guess I know.

GUILLERMO Oh. Sorry.

RICHARD Not your fault. People have no manners.

GUILLERMO None.

ANDY appears at the office door.

ANDY Ah, Richard. I know I said you can smoke out here, but some of the staff are complaining. Do you mind going outside next time?

RICHARD No. Not at all. Uh, can I finish this one?

ANDY I guess. Hey, Guillermo. How are you?

GUILLERMO Oh, I don't know.

ANDY I hear great things. The actors are thrilled; the designers are delighted. Everybody's very excited.

GUILLERMO Oh. Really? That's… something.

ANDY Yeah. *(to RICHARD)* And you guys okay?

RICHARD Oh yeah, having a great time.

ANDY Really? You sure?

RICHARD Yeah, we're laughing our heads off.

ANDY Okay. Well, if you want to talk to me—about anything—my door is always open. Really. I mean that. *(pause)* You sure you're okay?

RICHARD YES.

ANDY And… the ciggie. Right? No more smoking here? Right.

ANDY goes.

RICHARD He said I could smoke here. I tell you, it's the biggest profanity imaginable these days, smoking. You could fuck a dead dog in this theatre and nobody will say anything. But smoke one cigarette…

GUILLERMO Tons of letters. Listen, I have to get back. Sorry about the part.

RICHARD Sorry about the Trotsky.

GUILLERMO And sorry about your show.

RICHARD And sorry about _____ *(guest)*.

GUEST enters from fire-escape doors.

GUEST Guillermo. There you are. Listen, about that last scene…. Hey Richard!

RICHARD Hey! How are you? How's it going?

GUEST Great. Fabulous. I'm having a great time with this guy.

GUILLERMO Yeah, but what else are you going to say? I'm standing right here.

GUEST So listen, you know that bit I did before that you said reminded you of "Battleship Potemkin"? I thought I could do another version in this scene…

GUILLERMO That's a great idea. Or maybe…. Do you know "Andrei Rublev," the Tarkovski film.

GUEST Yes, the icon painter… and the little boy…

GUILLERMO Yeah. Oh my God, it's so fabulous…

GUEST Like a soul captured…

They exit, talking excitedly and laughing. RICHARD finishes his cigarette. Sighs. He does not look happy. He starts to close the door. He screams. The door closes.

Wendy Lill *Genie*

2003
Mary Vingoe: Director
Paul Fauteux: Mike
Jovanni Sy: Joe McNutt
Jenny Young: Alice

⌑•⌑

ALICE, 24, addresses the audience.

ALICE Alice Hall is having a baby. No, no, Alice and Mike are having a baby. We are pregnant. Doesn't that expression just kill you? We're pregnant. We. *(She giggles.)* Joint effort. Teamwork. Look at me. Us. *(She rubs her hand around her womb in awe.)* On my way to work today, passing people on the street, women in spike heels and tight skirts, kids with pierced noses and green hair, tiny old women, little guys yanking at each others coats... and I thought, how can things just go on as if everything's normal – when in fact there is this new life, this miracle growing inside me. Right here. New life. Baby One.

Then my cell phone rang. *(She listens.)*

Light up on MIKE.

MIKE Alice calls.

ALICE The clinic just phoned and want us to come in and talk about the results of a prenatal test.

MIKE What prenatal test? I'm in the middle of a team meeting on the spotted whale project.

ALICE Screw the spotted whale.

MIKE All right.

An office. MIKE and ALICE sit. Joe MCNUTT enters, shirt-sleeves, mid-thirties, manila file-folder in hand.

MCNUTT Alice Hall? And you're... *(checks file)* Mike? *(hand out)* Joe McNutt, I'm the genetics counsellor here. Still nice outside?

MIKE Yeh.

MCNUTT I was hoping to get to my son's baseball game tonight if the weather holds.

MIKE So what's this all about?

MCNUTT Your MSS results.

MIKE Our what?

MCNUTT Sorry for the jargon. Maternal serum screening. Standard prenatal testing now… that blood test after the urine sample – gives us a chance to peek at the fetus early on to see if there is anything we may need to be concerned about. *(opens files)* How old are you, Mike?

MIKE Twenty-seven.

MCNUTT Alice?

ALICE Twenty-five.

MCNUTT How long have the two of you been married?

ALICE Four months.

MIKE The wedding presents are still piled up all over the dining room.

MCNUTT I remember what that was like.

>   *MIKE and ALICE growing uneasy as MCNUTT writes.*

MCNUTT Do you both work?

MIKE I'm a marine biologist.

MCNUTT Really! And what kinds of things do you work on?

MIKE Ah, well… um… right now I'm part of a research project trying to save the spotted whale population in the Bay of Fundy.

MCNUTT Fantastic. And Alice?

ALICE *(curt)* Fitness instructor.

MCNUTT That's great. *(keeps writing)*

MIKE So what exactly are we here for?

MCNUTT Well what the MS test does is let us see if there's any higher chance of an anomaly in the fetus.

ALICE Anomaly?

MIKE It means an irregularity, a difference.

MCNUTT That's right.

MIKE *(cautious)* So ah… what sort of anomalies?

MCNUTT Possible anomalies we're able to test for now are such things as neural tube disorders, spina bifida, cleft palate, the Trisomies, 15, 18 and 21. We are even able to detect a crossed left finger or whether someone is right- or left-handed.

MIKE Really.

ALICE holds her hands on her stomach.

MCNUTT It's incredible what can know now. I just read in a journal this morning that there are two-hundred new prenatal tests on the market. You must know from your own work in biology, if you're doing population diversity stuff, that since cracking the DNA code, the genie's right out of the bottle.

MIKE Yeh.

ALICE *(internal)* Is this my body they're talking about?

ALICE clears her throat.

(looks pointedly to MIKE) So…

MIKE So what do you think you've found?

MCNUTT The numbers are showing high for Trisomy 21.

ALICE What?

MCNUTT Down's syndrome. With Down's, the genetic abnormality takes the form of an extra chromosome. There's no reason to worry at this point. This test is just preliminary.

ALICE *(internal)* Baby One? Are you listening?

MIKE Down's.

MCNUTT We don't know anything for sure.

ALICE *(internal)* The night we made love, the night we conceived, I screamed at him about who'd clean out the kitty litter. I was feeling hateful and petty. It's because of…

MIKE *(internal)* Uncle Norman.

MCNUTT And I also want to caution you about jumping to any conclusions…

MIKE *(internal)* Sluggo and Fatso. Forever.

ALICE *(internal, looking at MIKE)* What is he thinking? That night, he just stood there with that beautiful smile, teasing me, pulling at my t-shirt, saying "If you come to bed with me now, I'll clean out the kitty litter for the rest our lives."

MIKE *(internal)* Ohmigod. Uncle Norman and I shared the bathroom in the basement for five years. Maybe I caught it from him? Listen to me. I am a scientist… how can I be so stupid? Alice?

MCNUTT Like I said, this is just a preliminary test that we do; we'll need to do an amniocentesis to confirm. I just wanted to ask you some questions and answer yours, so when you leave here you can make some informed choices. Okay with that?

MIKE Sure.

MCNUTT Is there any Down's in your family, Mike?

MIKE My uncle Norman.

MCNUTT On your mother's side or your father's side.

MIKE He's my mom's brother. I call him Sluggo. He calls me Fatso. Just one of those little family things.

ALICE Uncle Norman was at our wedding! I danced every fast dance with him.

MIKE He's a real card.

MCNUTT So you have some familiarity with Down's.

ALICE *(internal)* Why does he talk like that? Like we're under a microscope?

MCNUTT And your family, Alice? Any Down's syndrome?

ALICE No.

> *MCNUTT taking notes.*

(internal) What is he writing about us?

MCNUTT Any other genetic defects that you know of in your families? Mike?

MIKE Ah... no.

MCNUTT Alice?

ALICE *(internal)* What if I told him that my brother can't find a job? That my dad spends every night at the casino, my sister's bombing out as a stand-up comic. Will he write that down?

MCNUTT Alice?

ALICE And that my mother committed suicide. And that my whole life was one big defect until Mike came along and...

> *MIKE grabs her hand and holds it.*

MIKE *(whispers)* Alice?

ALICE Ah... no.

MCNUTT You're both in good health?

MIKE Yes. You know, it's funny. I never even thought about something like this. I mean Alice and I are both young. I thought you just got together and got pregnant and then nine months later... had a baby.

MCNUTT It's a whole new world. Now we can tell right down to the colour of the hair. It's incredible what can be done. Some scientists have been able to pull together enough bits of DNA to build a wooly mammoth.

ALICE What are you talking about?

MIKE Alice...

MCNUTT Though who knows where something like that would be able to live these days.

ALICE (internal) Baby One. Are you… all right? Is there something… wrong with you?

MIKE (internal) Sluggo and Fatso forever. How many thousands of times did I hear that stupid expression. And yet I love him. He's family. But I don't know…. And could Alice handle it? Would it break her? Would it break us? What do we really know about each other? I'm scared…

MCNUTT Just a few more questions. Any pregnancies before this one?

ALICE (internal) When I was 16, but Mike doesn't know. My mom died and I tried to throw myself away… just like her. An ocean of drugs and a string of guys… don't even know who it was for sure…

MIKE Alice?

MCNUTT I know it's a lot to process.

ALICE No.

MCNUTT Do you folks go to church?

MIKE What?

MCNUTT Well sometimes religious considerations enter the equation.

ALICE (internal) What equation? Baby One? Are you there? Are you all right?

MCNUTT Not since Confirmation.

ALICE Excuse me. Why are we talking about church? Ten minutes ago, this baby, this life inside me was a miracle. I was a miracle. We were a miracle. Mike?

MIKE Listen, aren't there some risks with amnios?

MCNUTT Well it is a somewhat invasive procedure. The process does involve extracting a tiny bit of fluid to grow a culture… so there is a slightly higher risk of inadvertent miscarriage.

MIKE How much higher?

MCNUTT Maybe two percent.

MIKE That's not very high. What are the naturally occurring numbers for Down's in the population?

MCNUTT Right now the numbers are about one per thousand. But with the strides being made in the field of genetics, in advanced prediagnostic screening, we're already seeing a drop in the number of births.

ALICE Why is that?

MCNUTT Well, I guess because more people are choosing to terminate – when offered an informed choice.

ALICE Why doesn't he say abortion? Why don't you say no more Uncle Normans? Mike, whatever happens we have each other, we can handle it.

MIKE Alice, just let the man talk.

MCNUTT Well, I don't want to pull any punches. Statistics show that couples who have children with special needs have a higher rate of divorce… it's very hard to get the services you need…

MIKE Yeh, you don't need to tell me about it. I know, it's hard, Alice.

MCNUTT Well, if there's no more questions, I'll leave the two of you… you obviously need some time together. Just remember that you're young, you've got your whole life ahead of you and whatever happens with the amnio, you've got lots of time to make other babies. It's a lot to take in on a Friday afternoon. Take the weekend to think about your choices and call me Monday morning and we can go from…

ALICE *(internal)* I don't want to choose.

MCNUTT Pardon?

ALICE I don't want to choose.

MIKE Thanks.

> *MCNUTT exits.*

ALICE Mike?

> *MIKE and ALICE look at each other.*
>
> *Lights out.*

David Macfarlane   *The Prank*

2003
Andy McKim: Director
Joe Ziegler: James Foxbright

⌑ • ⌑

We see FOXBRIGHT, seated. He is intently reading a letter, and continues to do so, head lowered, as the HOST reads stage directions to the audience.

HOST   The second-floor hallway of a house. It is not grand. But it has a dignified, slightly gloomy aspect, and is furnished with old, too-grand furniture – the inheritance from a wealthier generation.

Seated in a chair, in the middle of the hallway, we see Foxbright. He inhabits the blurry domain of middle-age. Beside him, the hall closet is open, and the floor is strewn with the things he is sorting out. It is the day after his mother's funeral.

FOXBRIGHT continues to read for a few moments, engrossed. He chuckles quietly at what he is reading. Eventually he notices the audience. He addresses it directly.

FOXBRIGHT   Letters. Shoeboxes full of them. Letters I wrote from boarding school. Once a week. To Mother.

MRS. FOXBRIGHT   You know, my son was normally not very good at writing to me. Not very good at writing, really. Odd, that he would become a journalist. Well, perhaps not.

But there was one letter. One that I really loved. This one. The one about Le Brun and his famous prank.

FOXBRIGHT   Remarkable that she kept them. My letters. *(looks at the mess around him)* Well, not really. There weren't many things that she threw out. *(holds up wooden racquet in press)* Her racquet. First team, tennis. Cathcart Ladies College, 1947. *(holds up sweater)* The sweater she knit for me when she decided that if I were going to a skating party in grade four, I should have a proper Canadian skating sweater. It was the only thing she ever knit. It took three years. Note caribou.

And here, here in the collected letters of J.W. Foxbright—from the Arlis shoebox number four—my letter to Mother about Le Brun's famous prank.

MRS. FOXBRIGHT   I gather that by way of ancient tradition, new boys were expected to "pull" the occasional prank. It was difficult for me to make the connection between the encouragement of mischief and the amount of money I was paying for my son's education. Still, connection, apparently, there was. Pranks were thought by the faculty to be good things – evidence of pluck.

FOXBRIGHT She mentioned the story just the other day. It was at the hospital. The nurse—the one who made the mistake of asking if Mother wouldn't have a little more of her cream of celery soup—had just been chased from the room with a pretty withering stare. And, out of the blue, Mother asked about Le Brun. She said…. She said she had something she needed to write. *(He flips back through the pages of the letter.)* She loved this bit. Where is it? Ah yes. *(He reads.)* "The icing. The icing on the goddamn cake…" *(laughs fondly—a little sadly—at the memory)*

God, I was homesick.

I was in third form. My first year away. Bishops College School. *(sings)* "Oh true to thee dear Bishops. We strivest as thou wishest." An anthem that Le Brun felt could be improved. *(sings)* "The masters are a little thick. But not half as thick as Bishopric."

Once, during one of Mother's very rare visits to the school, I pointed Le Brun out to her.

MRS. FOXBRIGHT God save us. A round, pale figure. I recall small teeth – all of which appeared to be identical in size, and with identically-spaced gaps between them. His eyebrows were high and arched, almost as if they'd been plucked. His thick eyeglasses, along with their taped-together armatures, appeared to be wrapped around his face, more than set on his bulbous nose.

Le Brun was not… an attractive child.

LE BRUN I was something of a misfit, I grant you. By way of understatement, let me put it this way: looks were not my strong suit. I was, however, clever. No – more than clever. I was intelligent – more so than my peers; they could all see that. More so than most of the masters, actually; anyone could see that. I read constantly – though never books that had anything to do with what we were studying. My particular area of interest was the Second World War. I was famous for correcting masters.

MASTER Mutter, mutter… *("bit of a show, Jerry, howitzers, word from HQ")*

LE BRUN I believe, sir, that you'll find that the Fifth Army went in at Salerno without any preliminary aerial bombing.

MASTER *(rising in volume and irritation)* Mutter, mutter… *("devil of a time, Bosch, damnable Eye-ties, tank corps excellent lads")*

LE BRUN More likely, the 141st would have used 81 mm mortars at the Rapido River.

MASTER *(rising)* Mutter, mutter… *("artillery barrage, air campaign, 0800 hours, hell of a bombardment")*

LE BRUN Not just British troops. It was the Brits, along with the Poles, who finally took Cassino.

MASTER *(exploding)* Don't tell me about the German attacks at Messina, Le Brun. I was bloody-well there.

LE BRUN Counter-attacks, sir.

FOXBRIGHT Le Brun's prank, I must say, had the sparkle of brilliance to it. It involved a pig. A rather big pig. I can't now remember—nor is my letter to Mother very informative on this point—how Le Brun had convinced a local farmer to… rent us the pig for the night. But the plan Le Brun had outlined to me in advance of our carrying it out—in a barnyard, at about three in the morning—had conveniently skimmed over the difficulty of actually catching a frightened, strong, big pig. And putting it in a burlap sack.

LE BRUN It's true, I admit. A slight miscalculation. Luckily, it did not prove entirely disastrous – even though the pig's resistance was more stubborn than anticipated. *(sounds of pig, LE BRUN wrestling with squirming weight)* What became apparent to us—that would be Foxbright and myself—is the law that governs the behaviour of a parrot when a blanket is put over its cage cannot be applied with complete success to a distraught and uncomfortable pig.

YOUNG FOXBRIGHT *(struggling with weight and movement of imagined pig in burlap bag, and providing sound effects of the pig)* It heaved. *(squeal)* It buckled. *(squeal)* It kicked. *(squeal)* It – *(pause)* – squealed. *(really loud squeal)* Loudly enough to wake the dead; but not, apparently, loudly enough to wake our teachers. It seemed to me impossible that lights were not flicking on in the nearby houses of the masters as we passed them in our approach to the looming darkness of the school. But no lights appeared.

MRS. FOXBRIGHT Evidence, so I can only assume, of the chronically alcoholic nature of their teachers' domestic lives.

YOUNG FOXBRIGHT The plan was this: we would go into the school quickly in the dark, like commandos. We would do what we had to do as fast and as silently as possible.

LE BRUN Speed is of the essence. Cyanide capsules will be used in the event of capture. And it's ix-nay on radio contact. If all goes well, we'll be back in our beds before all hell breaks loose.

MRS. FOXBRIGHT I can just picture it. He described it very well in the letter. Now, let's see. There was Hume. Hume was head prefect. Noted for his impossibly high marks, courtly manners, excellent public speaking and general maturity, he had a squash player's lithe body. He had blonde hair, intelligent, brown eyes, fine, patrician features – all characteristics that would have been dazzling had they not somehow added up to… predictability. One had the impression upon meeting Hume that he'd been met before.

Hume shared a room with another prefect – a large, good-natured Jamaican whose name, improbably, was Locke. A Negro, as was said, perfectly reasonably, in those days.

FOXBRIGHT Their room was on the second floor of Robinson House, in about the middle of the hall. At one end was the apartment that Philip Hanbury, the elderly housemaster and the absurdly English head of the French department, shared with his frail, nervous wife, Lilly.

YOUNG FOXBRIGHT *(struggling with weight of pig)* At the other end of the hallway were the worn stone stairs, up which, in the pale red grow of the exit lights, we struggled with our squirming bundle.

And there, at the top of the stairs, behind the door on the landing, Le Brun had hidden an old hockey stick and a coil of rope. *(low gruntings)*

LE BRUN *(struggling with weight of pig)* The objective—after, that is, we blow up the Reichstag and re-supply the Dutch underground—will be the insertion of one large and really annoyed pig into the room of the head prefect.

YOUNG FOXBRIGHT Then?

LE BRUN Ah, that's the genius of it, Foxbright. Then, we lash their door closed with the hockey stick and the rope.

YOUNG FOXBRIGHT And then?

LE BRUN Then we run, you idiot. What do you think we do?

FOXBRIGHT At the time, Le Brun's answer had seemed as obvious as my question had seemed foolish. And yet, as things turned out, I had put my finger on the one serious flaw in the plan.

MRS. FOXBRIGHT They made their way, somewhat awkwardly I'd have to think, down the hallway. They must have been an unusual sight. And the fact that they were carrying a pig, in a bag, would have been the least of it. Most striking, I'm sure, to the casual observer, would have been their appearance. Their efforts in the barnyard had left them covered from head to toe in what they optimistically thought of as mud.

LE BRUN We opened Hume and Locke's door. Their room was dark. We could hear their breathing. The struggling bulges of burlap did not clearly reveal which was the front and which was the backside of the pig. With some difficulty we emptied the contents of the sack into the room.

We closed the door. We twisted the rope around the door handle. We secured the hockey stick across the doorjamb so that it could not be opened from within.

But… contrary to my careful planning… we did not run.

FOXBRIGHT How could we? How could we have imagined that we would? The point of the exercise, or at least the greatest pleasure we would take in it, would be lost if we simply made our escape—racing down the hallway, flying down one flight of stairs, scurrying into our dorm, and climbing into our beds—before anything really happened.

So we stayed, and staying, we could hear, through the scarred wooden door, the low, curious snuffling of the pig. *(snuffling sounds)*

MRS. FOXBRIGHT Suddenly, it snorted. *(loud snort)*

YOUNG FOXBRIGHT We could hear the sound of the prefects rising from the depths of sleep. And their noise, a kind of ascending moan—part complaint, part surprise, part bewilderment—must have made the pig even more anxious than it already was.

We could hear it clattering on the hardwood floorboards. Then it banged into something, and then into something else.

FOXBRIGHT Hume, curled into his bed, must have arrived at the only reasonable explanation of what he heard coming from the darkness at more or less the same level as his head.

MRS. FOXBRIGHT That a dwarf with a very bad cold had somehow found his way into their room.

And then it panicked. *(loud squeal)*

YOUNG FOXBRIGHT Light at crack under door.

LE BRUN Screech of terrified pig.

YOUNG FOXBRIGHT Shouts of prefects.

LE BRUN Crash of lamp.

YOUNG FOXBRIGHT The banging, banging against the door.

LE BRUN This is too, too good…

YOUNG FOXBRIGHT   …said Le Brun

FOXBRIGHT We knew we were doomed. But we also knew that we had made the right choice in not running. No matter how much trouble we were going to get into, it was worth it. We wouldn't have missed what then unfolded for an eternity of detentions. It was worth staying put because at the instant when the hockey stick finally broke, when the door finally banged open and the pig finally shot out into the hallway, the door to Mr. Hanbury's apartment opened, too.

MRS. FOXBRIGHT Everything froze.

FOXBRIGHT The pig, confronted with the two directions of the hallway, considered its options; Mr. Hanbury, tying the band of his housecoat around his waist while holding his sharp nose in the air with the angle of disdain with which he routinely regarded French students, French textbooks, and, quite probably, the French; Lilly…

MRS. FOXBRIGHT *(interrupting)* …Lilly, Mr. Hanbury's terrified wife, only dimly visible in the shadows of the apartment, as if she were a ghost so timid, so wispily grey, and so withdrawn that the mortals she encountered easily ignored her fluttering, ineffectual haunting…

FOXBRIGHT The two prefects, mystified by a view that included the housemaster and his wife, a pig, and two new boys – two new boys, they may have noted in passing, who were covered in shit.

MRS. FOXBRIGHT The pig spotted the only opening in the hall that it could see and, skittering on the polished floor, made for it at once. This was beyond Le Brun's wildest dreams. The opening was the door to the Hanbury's apartment.

LE BRUN Mr. Hanbury flattened himself against the wall as the pig headed past him.

YOUNG FOXBRIGHT To the extent that she could, Mrs. Hanbury screamed. *(breathless screams of "Philip, Philip. It's a pig. Philip.")*

MRS. FOXBRIGHT Demonstrating the leadership qualities that had got them elected to their high office in the first place, Locke and Hume must have felt it incumbent upon them to protect their housemaster and his wife.

LE BRUN This was something of a bonus.

MRS. FOXBRIGHT The two prefects charged down the hall, after the pig.

YOUNG FOXBRIGHT And Mrs. Hanbury…

MRS. FOXBRIGHT Poor Mrs. Hanbury could be seen retreating further into the shadows in the face of this stampede.

LE BRUN Mission, as they say, accomplished.

FOXBRIGHT It took us weeks to run off our detentions. And every Wednesday, as the two of us plodded around the track, Le Brun said the same thing.

LE BRUN The icing, the icing on the goddamn cake.

MRS. FOXBRIGHT Not the most original turn of phrase.

FOXBRIGHT But there was something so Le Brunian in the way he made this pronouncement, something so gleeful in the way he turned the vivid scene in his memory as we ran our laps, that I used the expression when I wrote Mother about the incident. And now, here, almost forty years later, here in this empty house, here on a page of this old letter, are those same words. I remember as if it were just the other night: Mrs. Hanbury's plaintive cries—Philip, Philip—as a terrified pig and two teenage boys thundered toward her. And when I wrote Mother about it I felt sure that the precise wording of Le Brun's description of Locke's and Hume's gallantry would amuse her.

MRS. FOXBRIGHT *(She reads from the letter, while struggling to maintain her composure. Eventually her laughter overtakes her.)* God, I laughed when I read it. Can you imagine? Where is it, now? Ah. What my son wrote to me was…. "You'll have to excuse my French, Mother. But the icing…. But the icing…. Was that Hume… Locke…" *(uncontrollable giggles, drops letter)*

FOXBRIGHT *(picks up letter, reads)* "The icing, the icing on the goddamn cake was that they were both completely fucking naked."

Pause.

The obituary departments protested, of course. There were regulations about language. But she told me to tell them that she had taken great care in writing it herself, and that since she was now dead, revision was out of the question.

Apparently, no one had taken this line of reasoning before. And so they published it, without alteration.

MRS. FOXBRIGHT Foxbright. Katherine, C. The only daughter of the late Sam and Margaret Newling. Pre-deceased by her husband, Freddy. A loss she somehow managed to bear. *(long pause, ironic stare)* Mother of her beloved son, James. Mrs. Foxbright attended Cathcart Ladies College where she excelled at tennis. Following a brief career in knitwear, she settled down to a quiet life enjoying the icing on the goddamn cake.

Book cart in the Tarragon Theatre Lobby.

Book cart designed by Ken Garnhum and made possible thanks to the generous support of Shelagh Hewitt-Kareda, Playwrights Canada Press, Talonbooks, Henry Bertrand, Mallory Gilbert and Andy McKim.